No Problem Here

No Problem Here

Understanding Racism in Scotland

Edited by

NEIL DAVIDSON, MINNA LIINPÄÄ,

MAUREEN McBRIDE and SATNAM VIRDEE

Luath Press Limited

EDINBURGH

www.luath.co.uk

First published 2018

Reprinted 2019, 2020

ISBN: 978-1-912147-30-4

The authors' right to be identified as the authors of this book under the Copyright,
Designs and Patents Act 1988 has been asserted.

The book is made of materials from well-managed, FSC®-certified forests and
other controlled sources.

Printed in Great Britain by Ashford Colour Press Ltd

Typeset in 11 point Sabon by Lapiz

Contents

CONTENTS

Acknowledgements

THERE ARE MANY PEOPLE whom the editors would like to thank. First, all of the contributors for their enthusiasm for this project, as well as for their patience as the book was being finalised. For the chapters which are based on empirical research, we are extremely grateful to all participants who gave up their time to engage in their respective projects. We hope that we have done you justice.

As the idea for this collection came about following a conference entitled 'Racism: From the Labour Movement to the Far-Right' held at the University of Glasgow on 5-6 September 2014, we would like to thank everybody who helped with the organising of the conference and all who attended and participated in discussions. Your insights undoubtedly helped to shape our thinking and our approach to the collection. We are extremely grateful to the Economic and Social Research Council (award number ES/K002198/1) and the then Dean of Research of the College of Social Sciences – the late Andy Furlong – for the generous financial assistance they provided to hold the conference.

Neil Davidson
Minna Liinpää
Maureen McBride
Satnam Virdee

Introduction: Understanding Racism in Scotland

Neil Davidson and Satnam Virdee

IN CONTRAST TO ENGLAND, there has been relatively little public discussion about the historical or contemporaneous structuring power of racism in Scotland. Over many decades, this silence has come to be interpreted as an indication of its absence by much of the Scottish elite, including its political parties, helping to consolidate a now powerful myth that there is 'no problem here', that in that memorable Scottish phrase 'We're a' Jock Tamson's bairns'. We contend that this narrative of an absent racism in Scottish history has become even more entrenched in the course of recent developments (such as the rise of the SNP and the independence referendum) because it is able to nest so comfortably within the new common sense of Scottish politics, the dominant story that has been forged, by the SNP and others – that the Scots are in some sense different from the English – more egalitarian, more likely to place an emphasis on collectivism over individualism and on government intervention over self-reliance. And the regular public statements made by successive First Ministers welcoming increased migration in contrast to the increasingly shrill pronouncements emanating from party leaders in Westminster seem only to have further reinforced the myth that Scotland does not have a serious racism problem.

On one level, such elite rhetoric is welcome, particularly when contrasted to what is unfolding today across large parts of Europe in relation to the refugee crisis. However, this mainly SNP-led re-imagining of Scotland as different (and arguably more progressive) than England has been crafted in such a way that the historical role which Scotland played in Atlantic slavery and colonial conquest has been consigned to what George Orwell referred to in *Nineteen-Eighty Four* as the 'memory hole', thereby giving the impression that it never happened. Or, on those rare occasions when such episodes are forced out into the open, they are implicitly projected back onto a reactionary British/English establishment. This suggests not only a degree of intellectual dishonesty but an unwillingness to confront the legacies of empire and racism in which Scotland is implicated.

Further, those broadly sympathetic public statements made by elite politicians in Scotland about migration and the 'new Scots' – are too often taken at face value – including by parts of the Left – and this carries with it the danger of underestimating and thereby disabling the contemporary struggle against racism that is required. It is crucial to remain alive to the disjuncture between elite discourse on migration and the lived reality of racialised minorities in Scotland. Everyday racism remains a deeply structuring force distorting the lives of those we know as the 'black and brown Scots'.

From racist harassment in the community, to systematic discrimination in the workplace, these so-called new Scots remain a class apart – one that is seen as somehow not quite Scottish. And on occasions – just as in England – this failure to imagine this group of Scots as 'truly Scottish', as 'unhyphenated Scots' can lead to violence and sometimes murder. From the racist killing of Surjit Singh Chhokar just prior to the advent of devolution in 1998 – a murder which required three trials before a conviction was finally achieved in October 2016 – to the death of 31-year-old Sheku Bayoh while being restrained by 15 police officers in Kirkcaldy during May 2015, racism remains a significant on-going problem in Scottish society, irrespective of the other more progressive transformations that are currently on-going.

In this volume, we wish to dig beneath the conventional 'race-blind' narratives that Scotland and its elites have crafted over many years, to perhaps unsettle them a little, so that we might begin to open up a space for writing a historical sociology of racism in Scotland, a historical sociology that might help us to uncover and perhaps finally come to terms with this hitherto occluded underside of Scottish history? The essays that follow were first presented at an international conference organised by the editors and held at the University of Glasgow in September 2014 (Davidson, Liinpää, McBride and Virdee, 2015). That event successfully brought together academics and activists of various sorts – although we are obviously aware that these are not mutually exclusive categories – to discuss racism in Scotland and related issues. The authors included here are about half of those who gave papers on the day and represent the full range of approaches taken by the speakers. The book consists of three parts.

Part 1 situates the discussion of race within the broader historical context of Scottish and British national identities. Scotland's disproportionately large role within the British Empire, particularly in relation to slavery, is gradually becoming more widely known. In Chapter 1, Minna Liinpää surveys this historical record before analysing how these aspects of the Scottish past are played down in official discourse of 'civic' nationalism – a category which she in any case regards as problematic – expounded by the SNP and the independence movement more generally. In Chapter 2, Allan Armstrong shifts the focus from Scottish to British identity, and the way in which versions of the latter can be found virtually across the spectrum of political opinion, including even some aspects of Scottish nationalism. In what is the most directly political intervention here, Armstrong links the notion of Britishness as an identity to the political project of Unionism and defence of the UK state from the era of 'Home Rule all round' to the present.

Part II is concerned with one very specific aspect of Scotland's imperial past: the Irish Catholic presence in Scotland. Quite apart from its intrinsic importance, this issue reminds us that, however different the specific circumstances today, current debates over race and migration need to be informed by the long-term history of these issues. In Chapters 4 and 5, Jim Slaven and Maureen McBride respectively deal with historical and contemporary aspects of the Irish Catholic experience, the latter drawing on her own field work. Both authors reject as misleading the notion of 'sectarianism', not least in the way it draws a false equivalence between the attitudes of Protestants and Catholics; both are equally clear that the actual issue here is racism towards people of Irish Catholic descent and that this was an indigenous Scottish development rather than one imposed by the British state. The revival of Orange and Loyalist rhetoric by the Conservative and Unionist Party in the British General Election campaign (which took place after the chapters had been finalised for this book) indicate that this issue is certainly not a purely historical one. In Chapter 5, Alex Law is as sceptical about the notion of 'sectarianism' as Slaven and McBride, but from a different perspective. In effect, Law argues that, whatever may have been historically the case, in contemporary Scotland 'sectarianism' functions as the basis for a classic middle-class moral panic, focused on the behaviour of male, working class football fans, who require to be subjected, not merely to Elias's civilising process, but to a veritable 'civilising offensive' embodied in the Offensive Behaviour at Football and Threatening Communications (Scotland) Act (2012).

Whether or not the type of racism directed at people of Irish Catholic descent is now entirely historical in nature, it is clear that other racisms are very much present in Scottish society. Part III consists of three case studies of groups which are subject to racism, followed by a further three of what racism means in important areas of social life, explicitly addressing policy questions. In Chapter 6, Nasar Meer discusses what we can learn about racial discrimination in Scotland through examining the self-reporting of Black, Asian and Minority Ethnic communities. There is no doubt that, among these communities, the cutting edge of racism in Britain today is experienced by Muslims: in Chapter 7, Paul Goldie draws on his own field work to highlight the situation in Glasgow, in part through interviews with non-Muslim 'white' Glaswegians which explore their attitudes to Muslims and reveals the type of deep seated but rarely-recognised problem of racism to which we have already alluded. The situation of Muslims is at any rate fairly widely discussed, that of Roma and Gypsy/Traveller people, far less so. In Chapter 8, Colin Clark attempts to rectify this absence, building on his own previous work on the subject, but also shows how even very specific forms of racism have features in common with all others. The situation of Roma and Gypsy/Travellers is also discussed in Chapter 9, where Gina Netto discusses the issue of housing, like Clark building on her own earlier research. But this chapter, along with the two that follow, is primarily concerned with the general effects of racism rather than its impact on specific racialised groups. Chapters 10 and 11 are both the work of individuals active in the Coalition for Racial Equality and Rights (CRER), with Carol Young focusing on the difficulties of achieving racial equality in the public sector and Jatin Haria dealing with the effects of racism on access to employment.

Finally, a concluding chapter by Minna Liinpää and Maureen McBride reviews the themes discussed in the book from a vantage point in early 2017, three years since the original conference at which the majority of chapters were first delivered. In particular, they note that the difference in voting patterns in Scotland and England during the Referendum on membership of the European Union has encouraged the very complacency about racism in Scotland that the book seeks to address.

The chapters which comprise this book vary in approach, but even the most empirically based give some consideration to conceptualising racism and even the most theoretical have some implications for policy. We believe that this three-sided approach involving theoretical understanding, empirical data and policy formation is likely to be the most effective in tackling the problem of racism, which as the contributors demonstrate, is assuredly present in Scotland.

Part I:

The Historical Legacy of the British Imperial State

CHAPTER I

Nationalism and Scotland's Imperial Past

Minna Liinpää

Introduction

ALTHOUGH MORE ATTENTION has been paid to Scotland's role in managing and profiteering from the British Empire's slave economy than before – and the current movement to remember this part of Scotland's history is gaining ever-increasing momentum – there is still a long way to go in terms of recognising and addressing this part of Scottish history. Human rights activist and Professor Emeritus in the School of Life Sciences at the Heriot-Watt University, Sir Geoffrey Palmer, for example, has called for more robust teaching with regard to Scotland's role in the Empire at schools (Denholm, 2014). Furthermore, Scotland's violent history has received growing media attention recently as numerous newspaper articles have sought to highlight Scotland's role in the slave trade (e.g. BBC, 2009; Wade, 2014; Leadbetter, 2014; McKenna, 2015; Ross, 2016; McLaren, 2017; Campsie, 2017; Garavelli, 2017).

History matters, especially for nationalism studies, as nationalist narratives often rely on origin and other myths to legitimate nationalist rhetoric in the present. The Scottish National Party (SNP) and its leading figures routinely appropriate historical events and figures that suit their political needs and agenda. Of course, it is nothing new that political elites make use of historical myths or common ancestry to forge a feeling of commonality (Kearton, 2005) or an 'imagined community' (Anderson, 2006). However, what is of interest is the question of *which* myths are remembered and *who* is included in this perceived 'common ancestry'. That is, not every historical event is drawn on when composing the 'national story'; rather, there is a selective and fluid process of remembering. Indeed, Kidd and Coleman (2012: 62) note the 'fickleness' of Scotland's myths – that is, they have much less staying power than the nation whose putative 'enduring essence' they are meant to represent. Consequently, the myths appropriated today are different from those appropriated in earlier centuries (Kidd and Coleman, 2012: 62). Additionally, not all people were (or currently are) included in the historically constructed 'national community'. Indeed, in the late 18th and early 19th centuries an independent Highland tradition was created and imposed on the whole Scottish nation (Trevor-Roper, 1983: 16); thus, a synthetic vision of Scotland was created via this Lowlands appropriation (Mackenzie, 1993: 730).

Although the SNP has repeatedly professed to a so-called 'civic' imagining of the nation and, indeed, many academics seem to share this vision of a civic-minded Scottish nationalism, this chapter seeks to interrogate, and ultimately challenge, this understanding of the inclusiveness of Scottish nationalist narratives. In particular, it will seek to uncover some of the ways in which certain episodes of Scottish history have long been absent in the public domain, and consider how such 'national amnesia', as Tom Devine would call it, affects ideas around, and the relationships between, 'Scottishness', belonging and nationalism. This chapter will, firstly and briefly introduce Scotland's connections with the British Empire and the slave trade, focusing especially on the Caribbean. It will then move on to consider the ways in which history plays a major role in nation-building processes, especially focusing on the rhetoric used by the SNP. By way of illustrating this, the Scottish independence referendum will be used as a case study to highlight some of the narratives that key SNP figures have used in terms of referring to history. It will be argued that the SNP focuses on very specific strands of history at the expense of more uncomfortable episodes in Scotland's past. Furthermore, the ways in which history is appropriated in political discourse gives us an indication as to where the SNP imagines the nation's boundaries to lie; of who belongs to the 'national community'? The Homecoming franchise and the idea of 'Scottish diaspora' will be discussed as an example of the SNP's tendency to selectively appropriate history, as well as a case in point of arguing against the predominant view of Scottish nationalism as wholly 'civic'.

Before moving on, I want to point out that when referring to 'nationalism', my intention is not to reify the concept. There is sometimes a tendency in nationalism studies to refer to nationalism in ways that suggest that nationalism is a 'thing' in and of itself, i.e. that nationalism is an active agent capable of 'doing' and 'acting'. Naturally, nationalism does not lead a life of its own detached from people; it is a phenomenon which stems from and is created, changed and reproduced by people on both macro and micro levels. Thus, I use 'nationalism' as a short-hand expression, and my intention is not to ignore the active processes that make and re-make nationalist narratives. I have also taken the decision to mainly focus on the SNP and the ways in which they tap nationalist rhetoric. Although the SNP is by no means the sole proprietor of nationalist ideas in Scotland, they are nonetheless the most visible and audible in public life.

Scotland's role in the British Empire

Before the 18th century, Scots had mainly travelled to Europe to pursue economic, educational and other interests; subsequently, however, the British Empire became the principle outlet for aspiring Scots (Hamilton, 2012: 429). After the failed attempt at founding a colony called New Caledonia on the Isthmus of Panama in 1695 (also known as the Darien Scheme), the Scots redirected their efforts into the emergent British Empire (Hamilton, 2012: 424). Following the Union and the ending of formal institutional barriers of the Empire in the Atlantic, Scots quickly seized opportunities as migrants, doctors, plantation owners, soldiers, slave traders, merchants and appointed imperial officers and governors within the British Empire (Hamilton, 2012: 426). Scots played a central role in the managing and running of the Empire; indeed, they were disproportionately represented in the imperial endeavour when considering the size of the population. For example, between 1784 and 1785, while only one tenth of the population of Britain were Scots more than 47 per cent of the appointed writers, 49 per cent of the officer cadets and over 50 per cent of the assistant surgeon recruits in Bengal were Scots (Devine, 2003: 250-1). Furthermore, when the East India Company (EIC) issued their free merchants' residence permits – which allowed trade within the East as long as goods were not exported to Britain – between 1776 and 1785, 371 merchants were awarded the privilege, of which 60 per cent were Scots.

By 1813 there were 38 prominent private merchant houses in Calcutta, 14 of which were dominated by Scots. The Scottish officer class also had a dominant position in India because of the high proportion of Scottish regiments serving there: 14 Royal regiments garrisoned the Indian and EIC provinces between 1754 and 1784, and seven of these were raised in Scotland (Devine, 2003: 251). Scots also flocked to the Caribbean sugar colonies such as Jamaica, Grenada, Dominica, St Vincent and Tobago in their thousands (Hamilton, 2012: 429). However, Scots did not feel confined to the British imperial endeavour, but sought advantage in other European empires as well (Hamilton, 2012: 424). From the 18th century Scots had established powerful mercantile communities in India, the Far East, Canada, Australia and New Zealand while maintaining close links with the home country by trading with its cities, buying vessels from its shipyards, and bringing out new employees (Mackenzie, 1993: 724).

As mentioned in the introduction, the focus of this chapter will be on the Caribbean. In the 18th century, Adam Smith – although critiquing the colonial system – noted the West Indian colonies' importance to the imperial economy (Devine, 2003: 221). For example, sugar consumption in England and Wales increased about twenty-fold in 1663–1775 (mainly due to the newfound enthusiasm for tea drinking), and, in 1700, British islands accounted for about 40 per cent of all transatlantic sugar assignments, a figure which subsequently rose to 60 per cent by 1815 (Devine, 2003: 221). Thus, Caribbean sugar production became crucial for the British economy, and the production was built on two key foundations; firstly, on the evolution of the plantation system and, secondly, the use of black slave labour (Devine, 2003: 223). The Caribbean islands were 'slave societies' in that they depended on un-free, forced labour as without the slaves it would have been impossible to run the sugar economies, and by 1850 about 85 per cent the British West Indies' population comprised of black Africans (Devine, 2003: 224). Devine notes how the Caribbean was 'known as the graveyard of the slaves' as the suffering of the slaves was especially horrendous – for example, on the Codrington plantations in Barbados, between 1741 and 1746, 43 per cent of all African slaves died within three years of arrival (Devine, 2003: 224).

As mentioned previously, Scots came to the Caribbean in great numbers, and they were highly visible due to their positions in the white communities as plantation owners, merchants and their employees, clerks, bookkeepers and overseers (Hamilton, 2012: 429). Scots also served as attorneys, managing the estates for absentee landowners and thus occupied key positions of responsibility and wielded enormous power over the enslaved Africans (Hamilton, 2012: 429). Because there were hundreds of thousands of slaves, an increasing number developed artisan skills which meant there was little demand for white labour in the 18th century West Indies; instead, it was a destination for well-capitalised or literate and numerate Scots with connections to potential employers (Hamilton, 2012: 430). Those who left for the Caribbean were mainly young, single and male as the West Indies were not regarded as a place for families: the goal was to make money and return home (Hamilton, 2012: 430). Scots' success in the Caribbean was dependent on the regular supply of labour from Africa (Hamilton, 2012: 430). Although relatively few slave voyages originated from Scottish ports, there was nonetheless money to be made in slave trade, and Scottish investors, captains, surgeons, merchants and crew all worked to make the slave trade profitable (Hamilton, 2012: 430).[1]

Importantly, what took place was not merely an outward projection of Scottish capital, people and ideas: Scots brought the Empire home and, thus, Scotland was influenced by overseas engagements (Hamilton, 2012: 424). Not only did the Empire have an effect on Scots' lives abroad, it also featured and left a mark on the society and life back in Scotland. The Empire was about accumulating wealth for many Scots who traded in colonial commodities such as tobacco, sugar and slaves, which led to the proliferation of big companies – such as Houston and Company of Glasgow who imported sugar – and the so-called 'tobacco lords' (Hamilton, 2012: 433), the names of whom can be seen on street signs around Glasgow's city centre, and the Merchant City area especially. Consequently, this chapter of Scottish history is ever-present, and we are surrounded by it in our daily lives – as statues and signage. Even if we may not consciously reflect on it, we continue to speak the names of Glassford, Buchanan, Dunlop and Ingram in our everyday lives.[2] Thus, Glasgow played host to an increasingly powerful mercantile community which grew ever richer and provided employment opportunities for Scots (Hamilton, 2012: 433). However, the Empire did not only provide opportunities for importing, but presented an export market for Scottish commodities as well: between 1765 and 1795 there was a tenfold increase in exports of linen to Jamaica as coarse cloth was needed for clothing for enslaved Africans, and the slave economies also increased demand for Scottish

[1] Ships carrying slaves mainly originated from Liverpool, Bristol and London.

[2] See Smith's (2014) accessible blog post on the Empire and public spaces.

herring (Hamilton, 2012: 436). In addition, during the 18th century, some slaves were also brought into Scotland to work as servants for wealthy families (including the Glassfords).[3]

The Scots' close relationship with the slave economy carried additional as well as financial consequences. When Janet Schaw travelled to Antigua in 1774, her letters to home were subsequently published as the *'Journal of a Lady of Quality being the Narrative of a Journey from Scotland to the West Indies, North Carolina and Portugal in the Years 1774 to 1778'* (Devine, 2003: 240). In her letters she noted how the single men who predominated as estate managers and overseers often took younger slave women as mistresses. Dr Jonathan Troup, for example, arrived in Dominica in 1789 and discovered two of his Scots colleagues had six children each with slaves (subsequently, Troup soon had a string of mistresses as well) (Devine, 2003: 242). Therefore, to this day, there is a large Caribbean population with a direct link to Scotland. Indeed, many carry Scottish surnames, such as Campbell, Lamont and Grant, which were forced upon their enslaved ancestors by their Scottish slave masters. There were also black people of Scottish descent living in Scotland – one of the most famous black Scots being Robert Wedderburn, a radical anti-slavery advocate and son of a Jacobite Scot in Jamaica – which leads Hamilton (2012: 437) to note how notions of a previously 'white country' are misplaced with regard to the current controversy about non-European migration. Furthermore, many ordinary people of African, Indian and Scottish descent lived and worked and were educated across the country, the presence of whom 'challenges historians to think carefully about who they regard 'Scottish' in the late eighteenth-century Scotland' (Hamilton, 2012: 437). These connections are especially important, and should be kept in mind with regard to the discussion on Homecoming Scotland.

Finally, it is important to also note some Scots' contribution to the plethora of ideas which, alongside evangelical convictions and economic change, worked towards ending the slave trade in 1807, and led to the final emancipation in the British Empire in 1833. For example, in the 1791 address to the inhabitants of Glasgow, it is noted that 'the circumstances attending the African slave trade, must fill with horror, every person of common humanity' (Pinfold, 2007: 314) and that chattel slavery 'is a system so contrary

---

[3] See, for example, this newspaper advertisement in the *Edinburgh Advertiser* from 1769 (National Library of Scotland): http://www.nls.uk/collections/topics/slavery/pop-ups/slave-advert-1769.

to every sentiment of humanity and religion, that it must be rejected with abhorrence' (Pinfold, 2007: 322). This group of abolitionists is not representative, however; as Devine notes, the vast majority of Scots in the West Indies favoured the slave system and worked it for their advantage (2003: 248). Nonetheless, Scots who had served in the Caribbean (such as Rev James Ramsay, James Stephen and Zachary Macaulay) became key figures in the anti-slavery movement, and their views were fuelled by the abominable scenes they witnessed in the Caribbean (Devine, 2003: 248).

Nationalism and the uses of history

History plays a key part in nationalist narratives and processes of nation-building – it is, thus, important to consider what is (not) remembered and who is (not) remembered, as well as how history is understood and represented. Indeed, silences can be as revealing as – or, indeed, even more revealing than – the events, people and places that we choose to incorporate into our national stories. Ernest Renan has famously argued that 'forgetting, I would even go so far as to say historical error, is a crucial factor in the creation of a nation' (1990: 11). Thus, political and national projects use and remember history selectively 'to bolster contemporary political aims' (Kearton, 2005: 25). What is more, this is not a passive process of reflecting on the past but rather drawing on history to help actively shape 'a particular sense of national tradition and continuity' (Kearton, 2005: 25). And as Smith (2005) has argued, 'myths, memories and symbols' from a nation's pre-modern past have an important role to play in their nation-building projects. Renan goes on to say that 'a nation is a soul, a spiritual principle' and that there are two things that constitute that soul, 'one lies in the past, the other in the present': 'one is the possession of a rich legacy of memories; the other is present-day consent, the desire to live together, the will to perpetuate the value of the heritage that one has received in an undivided form' (1990: 19). Therefore, he points out of how history and shared memories contribute towards the feeling of togetherness today. In her wonderful essay, Himani Bannerji notes that the writing of history is not a transparent affair, but entails issues of representation which, in turn, entail issues of epistemology and ideology (1998: 287). She goes on to elaborate that 'representation' has a double-edge to it:

> By claiming to re-present someone, some moment in time, some situation – in fact all three, all at once – through our

reporting, recording, or narration, 'representation' implies both epistemological and (re)constructive responsibilities (Bannerji, 1998: 287).

Bannerji points to how remembering history, or representing the past (be it people or events), has a normative element to it; historical memories, which are often misrepresented, can serve specific political and ideological ends. Moreover, when she talks about 'responsibilities' she highlights the burden that those in powerful positions have with regard to representing the past in a fair and truthful manner.

As mentioned in the introduction, appropriating history to bolster political claims is by no means a rare occurrence. However, the ways in which the SNP and its key figures make use of history challenges the ways in which Scottish nationalist narratives are often branded as 'civic'. Although there is not enough space to go into great detail, it is important to note the tendency in nationalism studies to divide nationalisms into different 'types' – thus, they are often understood and conceptualised via dualistic categorisations; be it cultural or political, Eastern or Western or, importantly for this chapter, ethnic or civic. Furthermore, these dualisms are closely interlinked – while civic nationalism is often depicted as political and Western in origin, ethnic nationalism is seen as cultural and Eastern. According to Ignatieff, the core idea behind civic nationalism is 'that the nation should be composed of all those – regardless of race, colour, creed, gender, language, or ethnicity – who subscribe to the nation's political creed' (1993: 8) while, in contrast, ethnic nationalism veers toward authoritarianism as it 'presupposes an inherited commonality that must be imposed when it is not otherwise forthcoming' (Xenos, 1996: 215). Therefore, civic nationalism is characterised as 'liberal, voluntarist, universalist and inclusive', and ethnic nationalism is characterised as 'illiberal, ascriptive, particularist and exclusive' (Brubaker, 2004: 56). Civic nationalism is thus seen as being ahistorical and acultural; a voluntary association of culturally unmarked individuals for whom nation-membership is a chosen and not a given. This is in contrast to ethnic nationalism whereby membership is understood to be based on ethnicity (Brubaker, 2004: 59-61).[4]

---

[4] I, however, find such dualistic characterizations both theoretically and analytically unhelpful. There is no space to go into detail here, but Brubaker (2004) offers a good discussion of the shortcomings of such conceptualisations.

Scottish nationalism has been portrayed as demonstrating civic characteristics not just by the SNP and its key figures but by various academics and political commentators alike. As Kearton notes, the civic conception of Scottish nationalism is prevalent in academia (2005: 26). She goes on to highlight Tom Nairn's comment that the 'national movement [is] conducted exclusively in political terms – political, and indeed quite self-consciously civic and pacific terms' (cited in Kearton, 2005: 27). TC Smout (also cited in Kearton, 2005: 27) argues: 'Modern Scottish identity is much more firmly allied to a sense of place than to a sense of tribe.' Similarly, for McCrone 'Scottishness falls at the 'civic' rather than the 'ethnic' end of nation-ness' (in Kearton, 2005: 27). Thus, as Hamilton notes (cited in Leith, 2008: 83), there emerges a consensus in much academic writing seeing Scottish nationalism as civic and inclusive, and the SNP as 'resolutely civic in [its] orientation' supporting a Scotland 'where membership is a legal concept and not one based on ethnic exclusion'.

During the referendum campaign, for example, the SNP sought to evoke a sense of belonging to the national community based on 'non-ethnic' characteristics such as descent or place of birth. In the SNP's White Paper on Independence – or the Future of Scotland as it was officially called – (then) First Minister Alex Salmond made the often heard argument during the referendum campaign of how voting for independence is about democracy; it is about 'the power to choose who we should be governed by and the power to build a country that reflects our priorities as a society and our values as a people' (2013: viii). The referendum was also framed through the idea of social justice.[5] (Then) Deputy First Minister Nicola Sturgeon, for example, said in her spring conference address in 2013 that 'if we are to build a better, more democratic, just and prosperous country for our children to inherit, then let me tell you this – Independence is not optional. Independence is essential'. Thus, both Salmond and Sturgeon sought to steer away from identity politics by suggesting that the fundamental meaning behind the referendum – and the fundamental reason for voting yes on independence – were to do with advancing social justice (i.e. building a more equal and socially just society) and democracy (i.e. taking political decisions locally). Furthermore,

---

[5] Further, the social justice arguments were closely anchored to Scotland's enlightenment history; that is, the SNP argued that there is a long, historical tradition of striving for fairness and equality in Scotland. Since the enlightenment period and Scotland's involvement in the slave trade overlap, it is telling the focus of SNP's historical remembering is on the former.

there was a strong suggestion that regardless of where you come from, you should be able to take part in making this decision, as highlighted by Alex Salmond in an interview with a Polish expat magazine:

> There is, I believe, a universal law, which is that the people who live and work in a country are the best ones to decide its future. It's nothing to do with background or origin (Macguire and Bator-Skorkiewicz, 2014: 27).

Similarly, Nicola Sturgeon emphasised the role that all 'people of Scotland' have in taking part in the process of building Scotland's new chapter: 'My case for independence is based on confidence, it's based on belief, it's based on hope and it's based on an unshakable knowledge that we in Scotland – all of us, regardless of where we come from – if we work together, we can build a better country' (Sikh Channel, 2014). Furthermore, belonging to Scotland was defined in terms of residence and commitment to the country: 'I believe in independence because I believe it will be better for all of us if decisions about Scotland are taken by the people who care most about Scotland – the people who live and work here' (Salmond 2013: ix). Indeed, Salmond goes on to spell out his vision of the independence project in clear terms: '... our current democratic journey provides a helpful context – as we decide our future in a context based entirely on consensual, civic, non-ethnic and peaceful principles' (Glasgow Caledonian University Speech in New York, 2014). Consequently, Scottishness is routinely framed as an open and all-encompassing identity in official political discourse:

> And all this nonsense about repatriating English – we value, absolutely value English people in Scotland, they're part of the community and it's perfectly satisfactory for people to be English and Scottish, Irish and Scottish, Pakistani and Scottish – it's one of the great things about Scottishness: it's a nonexclusive identity. And every single person who's part of our community will have equal status as a citizen, and equal rights and deserves equal respect (Alex Salmond, 'Morning Call', BBC Radio Scotland, 29 August 2014).

However, Kearton notes how 'ethnicity comes in through the back door of history' as 'a predominantly forward-looking civic conception of community is anchored around a historically grounded ethnocultural core' (2005:39). She, thus, argues that 'while Scottish nationalism is clearly further towards the civic end of an ethnic-civic spectrum, the understanding of Scotland as a civic nation is not unproblematic' (2005: 30) and 'while the Scots civic identity is inclusive in that (in theory) anyone can join, some of its recurring tropes have particular ethnic and cultural origins' (2005: 39). Curiously, however, the SNP use history in a way that the 'ethnic core is used to project an inclusive, forward-looking vision of the nation' (2005: 25). Thus, the multi-ethnic roots of medieval Scotland – consisting of Picts, Britons, Scots, Anglo-Saxons and Norse – are drawn upon as a rhetorical device to legit-imise the contemporary claim of Scottishness being an open and inclusive identity, and of Scotland being an ethnically diverse nation (Kearton, 2005: 27-28). Kearton notes how Salmond cites a chronicle from the 12th century which shows how the various ethnic groups fought in the Scottish army at the Battle of the Standard in 1138. Subsequently, he goes on to talk about the civic nationalism of the contemporary multi-ethnic Scotland (Kearton, 2005: 27-28). Similarly, in the run-up to the referendum, Salmond refers to two of the most talked about Scottish historical figures, Robert the Bruce and William Wallace, and uses their ethnic origins to argue for an inclusive vote in September:

> The two greatest heroes in Scottish history are Robert the Bruce and William Wallace. Firstly, Robert de Brus, his family were of Norman extraction. William Wallace, William le Waleys, means William the Welshman. His family came from Wales. So this is nothing to do with where you are from, this is about where you are. That is the argument, which will carry the YES vote in September (Macguire and Bator-Skorkiewicz, 2014: 27).

While there is nothing unique with Scotland's mixed origins, the key thing is that these are used in an attempt to legitimise contemporary ethnic diversity 'rather than glossed over in a nationalist narrative stressing the authenticity and continuity of the Scots ethnic group (Kearton, 2005: 27-28). None-theless, a very specific history is drawn upon, while some – more sinister chapters – are forgotten. Thus, the political project that uses history relies heavily on amnesia as well. While Salmond contends that he is 'happy to be the representative of a country whose most celebrated figure, Robert Burns – with the third most statues of any secular figure across the planet – is not a soldier, but a poet' (speech at Glasgow Caledonian University New York campus, 7 April 2014), he conveniently chooses never to mention that Burns came very close to moving to West Indies in order to take on a job as a book-keeper on a Jamaican plantation in 1786 (Morris, 2014).

'Homecoming'

Closely related to the ways in which Scottish history is used in nation-building, is the Homecoming franchise. The first Homecoming Scotland event – which spans across an entire year – took place in 2009 with the second Homecoming taking place in 2014 at the same time as the referendum. The events were run and managed by VisitScotland and EventScotland (which is part of the former), and were supported and funded by the Scottish government. Homecoming features a mixture of cultural and sporting events ranging from highland games, the Shetland Nature Festival to food and drink events. The themes that ran through the events in 2014 were 'active'; 'creative'; 'food and drink'; 'natural'; and 'ancestry', with the following 'products' listed under the last theme: 'Commonwealth', 'history', 'diaspora', 'anniversaries' and 'ancestral tourism' (About Homecoming Scotland, 2014). Thus, there was a great emphasis on so-called ancestral Scots 'to come home'. While the event website notes that 'contemporary Scotland blends a rich array of cultures from around the world', it nonetheless singles out 'several icons considered uniquely and recognisably Scottish' (Visit Scotland, 2014). Unsurprisingly, these turn out to be kilts, bagpipes, tartan, Highland games, the national flag and Gaelic. As such, Scottish culture is to a great extent framed through 'Highland culture'. Scotland's tourism relies on heritage (Bhandari, 2013: 3), and the objects of heritage in Scotland have the power to confer identity (McCrone, Morris and Kiely in Bhandari, 2013: 3). Of course, as mentioned before, it is not until fairly recently that Highland culture came to be quintessentially Scottish or represent 'Scottish heritage'. This entailed the 'invention of tradition' (see Trevor-Roper, 1983) whereby '(mostly) imagined and false Highland "traditions" were absorbed freely by Lowland elites to form the symbolic basis of a new Scottish identity' in the 18th century (Devine, 2012: 233). Sir Walter Scott, especially, was at forefront of advocating for 'Highlandism' and orchestrating the 'cult of tartanry' (Devine, 2003: 354). This culminated in King George IV's visit to Edinburgh in 1822 as Scott stage-managed a series of pageants with a Celtic and Highland flavour (Devine, 2003: 355).

As Mycock notes, the main focus of SNP-led government initiatives, such as the 2009 Homecoming, have been to encourage (affluent) Scottish diasporic communities from countries such as the US, Canada, New Zealand and Australia to 'come home' (2012: 63). While the term 'Blood Scots' was originally used in connection with the 2009 event, there was a swift change to 'ancestral Scots'. Thus, Mycock argues that the SNP's focus with regard to Homecoming is 'instructive in determining how Scottish nationality is understood by the SNP' (2012: 63). While the marketing of Homecoming 2009 was firmly directed towards Canada, the USA, New Zealand and Australia (Mullen, 2009: 9), other parts of the Commonwealth which are intimately linked with Scotland and its historical legacy – notably the Caribbean – were forgotten about. Indeed, Sir Geoffrey Palmer pointed out how no Jamaicans were officially invited to take part in the events even though many Jamaicans consider themselves to be part of the Scottish diaspora (Mullen, 2009: 9). Thus, there has been a lack of engagement with diasporic communities which relate to the violent legacy of Scottish colonialism as well as with the biggest Scottish-born diaspora in England 'who highlights links with the Union and a shared Britishness' (Mycock, 2012: 63). Following Homecoming 2009 the event was, however, subsequently framed in a more all-encompassing way with Alex Salmond arguing that the events 'captured the imagination of people around the world who have links to and ties to Scotland and more widely people who simply love our country' (Homecoming Scotland 2010: 2). While Homecoming is directly linked with Scotland's imperial past in that it urges Scots from the Commonwealth to 'come home', the more sinister chapter of Scotland's history connected with slave trade and plantations has been, to a large part, absent from public rhetoric. The SNP has not actively engaged with Scotland's imperial legacy in its constructions of an independent nation-state and there is 'scant acknowledgement of [the colonial legacy's] potential contribution in shaping contemporary Scottish national values or identity' (Mycock, 2012: 62).

Bhandari notes how genealogical tourism can advantage nationalist sentiment by offering an experience that reinforces the common cultural affinity to their ancestral land (Bhandari, 2013: 2). Thus, it is premised on the idea of embracing 'commonness', and the aspiration of 'root tourists' is the search for familiarisation and identification with others (Stephenson in Bhandari, 2013: 2). Via homecoming, the SNP are demonstrating what Brubaker terms 'homeland nationalism' by which he means nationalism which is:

...directed 'outward' across the boundaries of territory and citizenship, towards members of their own ethnic nationality, that is towards persons who 'belong' (or can be claimed to belong) to the external national homeland by ethnonational affinity, although they reside in and are (ordinarily) citizens of other states (1996: 111).

Such constructions of the nation do, however, bring the civic-ness that the SNP claim to propagate into question. What transpires through events such as Homecoming is that Scottishness is not solely an identity based on residency or on one's choice to live and work in Scotland but that ancestry – but only *some* ancestry – plays a key part in being Scottish as well. There is a sizeable population living in the Caribbean with direct familial links to Scotland. However, there is a selective view of Scotland's diaspora (Mullen, 2009: 8) which has led Sir Geoffrey Palmer to term those Caribbeans with a connection to Scotland as the 'forgotten diaspora'.[6] Consequently, Mullen notes with regard to Homecoming 2009 that 'the Scottish government has severed itself from the complexity of the nation's past and shown how it is keen to adapt a romantic Disney-like charade based upon the denial of historical evidence' and that 'for a country which has a long imperial past, a peculiarly white vision has been authorised and publicised' (2009: 10).

Considering the Homecoming franchise is revealing because it portrays the government's vision and understanding of Scottish history and heritage. Importantly, Hall urges us to think of heritage as a discursive practice: 'it is one of the ways in which the nation slowly constructs for itself a sort of collective social memory' (2007: 89). By storying their turning points into a single, coherent narrative, nations construct identities by selectively binding their chosen high points and memorable achievements into an unfolding 'national story'. This story, then, serves as the nation's 'tradition' (Hall, 2007: 89). Building on Raymond Williams' idea of 'selective tradition', Hall argues that 'like personal memory, social memory is also highly selective' and 'it highlights and foregrounds, imposes beginnings, middles and ends on the random and contingent'. Thus, social memory 'foreshortens, silences, disavows, forgets and elides many episodes which (...) could be the start of a different narrative'. Hall goes on to argue that the 'process of selective "canonisation" confers authority and a material and institutional facticity

---

[6] See Palmer's essay 'Forgotten Diaspora' for more of his experiences around the invisibility of the Caribbean diaspora; it can be found at: http://www.scotdec.org.uk/aadamsbairns/files/docs/unit2/theme2/activity2/support/2.21_forgotten_diaspora.pdf

on the selective traditions' – this, in turn, makes 'it extremely difficult to shift or revise' (2007: 90). Drawing on Benedict Anderson, Hall argues that 'even so-called "civic" states (…) are deeply embedded in specific "ethnic" or cultural meanings which give the abstract idea of the nation its *lived "content"'* (2007: 88-89; emphasis added). Consequently, national heritage is a powerful source of such meanings and 'it follows that those who cannot see themselves reflected in its mirror cannot properly "belong"' (2007: 89). Thus, heritage – or what is constructed as heritage – serves as a powerful link between history, nationalism and belonging.[7]

Encouraging steps

More recently, however, encouraging steps have been taken with regard to remembering and acknowledging Scotland's history more fully. Since 2001, Coalition for Racial Equality and Rights has co-organised Black History Month, which has included talks, debates and other events highlighting Scotland's links to transatlantic slave trade. During Homecoming 2014, the Scottish Government funded a conference entitled 'The Global Migrations of the Scottish People since c.1600: Issues, Debates and Controversies' which featured a panel on 'Scotland and Black Slavery', for example (The University of Edinburgh, 2014; see also Mullen, 2017). The Commonwealth Games which were held in Glasgow in summer 2014 provided a convenient arena for thinking and discussing Scotland's role in the Empire in public fora. Over the period of about two weeks, people from all over the Commonwealth gathered together in the 'second city of the Empire'. Before the games started, Humza Yousaf – an SNP MSP and the then Minister for External Affairs – noted that there are many reminders in Glasgow of 'Scotland's role in the UK's dark past throughout the city' (2014: 11). Furthermore, he went on to say that:

> I see the 2014 Commonwealth Games as a chance for us to learn lessons for our past, and look forward to a new relationship with the Commonwealth, which includes a large proportion of African and Caribbean countries. This new relationship will be built on partnership and collaboration, rather than a relationship where one country is superior to the others (2014: 11).

---

[7] See also Bemis's publication *New Perspectives on Heritage: A Route to Social Inclusion and Active Citizenship* – available online at http://bemis.org.uk/docs/new_perspectives_on_heritage. pdf [last accessed 3/11/2017].

He concluded by saying that he hoped that by acknowledging this particular part of Scottish history, 'Glasgow's Commonwealth Games will allow us to move towards a more positive future and a relationship with Commonwealth counties which is a partnership of equals' (2014: 11). In addition to Yousaf, former SNP MSP and MP Anne MacLaughlin used her Westminster maiden speech to support reparations to the Caribbean (Mullen, 2017). In his conclusion, Yousaf also mentioned the Empire Café as an example of the cultural programme that took place during the games and was aimed at examining Scotland's links with the slave trade 'over tea and cake' (Duffy, 2014b).

The Empire Café was an idea of author Louise Welsh and architect Jude Barber, and it was open for a week during the Commonwealth Games. The café which was based in the Briggait in Glasgow's Merchant City hosted readings, films, art installations and discussions around the theme of Scotland and slavery (Duffy, 2014b). In addition to the café, a street-theatre play entitled Emancipation Acts also took place during the games. This series of plays explored Glasgow's role in Caribbean slavery, its abolition and current calls for reparations (*What's On Glasgow*). Graham Campbell (activist and now SNP Councillor), who curated Emancipation Acts, noted that 'it is important for Afro-Scots now, as a lot of people are relatively new to this city, and knowing their ancestors played a big part in building the city from a long time ago, and that they really do belong, it is an important thing to tell them' (Duffy, 2014a). There was also an exhibition in Glasgow's Kelvingrove Art Gallery and Museum entitled *How Glasgow Flourished, 1714–1837*. Although the exhibition focused on Scotland's thriving economy, it nonetheless featured items relating to slavery, and the *Glassford Family Portrait*, which famously includes a black boy in the background – thus hinting to Scotland's role in the Atlantic slave trade – was prominently displayed, for example. Furthermore, in the opening ceremony of the Commonwealth Games, Pumeza Matshikiza, a South-African soprano, sang 'Freedom Come All Ye', an anti-imperialist song sung in Scots and written by Hamish Henderson in 1960.[8] As such, this choice of song seemed very symbolic in the context of holding the Commonwealth Games in Glasgow.

These events and discussions seem encouraging, especially following the controversy that surrounded the (then) Scottish Executive's booklet published in March 2007. The booklet marked 200 years since the abolishment

---

[8] You can find the lyrics here: http://www.educationscotland.gov.uk/scotlandssongs/secondary/thefreedomcomeallye.asp

of slavery in the British Empire, and it focused on Scotland's involvement in slave trade industry, and was especially aimed at primary and secondary school children. Paula Kirching, the main author of the booklet, noted how this part of history is not widely taught at schools, and when it is, there is a tendency to focus on London, Liverpool and Bristol (Money, 2007). However, the two original researchers who were awarded the funding to write the book by the Labour-Liberal Democrat Scottish Executive – Rev Iain Whyte and Eric Graham – were later dismissed from the job. It was reported that there was disagreement with regard to the content and style of the booklet, and Whyte commented by saying that in his view 'they wanted a particular slant that was not historical' and that he 'felt that they wanted certain stories that weren't possible to produce, to change the text in certain ways' which he was not prepared to do, and that 'the government always has a certain agenda and they felt that what we were producing wasn't what they wanted' (Money, 2007). Consequently, anti-racism groups, such as the Glasgow Anti-Racist Alliance (now known as CRER – Coalition for Racial Equality and Rights), criticised the publication for not going far enough with regard to discussing the current issues affecting black communities in Scotland (Money, 2007). Thus, the recent attention being paid to Scotland's role in slave trade is a promising step forward, but more remains to be done.

Conclusion

This chapter has traced Scotland's and Scots' imperial journey, and high-lighted how parts of this history have remained largely absent in nationalist narratives which otherwise rely heavily on the past. While the SNP is often hailed as exemplifying civic nationalist ideas in practice by its members, political commentators and academics alike, this view can – and should – be challenged. Although the SNP and its key figures do often steer away from identity politics in order to extend the boundaries of the nation to include those not born in Scotland or those without familial ties with the country, ethnicity does, in Kearton's terms (2005), enter through the backdoor of history. The Homecoming franchise, especially, acts as a case in point. More-over, there is a selective view of the 'Scottish diaspora', which leaves a con-siderable group of people – many of whom are from the Caribbean – outside the confines of the 'diaspora'. Even though progress has been made in terms of remembering and acknowledging Scotland's violent history within the

Empire via media attention and cultural and political events, for example, this is only the beginning.

An idea that has been suggested with regard to acknowledging Scotland's role in the Empire and the slave economies is to establish a permanent memorial devoted to Scotland and slavery. Michael Morris (from Liverpool John Moores University), for example, has argued that such a feature is long overdue, and suggested there should be a museum or a series of public artworks in those areas of Glasgow where the traders' wealth is especially obvious. He notes that 'it would stand in the best traditions of this city to fully acknowledge the enormous debt it owes to Atlantic slavery, and to seek ways that we might begin to repair an old wound that has never been allowed to heal' (Duffy, 2014a). Furthermore, there have been other ventures such as the Multicultural Homecoming events organised by BEMIS – Empowering Scotland's Ethnic and Cultural Minorities which aimed to celebrate Scotland's heritage beyond bagpipes, kilts and highland games. Thus, there is momentum and desire behind a movement towards a more all-encompassing representation of the past – and it is crucial to keep that momentum going. History matters, as do the ways in which it is remembered and appropriated: how we remember the past affects the contours and the content of the nation.

CHAPTER 2

'Britishness', the UK State, Unionism, Scotland and the 'National Outsider'[9]

Allan Armstrong

Introduction

SATNAM VIRDEE'S *Racism, Class and the Racialized Outsider* (2014) shows how the conception of 'Britishness', promoted by the Labour Party from its birth in the 1890s to its social democratic heyday in 1945–51, and beyond whilst in opposition, more often than not excluded the *racialised* **outsider.** This version of 'Britishness' was often associated with Christianity thereby excluding those of Jewish descent and later whiteness leading to the marginalisation of those of Indian and Caribbean descent. This article will develop the notion of the outsider, in relation to the UK state, to encompass the *national* outsider, with regard to people living particularly in Scotland, but also Wales and Northern Ireland. Whenever Irish, Scottish, or Welsh people have tried to assert a greater degree of national self-determination, which challenges the UK's constitutional set-up, they have often been treated as 'national outsiders'.

The use of the 'national outsider' analogy to the 'racialised outsider' does not imply an equivalent experience of repression or denial of democratic rights. In a similar manner, the use of the term 'wage slavery' can address a wide range of experiences of exploitation and oppression. It covers the relatively privileged, highly paid professional workers, who are capitalism's 'house slaves', mainly found in imperialist metropolitan centres; as well as

[9] This is an abbreviated version of an article by Allan Armstrong which can be viewed at: http://republicancommunist.org/blog/2015/10/20/britishness-the-uk-state-unionism-and-the-outsider/

the brutally exploited, very low-paid, fixed-term contract workers, who are capitalism's 'field slaves', mainly found in the plantations and mines of the 'Third World'. There has always been a possibility for the 'national outsider' to step in from the cold and take a full part as a privileged Scottish-British, Welsh-British or Ulster-British 'insider', in a way that was much harder for 'racialised outsiders'.

For one of the distinctive features of the UK's unionist constitution is that it has acknowledged the existence of these subordinate hyphenated 'national' identities. 'Britishness' encompasses the Scottish-British, Welsh-British, Irish-British (up to 1922) and Ulster-British (since 1922). It also covers those English, who either see 'Britishness' as form of 'Greater Englishness', or who recognise England's position within a wider UK made up of other nations (and part nation in the case of Northern Ireland – the Irish Six Counties). There are also some who consider themselves just to be British and 'Britishness' still has some pull in the former White British colonies. These British identities are a product of the particular unionist and imperial nature of the UK state. Unionism represents the politics which promotes the 'Britishness' needed to maintain this state.

There is no single form of 'Britishness'. States, even long-lasting ones like the UK, do not have the power to create a single national identity. National identities are always class contested. Thus there are different variants of each hybrid British identity, expressed in support for different parties, and in alternative versions of history and culture. Nevertheless, there is still an over-arching politics, which covers these – unionism – which stretches from the Left unionism upheld by some Marxist-Leninist organisations through to the far right unionism of Loyalism and British neo-fascist organisations.

In its attitudes towards the UK constitutional set-up, unionism has adopted three main forms, of which *conservative unionism* has been the most powerful. Conservative unionists have tried to balance the two poles of the various hybrid-British identities by further extending the existing administrative devolution to the constituent parts of the UK – Scotland, Ireland and later Wales. Such devolution was part of the original unionist state set-up (e.g. the Church of Scotland and the Irish Yeomanry). Conservative unionism has been most associated with the Conservative (and Unionist) Party (and, after the first Irish Home Rule Bill, with the breakaway Liberal Unionist Party); but it has also commanded significant support in both the later Liberal and Labour parties.

However, another significant strand of unionism emerged in the UK in the last quarter of the 19th century – *liberal unionism* (not to be confused with the conservative Liberal Unionists of that period). Liberal unionists have been prepared to concede political devolution, once called Home Rule. This form of unionism was developed first in the Liberal Party, initially in response to the demand for greater Irish self-determination. The Independent Labour Party and sections of the Labour Party later took this up.

Sometimes members of the Conservative Party have also supported liberal constitutional reform. In addition, a greater number of Conservatives have also accepted liberal unionist constitutional reforms they once opposed after they have been implemented, such as the devolved parliaments set up in Scotland and Wales after the 1997 Devolution referenda. In the process, this has become the new conservative unionism, to be maintained against further liberal unionist pressure.

The last significant strand of unionism, *reactionary unionism*, has its strongest base in Northern Ireland amongst the Ulster unionists and loyalists (including the Orange Order). Reactionary unionists are also found in UKIP and the Tory Right. They have been prepared to attack and undermine existing liberal constitutional institutions and practices.

Despite these political differences, conservative, liberal and reactionary unionists have all supported the continuation of Westminster supremacy, the Crown and Empire. The greater the acceptance of the British pole of the hybrid Scottish-British, Welsh-British, Irish-British and later Ulster-British backgrounds, the more willingly have these people taken part in the maintenance of the British Empire. They could do this in the armed forces and colonial administration, or as businessmen, missionaries and settlers. So deeply has the imperial notion of 'Britishness' penetrated, however, that even amongst many nationalists wishing to weaken their links with the existing UK state, imperial attitudes have remained. Hence the Irish Parliamentary Party's support for the First World War; early Sinn Fein leader, Arthur Griffith's support for a Dual Monarchy Empire (British and Irish); and today the SNP's official support for Scottish regiments and the British High Command. Another revealing indication of the strength of unionism has been the absence of any major political force advocating the abolition of the Union and the creation of a unitary Britain.

One consequence of any sharing of 'outsider' status, in relation to the UK and the current dominant idea of 'Britishness', is that this does not automatically lead to greater solidarity with others, such as Virdee's 'racial-ised outsiders'. There is a hierarchy with regard to the 'insider'/'outsider' sta-tus and to 'Britishness'. Thus, whilst those sharing 'outsider' status may more easily be drawn into struggle than those who uphold official state-promoted 'Britishness', there still remains a considerable job to be done to ensure that wider political solidarity amongst 'outsiders' actually occurs.

Clashing Unionisms in the Scottish Labour Party

From the end of the nineteenth century, the Independent Labour Party (ILP) emerged as a significant political force in Scotland. The ILP took over the liberal unionist mantle from the old declining Liberal Party and was strongly identified with Scottish Home Rule. The ILP became a key component of the Labour Party, particularly in Scotland. Scottish Home Rule remained a party policy, even if increasingly a paper one, in the inter-war period, but imme-diately before, during and after the Second World War, a political struggle took place within the Labour Movement, and between the Labour Party and the SNP, over whether or not meaningful Scottish self-determination should be enacted once the war was over.

The incoming post-war Labour government failed to democratise the existing Scottish-British relationship within the UK by introducing Home Rule. This was despite Labour formally having this as a longstanding policy. Furthermore, by the end of the war, the SNP was in a relatively strong posi-tion and was exerting considerable political pressure. This was highlighted by their May 1945 Westminster by-election victory. Robert McIntyre won what had previously been a Labour held seat in Motherwell. The SNP shared some economic and social policies with Labour. Therefore, it might have been expected that Attlee's Labour government could have been pressured into implementing Scottish Home Rule.

Yet, in the face of all this, the post-war Labour governments still relent-lessly pursued a conservative unionist constitutional strategy and faced down the pressures to introduce Scottish Home Rule. Labour's war-time role in coalition with Churchill's Conservatives probably contributed much to the shift from liberal to conservative unionism. Their managerialist desire to utilise a centralised UK state machine, the better to implement their post-war social democratic reforms, was another factor, The CPGB, then in its strongest position, also encouraged this slippage way from the earlier liberal unionism found for Scotland, which it had also supported in the 1930s. The centralised economic planning found in the USSR, another unionist state, inspired them.

Tom Johnston expressed this shift to conservative unionism most clearly. He had been a co-owner of the ILP's *Forward*, and a one-time supporter of Scottish Home Rule. However, he later became Churchill's appointed Scottish Secretary in the war-time coalition and, under Attlee's Labour administration, the post-war chairman of the North of Scotland Hydro-Electricity Board. He abandoned his earlier support for Scottish Home Rule. Nevertheless, successive Labour governments' retreats over Scottish Home Rule were still strongly contested. Despite the collapse of the SNP vote in the 1945 General Election, following the end of the war-time political truce between the Conservatives, Labour and Liberals, John MacCormick's Scottish Covenant Movement, campaigning for Scottish Home Rule, gained widespread support. This included local Labour Party and trade union branches in Scotland.

Why were the post-war Labour governments successful in their dismissive response to this Scottish Home Rule challenge? How was Labour able to obstruct any further popular widening of the notion of 'Britishness' to encompass greater national self-determination for those holding hybrid British identities? The answer lies in 'The Spirit of 45'. This provided very real benefits for the white male working class throughout the UK and by extension to their families. Labour's economic and social reforms, and the strong post-war economic recovery, trumped the political demand for Home Rule. There can be little doubt that the post-war Labour government's establishment of the Welfare State (building on the war-time coalition government's precedents) did provide the notion of 'Britishness' with its widest and most popular basis of support up to that time. The National Health Service was the 'jewel in the crown' of the UK's new social monarchist and imperial order. Here the word 'National' was designed to give the notion of 'Britishness' a popular dimension missing in its traditional associations with the Empire, Crown and Westminster.

Thus, the earlier economic and social underpinning of Scottish working class support for Home Rule no longer appeared so necessary. The new North of Scotland Hydro-Electric Board (operating in the Highlands and Islands), the all-Britain nationalised industries, such as coal, rail transport (with its administratively devolved Scottish 'region') and the all-UK Welfare

State, together provided secure jobs and social security 'from the cradle to the grave'. The post-war economic boom did the rest.

Labour's failure to democratise 'Britishness' in the 1960s and '70s

Just as economic and social reforms marginalised democratic political challenges in Scotland after 1945; so setbacks and failures in these fields led to the re-emergence of the Scottish democratic issue from the late 1960s. Furthermore, from then on, the inadequate political response of Labour led to a greater questioning of the conservative unionist UK status quo. This resulted in a falling off in support for the existing notions of 'Britishness', accentuated by the rapid decline of the British Empire. Support started to rise for the Scottish pole of hybrid Scottish-British identities.

In the face of renewed national democratic challenges, the 1974–9 Labour governments failed to democratise the notion of 'Britishness'. This would have necessitated a rebalancing of the hybrid British identities inherited from Labour's post-war 'Britishness'. It would have meant finding new relationships: between the UK's constituent units, through political devolution or federalism; within the British Labour Party and its subordinate offices in Scotland and Wales; and with the SNP and Plaid Cymru, parties organised solely at the national level.

From the mid-1960s, industrial decline began to undermine the post-war economic revival in much of Scotland. A decimated post-war SNP started to recover once again as a populist nationalist party with Left and Right elements. These divisions were often a reflection of the nature of the local communities in which the party organised. The political glue that held this politically diverse SNP together was combination of a commitment to future Scottish independence and an immediate programme of right social democratic economic and social reforms.

Initially, the 1964–70 Wilson Labour governments tried to counter this challenge through further administrative devolutionary measures, including the setting up of the Highland and Islands Development Board and other regional development agencies. This was very much in the tradition of Labour's immediate post-war conservative unionist approach. However, the growing economic gap between Scotland and, in particular, south east England – the hub of unionist political power, where Westminster, Whitehall and the City of London were located – gave the SNP a political opening to raise the issue of greater Scottish self-determination once more.

After Winnie Ewing's spectacular by-election win for the SNP in Hamilton in 1967, following Gwynfor Evans by-election win for Plaid Cymru in Carmarthen in 1966, the British ruling class began to take notice. In 1969, the Labour government appointed a Royal Commission (under Baron Crowther, then after his death, Lord Kilbrandon) to look into the matter. However, when Labour won back these two seats in the 1970 General Election, the Royal Commission abandoned any sense of urgency. It took until 1973 (and the by then not-so-new Edward Heath-led Conservative government), for it to report. The key feature of this report was that it raised the issue of liberal unionist reform of the UK constitution once again. It proposed political devolution for Scotland and Wales. However, the Conservative government decided to do nothing about it.

The two General Elections of 1974, which Labour won, provided a further jolt. In the March election, the SNP gained 7 seats and Plaid Cymru 2. By the October election the SNP held 11 seats and Plaid Cymru 3. In 1976, the Labour Party in Scotland faced a Scottish Labour Party breakaway led by Jim Sillars. This time the British ruling class and Labour government began to look seriously at those earlier liberal unionist devolution proposals from the Royal Commission. This led to the Scotland and the Wales Acts of 1978, designed to pave the way for devolution referenda in both nations.

However, 1979, the year when the two referenda were held, was at the tail-end of Callaghan's Labour government, which had lost its parliamentary majority. It was floundering in the face of a growing economic crisis. It had become increasingly obvious to the British ruling class that the UK's economic competitiveness in the world was continuing to decline. Through the Social Contract, backed by most trade union leaders, Labour had already undermined the recent working class challenge, although this was not seen as going far enough.

An increasingly confident Right, led by new Tory leader, Margaret Thatcher, was gaining more support from the British ruling class. Labour became split over its own liberal unionist devolution proposals. A revived conservative unionism found its voice in Labour. Key Labour Party individuals joined the Tories in opposing Scottish and Welsh Devolution. Despite winning a majority vote for Scottish Devolution in the 1979 referendum, a Labour rebel-initiated and Tory-supported parliamentary amendment prevented Devolution from being implemented. A broken Labour government was defeated in a vote of 'No confidence'. The issue of the 'national outsider' had not been resolved. It was to become even more strained under Thatcher's Tories.

The Failure of 'New Unionism' after 1997

From the mid-1980s, the British ruling class was once more facing mounting national democratic opposition. This emerged first in Northern Ireland (particularly during the Hunger Strike and its aftermath). Later, largely in protest against the impact of Thatcher's neo-liberal measures, the challenge extended to Scotland, particularly after the Poll Tax revolt, and to Wales. Eventually, in response to this renewed opposition, a 'New Unionist' strategy was developed to hold the UK together. This occurred over two phases, the first in 1994, when John Major's Conservative government wooed Irish Republicans and Ulster Loyalists under the Downing Street Agreement with the promise of a reformed Stormont. However, it took New Labour, elected in 1997, to implement this under the Good Friday Agreement (GFA) and provide more solid grounding for the Peace Process.

The second phase occurred when Tony Blair's government extended the 'New Unionist' constitutional settlement. Unlike the considerably less ambitious post-Thatcher Conservative proposals, aimed only at Northern Ireland, Blair's constitutional proposals covered the whole of the UK. The reinvigorated Peace Process designed for Ireland, north and south, was to be supplemented in Scotland, Wales and Northern Ireland, by 'Devolution-all-round'.

The main purpose behind the 'New Unionist' constitutional reform of the UK has been to create the optimal political conditions needed to maximise corporate profits throughout these islands. The 2008 Financial Crash provided the British ruling class, abetted by Labour (and the Scottish-British) Chancellor of the Exchequer, Alistair Darling, with the opportunity to exert its control over the financial sector of the Irish economy too. Since then there has been a constant tussle between Ireland and the UK, not just by prominent Irish establishment figures, but also by Sinn Fein, Stormont Depute First Minister, Martin McGuinness. The result of this has been to increase UK state political influence and British corporate economic control in the whole of Ireland.

One of the primary aims of the 'New Unionist' devolution deal in Scotland was to see off the SNP. Devolution offered the British ruling class the prospect of co-opting the SNP into the running of the Scottish component of the UK state. The possibilities of co-option have been demonstrated most spectacularly in the transformation of the formerly revolutionary nationalist Sinn Fein into the thoroughly constitutional nationalist coalition partners of the reactionary unionist DUP at Stormont. However, just to ensure that the SNP could not replace Labour (or a wider unionist alliance in Scotland), Holyrood was given a form of proportional representation to ensure it could never become the majority. Yet, against all predictions, and after the initial setbacks for the SNP in the 2003 Holyrood election (in the face of more radical challenges – the SSP, Greens and independents), it was able to form a minority government in 2007, and then a majority government in 2011. This government was pledged to seeking a Scottish Independence Referendum.

Why did Devolution not work out in the way that the British ruling class and the unionist parties had hoped? Back in 1995, then Shadow Labour Scottish Secretary, George Robertson, claimed that 'Devolution would kill Nationalism stone dead'. One of the major reasons why this did not happen was New Labour's undermining of the 'Britishness' once associated with 'The 'Spirit of 45'. By the time New Labour was giving its support to a new constitutional settlement – the Peace Process plus 'Devolution-all-round' – this was no longer linked to the maintenance of any Keynesian economic or social democratic welfare policies that could benefit the working class.

The shared neo-liberalism of Thatcher and Blair, or 'Blatcherism', had replaced the old 'Butskellism', which had underwritten the post-war British Welfare State. Its dismantling became a joint Tory/New Labour concern. Once in government, Blair and Brown went even further than Thatcher and Major, to the extent that Thatcher could say that her greatest political achievement as Prime Minister had been 'Tony Blair and New Labour'! Back in 1945, Labour's commitment to the Welfare State had trumped and marginalised the demand for Scottish Home Rule. But, since 2003, the demand for greater Scottish self-determination has trumped New Labour's liberal unionist constitutional reforms. These have brought very little economic or social benefit to a working class reeling under the impact of neo-liberalism imposed by successive New Labour, Con-Dem and Conservative governments. This is why the Labour initiated Devolution concessions have failed to stall the demand for greater self-determination.

During the Scottish Independence Referendum campaign from 2012–14, Labour 'No' supporters did try to invoke 'The Spirit of 45'. They failed miserably, because it was under New Labour, following the Tories, that this legacy had been undermined. Miliband's One Nation' Labour never really broke free from Blair's 'Tory-Lite ' New Labour. Furthermore, Miliband was more challenged by the neo-Blairites and the even further right, 'UKIP-Lite' Blue Labour, than by any residual Labour Left. This is why an SNP government could, with increasing confidence, claim to be the inheritors of the social democratic legacy of 'the Spirit of 45', and even that very icon of post-war Labour, the National Health Service, but with the 'National' increasingly understood as Scottish rather than British. Thus the SNP has been able to win support from disillusioned Labour supporters, who have seen their party abandon the post-Second World War social monarchist, unionist and imperial Welfare State settlement, which had underpinned their Scottish-British identity.

Despite the tameness of the SNP leadership's 'Independence-Lite' proposals and their probable willingness to have settled for 'Devo-Max' for now, if that option could have been included in the 2014 referendum, the British ruling class were not prepared to concede any constitutional reforms, which the mainstream unionist parties had not initiated themselves. 'Devo-Max' was seen as a second prize that would benefit the SNP more than the unionists.

The 'Devolution-all-round' settlement, put in place under New Labour had been expanded in Scotland and Wales under the Tory/Lib-Dem coalition government from 2010–12. However, the SNP government's independence referendum threat to this existing settlement led the Conservatives, Lib-Dems and 'One Nation' Labour to fall back on conservative unionism to minimise the concessions needed to hold the UK together. They jointly formed the 'Better Together' campaign, also known as 'Project Fear'.

The SNP government, with its constitutional nationalist politics has, however, at the same time as pushing the Scottish pole of a Scottish-British identity to its limits, also promoted a wider and more liberal unionist notion of 'Britishness'. Scots who chose to do so could still retain their Scottish-British identities, but more in the manner of those Swedes, Danes, Norwegians and others who are happy to share a looser Scandinavian identity. Scandinavians cooperate politically, economically and culturally through the Nordic Council. In the SNP scheme of things, a strengthened Council of the Islands (covering England, Scotland, Wales, Ireland and Northern Ireland) could take on a similar role to the Nordic Council.

Why does the SNP leadership promote both Scottish nationalist and British liberal unionist politics simultaneously? The SNP leadership wishes to create a ruling class by prising away leading Scottish capitalists from their unionist politics by prioritising the Scottish pole of their Scottish-British identity. They are trying first to win over the Scottish managerial levels of big business and those from a professional background to create a future Scottish ruling class. Their preferred method of achieving this is by the gradual accretion of powers devolved from Westminster, thereby opening up greater prospects for patronage. They have no desire to challenge fundamentally the anti-democratic UK monarchist, unionist and imperial set-up, nor indeed the wider global corporate order. They remain very wary of extra-parliamentary activities fearing these will alienate those influential people they want to attract.

So far, relatively few major capitalists have been won over; Sir Brian Souter, owner of Stagecoach, a major global transport corporation, being the best known. However, as British capitalism continues to decline, and as the SNP gains greater political leverage over the devolved institutions of the UK state, others could be won over. Gaining control of Scottish local councils and Holyrood is important. This all provides the SNP with access to additional patronage that can be used to lubricate this process. However, in a country like Scotland, with a relatively small indigenous capitalist class, the creation of a wannabe Scottish ruling class needs to be supplemented by winning support from other classes to boost the SNP's political project. The SNP masks its own class politics through the promotion of a form of social democracy designed to appeal to Scottish working class Labour voters. In this it has been very successful, greatly assisted by a Scottish Labour Party mired in careerism, corruption and a belief in its own entitlement.

Clashing nationalisms today and the Scottish Independence Referendum Campaign

Since the 1970s the racialised notion of 'White Britishness' has largely given way to cultural or ethnic notions of 'Britishness' in most parts of the UK. This has been adopted by Conservatives, Labour and Lib-Dems. It underpinned the politics of their 'Better Together' coalition. In contrast, the SNP government has moved beyond the party's own earlier largely ethnic nationalist version of 'Scottishness' to a broader civic nationalist version.

Civic nationalism rejects both racial and ethnic notions of who belongs to a nation, in favour of accepting all those who choose to live in the country, whatever their background. The effect of this was highlighted by the SNP government's promotion, for the Scottish Independence Referendum, of a franchise consisting of Scottish, other UK, Irish Commonwealth and EU residents living in Scotland and extending the vote to those over 16. During the independence campaign, the multi-ethnic nature of the 'Yes' campaign was very evident, ranging from Asians for Independence to English Scots for Yes.

Civic nationalism contains a universal element, through rejecting 'race' and ethnicity and desiring the integration of all who wish to reside permanently in the nation. This is not to deny that as long as current capitalist society, so prone to multifaceted crises, exists, both racist and ethnic nationalism are likely to re-emerge and undermine such civic nationalism. Universalism can only be fully realised in a world where nation-states no longer exist, and where capitalist social relations no longer predominate. Yet, despite the political and social limitations of any civic nation in a world still divided into UN-recognised 'nation'-states, racist and ethnic (or ethno-religious) attempts to subvert such a civic nation need to be opposed – just as the limited democracy found in a parliamentary system needs to be defended against corporate business attempts to undermine it, and military and fascist attempts to overthrow it. Up until now, the SNP leadership's civic nationalist politics have marginalised ethnic nationalist politics in Scotland. However, such politics still exist on the nationalist fringe.

Why is there less of a prospect for the development of a British civic nationalism? The difference arises from the particularly reactionary nature of the UK state, with its constitutional monarchy. This fronts the state's anti-democratic Crown Powers; its unelected House of Lords; its unwritten constitution; its undemocratic first-past-the-post elections; its privileged position for the City of London; its unionist denial of the right of self-determination to its constituent nations; and its continued imperial commitments, either on behalf of the British ruling class. A UK constitution, which does not recognise popular sovereignty, but is based on the anti-democratic notion of the sovereignty of the Crown-in-Parliament, does not recognise guaranteed democratic rights.

The open or tacit acceptance of the existing UK state and British constitutional framework soon undermines the progressive potential for parties which go along with this. Various social democratic parties have hoped to extend 'Britishness' to cover their working classes more fully. However, the more reactionary the local form of the UK state is, the more the 'Law of the Falling Rate of British Progress' takes over, and the sooner any countervailing tendencies towards increased inclusion are stymied and rejected. Thus, whenever the UK state faces politically challenging campaigns for constitutional reform, British-orientated Labour parties have united in defence of the UK and made common cause with the other unionist parties. This 'Law' can be illustrated in the pre-First World War Belfast branch of the ILP under William Walker. Later it was seen in post-partition 'Ulster' in the Northern Ireland Labour Party. Today, we see this 'Law' in operation in Scotland. British Labour, and particularly its Scottish Labour 'branch office', joined the Tories and Lib-Dems in 'Better Together', in order to oppose the exercise of greater Scottish self-determination.

The difference between civic and ethnic notions of nationalism is now highlighted in the Conservative government's proposed franchise for the forthcoming EU referendum. 1.5 million EU residents in the UK are to be excluded. In contrast, the SNP government successfully argued to include EU residents in Scotland in the vote for the Scottish Independence Referendum (as well as 16-18 year-olds), highlighting the more open nature of the 'Scottishness' they envisaged. The Conservative government's exclusion of EU residents (and others too) points not only their more restricted ethnic 'Britishness', but to the likelihood of stepped up attempts to create more 'outsiders'.

The threat of reactionary unionism

Liberal unionism was largely marked by its absence during the Scottish independence referendum. The main battle was between the forces of constitutional nationalism in the SNP and of conservative unionism represented by the Conservatives, Labour and Lib-Dems. However, the forthcoming EU referendum brings reactionary unionism (previously mostly confined to Northern Ireland) to the forefront.

UKIP is central to a wider reactionary alliance. UKIP has extended its politics beyond a right wing English chauvinism, in order to play to the reactionary elements still found in the various forms of hybrid 'Britishness' in Northern Ireland, Wales and Scotland. Orangeism, Protestant supremacy and hostility to state recognition of the minority Celtic languages all figure in this. UKIP has also opposed socially liberal laws on sexuality still supported by David Cameron. The Tory Right and other reactionaries do not like Cameron's social liberalism. Thatcher opposed such measures, so she remains an icon for the reactionary right. UKIP is the only party that covers the full extent of the UK state, since the Ulster Unionists made their final break with the Conservatives in 1985, in protest at the Anglo-Irish Agreement. Whereas conservative unionists largely accept the post-1997 'New Unionist' settlement, reactionary unionists are prepared to attack this from the Right.

Northern Ireland is very important to UKIP's reactionary unionist alliance, because the Ulster unionists have already demonstrated their capacity to undermine the institutions of the 'New Unionist' settlement there. They have often obstructed Stormont, both aided and pressured by the street forces of reactionary and neo-fascist loyalism. UKIP has been courting these forces in Northern Ireland for some time, winning over several former Ulster Unionist and Orange Order members, and making appeals for Traditional Unionist Voice and PUP vote transfers. UKIP now has an MLA at Stormont and 4 local councillors. UKIP is trying to broaden its support in Northern Ireland, amongst unionists and loyalists, by taking the leadership of the anti-EU campaign. They are also standing in the May 2016 Stormont elections to woo reactionary unionists and loyalists with the promise of the reintroduction of policed posts along the border, in the event of a 'No' vote in the in the EU Referendum. The post-Good Friday Agreements are seen as making too many concessions to Irish nationalists and the Irish government, so reactionary unionists want Partition to be reinforced once more.

This all has a bearing on the political situation in Scotland, despite the SNP government having no vision beyond Scotland. Indeed, its own 'Independence-Lite' proposals are based on the continuation of the remainder of the UK – or rUK. The SNP also wants to leave the Crown Powers, the City of London, the British High Command (and NATO) with key roles within its future 'Independence-Lite' Scotland. Just as all these external forces would make their reactionary weight felt in Scotland, so the continued existence of Northern Ireland will continue to have a reactionary impact. The SNP leadership does not acknowledge the nature of the political threat from reactionary unionism, with UKIP acting as an important transmission belt from Northern Ireland to the wider UK. This is because the SNP leadership makes no fundamental critique of the operation of the UK's constitutional order beyond Scotland's own borders, since it does not want to challenge the wider UK state. A future rUK, along with the USA and the EU bureaucracy, are seen as allies. Therefore, when it comes to any non-Westminster, non-Scottish political issue with ramifications in Scotland, the SNP government either ignores or downplays this.

One consequence of this is that the SNP has accepted the unionist-promoted view that Scotland still suffers from some deep-seated historical problem labelled 'sectarianism'. Exaggerated claims are made for the impact of Scotland's religious divisions. Others say that modern 'sectarianism' now focuses, not so much on church allegiances, but more on support for particular football teams. Using the misguided 'sectarianism' model, the SNP government has been trying to clamp down on its 'manifestations' through the Offensive Behaviour Act. This is targeted primarily at football supporters and public houses. Yet, there is nothing religiously sectarian about most of the songs or wall-displays that have led to prosecutions or warnings under this act. What is called 'sectarianism' in Scotland today represents the overspill of a political divide first enforced by the UK state in Ireland as a whole, but then maintained within Northern Ireland after Partition.

From the 16th until the 19th century, religious affiliation certainly had significant economic, social and political ramifications in most European countries, including Scotland and England. Yet many other countries, such as Spain, France and Germany had a far more violent history of religious oppression and conflict than Scotland. So, why is this now largely a thing of the past there while 'sectarianism' continued in Scotland? The immigration to Scotland from both ethno-religious communities in Ireland, during the Industrial Revolution and in the aftermath of the Great Famine, gave 'sectarianism' a new lease of life over here. The consequences of the methods required to maintain British unionist control over Ireland were imported into Scotland. Today there is political divide in Scotland between those who, on the one hand, consider themselves Scottish-British or Scottish-British with 'Ulster' British roots; and those, on the other hand, who consider themselves Scottish with Irish roots, alongside those who see themselves as Scottish (or have other hybrid-Scottish identities) but who now also reject 'Britishness'. The loyalist rampage in Glasgow on 19 September 2014, the day after the Scottish Independence Referendum, made it clear that they also see, not only the Scottish-Irish as 'outsiders', but also those who consider themselves Scottish and not British.

Furthermore, the SNP still retains some British elements within its Scottish nationalism. These tend to vitiate the otherwise more civic nationalism found in the movement for Scottish self-determination. The SNP government's support for Scottish regiments, for example, which have loyally served British imperialism from Culloden to Crossmaglen, and from the Heights of Abraham to Helmand, has led them to deny the nature of the global imperialist order and its current military upholder, NATO.

SNP MPs', MSPs' and councillors' practical acceptance of their role in wielding Westminster's devolved austerity axe (whilst still managing to claim they offer more protection than the unionist parties) could also undermine civic nationalism in the future. Those hardest hit and alienated by austerity could fall prey to the allures of scapegoating – whether it be on a racist or ethnic (e.g. anti-migrant or anti-English), or social basis (e.g. welfare recipients). If reactionary unionism in Northern Ireland, and conservative unionism in England and Wales are currently dominant, then Scotland and 26 Counties Ireland have shown a different politics, which can attract large numbers. The multi-ethnic nature of those mobilised during the Scottish referendum campaign, and the broad franchise that was extended to them, has strengthened the notion of 'Scottishness' based on civic national principles. This is in sharp contrast to the exclusive 'Britishness' being promoted by conservative and reactionary unionists, with very little opposition from liberal unionists, who are in wholesale retreat.

The recent referendum to make gay marriage legal in 26 Counties Ireland has also broadened the notion of 'Irishness', reconnecting with the original Irish republican wish to widen the popular basis of 'Irishness' by uniting Catholic, Protestant and Dissenter, but on a new social basis. The impact of this spilled over the Border, leading to a demonstration of 10,000 in Belfast supporting gay marriage. The Water Charges struggle (so reminiscent of the Anti-Poll Tax struggle) also has the potential to bring about greater unity, provided it is not diverted into purely electoral politics for party advantage in the forthcoming Irish General Election. Such developments could also begin to challenge the very restricted ethno-religious concept of 'Britishness' defended by those reactionary Ulster unionist representatives of the 'Ulster'-British. However, only socialist republicans advocating an 'internationalism from below' approach, encompassing Scotland, England, Wales and the whole of Ireland will be able to make these links.

The SNP and the prospects for a Labour revival in Scotland

The SNP leadership wanted to make a post-2015 Westminster General Election agreement with a Miliband-led Labour government. However, his conservative unionism was so entrenched that he announced he would rather have a Tory government than have to make deals with the SNP to implement his own 'One Nation' Labour manifesto. In bowing to Cameron, Miliband signed Labour's own death warrant. This followed the near fatal damage Labour experienced in Scotland, when they acted as Cameron's principal 'Better Together' agent. It was the SNP landslide victory in the May 2015 Westminster General Election, on the basis of more traditional social democratic and anti-austerity politics, which paved the way, by example, for Jeremy Corbyn to win the Labour leadership election in September. This is barely acknowledged by those on the Labour Left wishing to divert attention from the wider political significance of Scotland's 'democratic revolution' for the UK.

The SNP leadership hoped that the new Corbyn-led Labour Party would be different from that of Miliband, especially in regard to any extension of Devolution. However, Corbyn has failed to acknowledge that he would back a further referendum, if the SNP won the 2016 Holyrood election with that demand in its manifesto. As with CPGB, faced with the demand for Scottish Home Rule after World War Two, and the SWP faced with the demand for Devolution in the late 1970s, so there are still Left unionists who believe that the UK set-up underwrites British working class unity. In this spirit they proffer their advice to Corbyn.

Corbyn faces a significant neo-Blairite opposition. He will find great difficulty commanding the support of many of his party's MPs or of the party machine for his own neo-Keynesian and social democratic proposals. Len McCluskey (UNITE) and Sir Paul Kenny (GMB) are plotting behind the scenes to undermine these, as their shared support for Trident renewal highlighted. McCluskey's left posturing and occasional nods towards Corbyn are designed to manoeuvre himself into a better position to achieve his long-standing aim to restore the trade union bureaucracy's privileged role within the Labour Party. He would ditch Corbyn overnight, if any plausible candidate emerged, prepared to cut a deal with him. The likelihood of Corbyn leading a substantial Labour revival in Scotland remains slim. On issues like Trident, the SNP leadership can still deliver the votes of MPs on the party's right wing, something Corbyn is unlikely to be able to achieve with Labour.

Taking the 'democratic revolution' forward

As a result of the 2012-4 'Yes' campaign, Scotland entered the first phase of a 'democratic revolution'. 97 per cent registered to vote, whilst 85 per cent actually voted. Vibrant and well-attended meetings and a new independent social media countered the unionists' 'Better Together' campaign and the mainstream media offensive. Although the unionists technically won the 18 September referendum, they are very aware that things went far beyond what they had originally anticipated, when they conceded a referendum to see off the prospect of Scottish independence for a generation. This is why so much effort is being put into attempts to roll back this 'democratic revolution' and to contain it within the conservative and reactionary institutions of the UK state, particularly Westminster. First came Lord Smith's enquiry to sideline the empty federalist promises made by Gordon Brown and others. Then came Cameron's official government response, which was to dilute even Lord Smith's limited proposals. This was coupled to his attempt to win over UKIP support in England by falling back on English chauvinism; and to create two tiers of MPs at Westminster, under the guise of 'English Votes for English Laws'. As well as the Ulster unionists, Michael Forsyth, once Thatcher's leading advocate in Scotland, has been horrified at this attempt to drastically curtail a shared 'Britishness'.

Since the SNP's electoral triumph in the May 2015 Westminster General Election, there has been a combined unionist focus on 'house training' their MPs. The British ruling class is particularly adept at taming political opponents. This can be seen in the domestication of the once revolutionary nationalist Sinn Fein. It has become a thoroughly constitutional nationalist and is now part of the machinery needed to maintain the post GFA neo-partitionist order in Northern Ireland.

Unlike Sinn Fein, the SNP has always been a constitutional nationalist party, with a greater resemblance to the pre-First World War, Irish Independence Party (IIP). However, the SNP today, like the IPP back then, have accepted their mandate as coming from being elected national representatives at a Westminster based on the sovereignty of the Crown-in-Parliament, and not by upholding the principle of the sovereignty of the people. At the end of the day, there is a limit to what can be done by 56, 55, 54 or however many MPs in Westminster, just as there was for the 80+ IIP MPs before the First World War. Westminster is one of the most powerful institutions for subverting any radicalism, as the fates of many one-time Labour firebrands have shown.

Meanwhile, beyond Westminster and Holyrood, the Scottish Independence Referendum Campaign led to the large-scale involvement of people not under the control of the official 'Yes' campaign. This included the Radical Independence Campaign (RIC). RIC was able to organise conferences of 800 (2012), 1100 (2013) and 3000 (2014) in Glasgow. It initiated the very successful voter registration drive in housing schemes long abandoned by a complacent Labour Party. The radical threat represented by such independent political organisation has produced the other wing of the attempt to roll back Scotland's 'democratic revolution'. Many in the SNP leadership are not at all happy with the continued existence of 'Yes' forces beyond the party's control, and even more dangerously, with the ability to mobilise people for actions which threaten their desire to create a wannabe Scottish ruling class ready to cut its own deals in the global corporate order.

The SNP leadership has tried to hoover up all the 'Yes' voters in a massive recruitment drive. They are meant to act as cheerleaders for their new MPs, and their anticipated bigger numbers of MSPs after the May 2016 Holyrood election, and councillors after the 2017 local elections. As with the unionists, the SNP focus is primarily on the UK state's institutions, all of which operate under the sovereignty of the Crown-in-Parliament. Given the privileged role the City of London enjoys under this set-up, this makes it even more difficult for the SNP to challenge austerity in practice as opposed to rhetoric.

Another distinctive feature of the wider 'Yes' campaign was its reliance on the social media, with several influential websites and blogs. Amongst those taking part, was a relatively small number of 'Cybernats' who specialised in online abuse and threats to 'No' supporters. Unionist propaganda directed against the 'Cybernats', downplayed the continued threats emanating from 'Project Fear', as well as the 'Cyberloyalists' also resorting to abusive tactics online. However, in the aftermath of 'defeat' in the Scottish independence referendum, many 'Cybernats' have turned their fire on anyone, including 'Yes' voters, who dare to criticise the SNP. What is also becoming more evident is that, in their retreat into a nationalist 'laager' (as in the Scottish Independence Campaign – or the 45 per cent), some also want to move from the civic Scottish nationalism, which underpinned the 'Yes' campaign, to a more ethnic and anti-English Scottish nationalism. This can also be seen in some of the actions and statements coming from Scottish Resistance. Tommy Sheridan and his supporters in Solidarity are now looking for support in these quarters. Sheridan's political drift from Left nationalist (following his earlier Left unionist phase in Militant) to populist nationalist has been one of the dire consequences of the split in the Left in Scotland since 2006, in the aftermath of 'Tommygate'.

In contrast, RISE – Scotland's Left Alliance represents an attempt to resurrect a Left, building on Scotland's 'democratic revolution' and Scottish internationalism. RISE, like the SSP before it, is itself an alliance of Left nationalists and socialist republican internationalists. To be successful, RISE will have to challenge populist nationalism, in order to ensure that people do not turn in this political direction, once the SNP leadership falters. RISE will also have to take on board the republican principle of acknowledging the sovereignty of the people, a principle first adopted by RIC in May 2014, to develop a political strategy that does not end up tail-ending the SNP. It is also vital that RISE has a political perspective, which includes England, Wales and Ireland, as well as the EU. RIC provided the precedent by bringing in speakers from England, Wales and Ireland (including Bernadette McAliskey), as well as from Greece, Spain, Catalunya, Euskadi and Quebec. RIC sent speakers to England, Wales, Ireland (north and south), Catalunya and Greece. It organised a series of demonstrations to support the Greek people against the EU 'coup' directed at the elected Greek government. This internationalist approach needs to be further developed.

UKIP has clearly understood the need to address the current political crisis engulfing the UK state at an all-UK level. Their reactionary British 'internationalism from above' is designed to maintain the unity of the constituent units of the UK state – England, Scotland, Wales and Northern Ireland – through the defence of all its most reactionary features protected under the Crown Powers. The forthcoming EU referendum provides UKIP with another basis for moving politics to the Right and promoting their version of 'Britishness'. This involves the UK's removal from the EU and the creation of new 'ethnicised outsiders', anticipated in Cameron's limited franchise for this referendum.

The best way to counter all forms of unionism, and challenge the constitutional nationalist and neo-liberal SNP government, is to promote the break-up of the UK state and its alliance with US imperialism. Such an approach can also oppose that fount of reaction, the current Northern Ireland set-up, from which reactionary unionists currently draw much of their sustenance. Similarly, we need to unite with those in the EU challenging the Troika; those advocating national self-determination on a civic national basis in Spain and elsewhere; and those migrant workers currently under attack. In the process, 'Britishness' and the category of the 'outsider' need to be brought to an end. Only the break-up of Britain will open up the road to a genuine internationalism and the socialist transformation of society.

Part II:

Anti-Irish Racism and Sectarianism

CHAPTER 3

The Irish Experience in Historical Perspective

Jim Slaven

Introduction

THIS CHAPTER WILL offer a historical perspective on the process of racialisation which impacted on the Irish community in Scotland. Traditional accounts of the Irish experience have tended to focus on the role of the Catholic Church in the assimilation process or involved localised studies of the community in specific geographical locations. Less has been written on the role Irish immigration (and their place as a racialized Other) played on the development of notions of Scottishness (and Britishness). I will also explore the key role Scots played in the development and promotion of racialism during a vital period of class and state formation.

Wha's like us?

Discussing the Irish experience in Scotland in a historical perspective is a strangely challenging endeavour. Not because there is not a wealth of historical material to be researched or empirical evidence to be analysed. It is challenging because the Scotland it reveals does not easily correspond with the way Scottish people view their history, particularly in relation to race, racism, imperialism, state and class formation and nationalism (both Scottish and British). The political decline of unionism in Scotland and a body politic dominated by Scottish nationalism has reinforced Scotland's view of itself and its history as distinct from England.

The focus on Scottish difference from England and Englishness also underpins much of the indigenous historiography (Devine, 2012). Indeed much coverage of racism in Scotland has highlighted Scotland's perceived good record in this area (Fraser, 2015). This is particularly the case when you only consider the issue of racism as being relevant to immigrants from 'New Commonwealth' countries. Of course the vast majority of these immigrants settled not in Scotland, but in England. It is also true that the vast majority of these immigrants were black. Attempts to limit discussion of racism to either this timeframe or the black/ white paradigm only encourages a 'no problem here' mentality in Scotland (Donald, 1995).

At the outset we should be clear that 'race' is a social construct. That is not, of course, to deny the obvious fact that migrants have travelled to Scotland over the centuries. Neither is it to deny that many of them have suffered racial discrimination, from individuals and institutions. It is merely to be clear that the ideology of racism does not operate in a vacuum. The place of racialised migrant labour in relation to (and reproduction of) the capitalist means of production should be front and centre. It is also to highlight the way racism interacts with other economic and political ideologies. In the case of the Irish in Scotland, for instance, their economic and political exclusion was justified on the basis of 'race' (Miles, 1982).

The New Labour project of 'devolution all round' has served to reinforce the view of a resurgent 'Celtic' nationalism dragging power away from the imperial centre. This process of state reconfiguration has provided the policy backdrop which has led to a reimagining of Scotland's place in the Union along Scottish nationalist lines. This narrative places England in the role of Scotland's historic Other. However it was not always thus.

Double-barrel racism

By the beginning of the 19th century significant numbers of immigrants from Ireland were arriving in Britain. In Scotland, like elsewhere, these immigrants came mainly from rural Ireland and were making their way to ever expanding urban centres. The industrial revolution in lowland Scotland brought with it a huge demand for low cost labour to build the canals, railways and roads, and work in the factories and mines. The Irish who arrived in Britain were arriving into host communities with pre-existing ideas of the Irish and Irishness. These ideas were based around specific discourses about racialism, national identity and state formation based not only on centuries of British occupation of Ireland but also underpinned by cultural and scientific racism (Hickman, 1995)

Etienne Balibar has argued that in France the 'Arab-Islamic' community tend to suffer a double hit of discrimination (Balibar, 1991). As they are seen in a colonial racist context to be inferior while at the same time their religion marks them out for cultural racism and cast as alien. A similar process has impacted on the experience of the Irish in Scotland (Hickman, 1995). That both racism framing the Irish as inferior, in the context of Britain's long colonial relationship with Ireland, and racism framing the Irish (Catholic) as alien from the British/Scottish (Protestant) occurred. This overdetermination of exclusion based on religion combined with an exclusion based on race posited the Catholic Irish as a racialised Other in Scotland (Virdee, 2014).

There are differences and connectedness between these two forms of racism and difficulties in identifying the precise boundaries between each as they often overlap and coexist (Silverman, 1993). Despite this the distinction is worth preserving as historically anti-Irish racism has applied both of these forms of racism, viewing the Irish (in the context of colonial rule) as inferior and also through racialised religion as alien. It allows us to place the experience of the Irish in Scotland within the historical context of a particular strain of Scottish (and British) thought. Furthermore this historical approach offers an insight into the development of Scottish (and British) cross class national identity which places the Catholic Irish as the Other during the process of (British) state formation.

In a Scottish context this is significant as the role of the Other in the formation of Scottish national identity had been occupied by the English until the 18th century. The Scottish embrace of Protestantism, political union, imperialism, British state formation and then British national identity (albeit with a Scottish nationality within it) had profound implications for not only Irish immigrants but for Scotland and the story Scotland tells itself in the context of a resurgent nationalism. Although out with the scope of this chapter the role of state strategies of developing cross-class identification with the nation state in the 19th century and the role of the Catholic Church in 'incorporating and denationalising' the Irish community are also crucial (Hickman, 1995).

Carlyle's boat

It should also be acknowledged that during the 19th century the development of British nationalism was paralleled by the development of a particular sort of Irish nationalism (Nelson, 2012). To understand one it is essential to understand the other. Leading Scottish intellectual and political commentator Thomas Carlyle, writing in the context of the national crisis in 1839, was able to claim 'Ireland, now for the first time, in such strange circuitous way, does find itself embarked in the same boat with England, to sail together, or to sink together' (Carlyle, 1899). The boat serves as an allegorical representation of the union between Britain and Ireland, and Carlyle gives us a useful insight into the dialectical relationship between the two islands and the two emerging nationalisms (Martin, 2012). The way Scotland (and the British state) saw itself during this period was often in relation to Ireland, through their respective nationalisms and through categories of race, nation and class.

Those Irish arriving in Scotland were arriving in a country which had changed dramatically over the previous centuries. Each significant change, religious, political and cultural, had widened the gulf between indigenous Scots and the arriving Irish. The Reformation, the act of union and the industrial revolution had each driven Scotland closer to the imperial centre and further from an understanding of the Ireland the immigrants were leaving. These factors meant the Irish arriving in central Scotland were perhaps geographically only crossing a short stretch of water but by every other standard it was another world.

Following the Reformation, Scotland had embraced their new reformed faith enthusiastically. Indeed the Reformation itself was a largely peaceful affair in Scotland compared to the Thirty Years War fought out in central Europe between 1618 and 1648. In Scotland, with the exception of St John Ogilvie, no priests were executed and no large scale civil conflict resulted (Cooney, 1982). Catholics 'simply melted away' (Gallagher, 2013) with the exception of communities in the north east and Gaelic speaking West Highlands. Between 1680 and 1800 the Catholic population of Scotland fell from 50,000 to 30,000 (Gallagher, 2013).

In 1707 Scotland entered into a political union with England, then became one of the first countries to industrialise. All of this occurred at a time when, in terms of religion, Ireland remained loyal to Rome while occupied by Britain and economically destitute. Not only was Ireland not reconciled to its political and economic situation, at various periods it was in open rebellion. At least in part as a legislative response to this rebellion and perceived 'Irish receptivity to French ideas', in 1800 Ireland was brought directly under the control of Britain with the Act of Union (Foster, 1988).

While, following Scotland's political union in 1707, the Scots had been able to retain their own legal, educational and religious institutions; Ireland was to be controlled almost totally by London. So while the political union, and a degree of autonomy through national institutions, had seen Scotland move closer to England and the British imperial project the 1800 Union with Ireland had the opposite effect.

The 1800 Act of Union on one level merely institutionalised the de facto control of Ireland by Britain but it also reorganised the British state, absorbing the Irish, with all their difference, directly into the British state. In other words it absorbed a colony directly into the imperial nation. With this came a new name, 'The United Kingdom of Great Britain and Ireland'. As has been argued by Martin even the new name itself is a pointer to problems to come. The 'United Kingdom' signifies the unity between the nations of Scotland, England and Wales while Ireland follows a conjunction. This reading of even the state's name highlights the contradictory position of the Irish. Incorporated into Britain politically and economically but still colonised and considered alien. The Irish were constructed as religiously, culturally and racially Other (Martin, 2012).

The 1800 Act of Union made Britain's direct control over Ireland, economically, politically and in terms of suppressing rebellion, easier. However the corollary of that was that any attempt to confine Irish difference and revolutionary potential to the island of Ireland was impossible (Martin, 2012). This led to the Irish been seen as a threat to 'national security' in what has been describes as 'the first war on terror' (Martin, 2012). The process of problematising (and racialising) the Irish serves a key role in cementing the modern state's legitimacy over the use of force. Particularly in the context of political violence in what Foucault describes as the 'pact of security' (Foucault, 2007). This debate about 'security' and 'terror' in part underpinned the development of a British (state) ideology which incorporated Scotland, England and Wales in a 'one nation' narrative able to reproduce 'one people' (Althusser, 2014). The implications on this focus on Irish 'terror' and security were as relevant in Scotland as elsewhere in the state (Cathain, 2007).

These changes led the British political and intellectual elites to think through the implications of these changes. Traditional markers of difference between Britain and Ireland such as religion, nation and race had to be rethought in the context of Irish absorption into the newly expanded imperial nation. How was this incorporation of the Irish to work? Was assimilation possible/desirable? How could Irish difference be tolerated within the newly constituted British nation? And what to do about Irish anti-colonialism now absorbed into the colonial centre? These are the questions which dominated political discourse in 19th century Britain.

Scotland and the alchemy of race

As Kidd points out 'racialism was an omnipresent factor in 19th century intellectual life' and this meant that 'race had a spectacularly different range of meanings for Scots of the Victorian era compared to that held by their descendants in the second half of the 20th century' (Kidd, 2006). These debates about race and racialism, inclusion and exclusion into the state played an important role in how the Scots imagined and re-imaged themselves in the context of a developing and racialising British (and Scottish) nationalism. These debates about racialism did not just affect Scotland; Scotland affected those debates. Leading Scottish scientists and intellectuals were central to the advancement of what Appiah describes as a system of knowledge, particularly scientific knowledge, that 'divide human beings into a small number of groups, called 'races', in such a way that all members of these races shared certain fundamental, biological heritable, moral and intellectual characteristics that they do not share with members of any other race' (Appiah, 1995).

While it is important to point out that, like race itself, 'whiteness' is a social construct. Also, like Scots, the Irish in 19th century did not describe themselves as white it is also important to see this process of racial categorisation as being about more than colour. Recognising what Jacobson describes as 'the alchemy of race', the strange process where apparently white people were denied their whiteness by those defining it as Protestant, Saxon and British. This process led to a system of racial classification where 'one might be both white and racially distinct from other whites' (Jacobson, 1998). In 19th century Scotland these debates about racial categorisations took on added importance as Scotland enthusiastically embraced the idea of Britain. Racialism, along with shared Protestantism, the economic gains of industrialisation and empire, and the inclusion of Scotland into a broader Britain wide party political system at Westminster, played a significant role in cementing Scotland's place in Britain. The idea of Scotland being racially other than Celts was a powerful part of the process (Kidd, 2003). Scotland was to be British (albeit with Scottish nationality within it) and Scotland was to be Protestant and Teutonic (sometimes Saxon). In other words Scotland was to be like the English and unlike the Irish.

Therefore Scotland's attitude to the Irish race cannot be disentangled from Scotland's view of its own race and Scotland's role in developing racialism. Race and racialism were significant in the way Scotland thought about itself and others. That is not to say these thoughts were fixed or consistent. Race had varied, situational and often contradictory definitions (Mandler, 2000). Ranging from radical polygenists who believed the difference between races was so great that the bible's story of Adam and Eve was insufficient to explain human origin. While many others viewed racialism as an important, and new, scientific discovery they stuck to a monogenist explanation of human origin, for fear of being labelled atheists (Kidd, 2003).

It should be stressed that although race was a common topic in intellectual life in Scotland in the 19th century this was not in itself a response to Irish immigration. Rather Scotland's fascination with racialism can be traced back to the Scottish enlightenment in the 18th century. Henry Home, Lord Kames, in his 1774 work 'Sketches of the History of Man', begins to question the biblical explanation of the origins of humanity (Kidd, 2003). This laid down a challenge that was enthusiastically taken up by those in the mainstream of Scottish intellectual life over the next century and a half.

'Race is everything'

Prominent among these thinkers was Dr Robert Knox, who has been described as the 'founding father of modern racism' (Lorimer, 1996). Knox had been one of Scotland's leading anatomists, with his lectures attracting hundreds of spectators, before he was exposed as being a central figure in the scandal of Irish immigrants, Burke and Hare (Edwards, 2014). Moving to London Knox would go on to write one of the most infamous racialist and anti-Irish (and more broadly anti-Celtic) works of the time, *The Races of Men* (Knox, 1850). The purpose of The Races of Men is clear as Knox states 'the object of this work is to show that the European races, so called, differ from each other as widely as the Negro does from the Bushman; the Caffre from the Hottentot; the Red Indian of America from the Esquimaux; the Esquimaux from the Basque' (Knox, 1850).

For Knox, who argued 'race is everything in human history', it was not enough to show that the Irish were racially inferior in Scotland (Knox, 1850). He claimed race, that is the inferiority of the Irish race, was responsible for Ireland's problems also and he suggested a solution: ethnic cleansing:

> The source of all evil (there) lies in the race, the Celts race in Ireland. The race must be forced from the soil; by fair means, if possible; still they must leave. England's safety requires it. I speak not of the justice of the cause; nations must ever act as Machiavelli advised: look to yourself. The Orange (Order) of Ireland is a Saxon confederation for... clearing the land of all papists and Jacobites; this means Celts (1850: 10).

Knox continues that the Encumbered Estates Act, introduced at Westminster at the end of *An Gorta Mor*, 'aims simply at the quiet and gradual extinction of the Celtic race in Ireland' (Knox, 1850).

Knox was far from alone in his views of the Irish. Thomas Carlyle, one of Britain's leading public intellectuals of the time and Scottish Presbyterian, wrote the following about 'these poor Celtiberian Irish brothers' in *Chartism* (1839):

> Crowds of miserable Irish darken all our towns. The wild Milesian features, looking false ingenuity, restlessness, unreason, misery and mockery, salute you on all highways and byways. The English coachman, as he whirls past, lashes the Milesian with his whip, curses him with his tongue; the Milesian is holding out his hat to beg. He is the sorest evil this country has to strive with. In his rags and laughing savagery, he is there to undertake all work that can be done by mere strength of hand and back; for wages that will purchase him potatoes. He needs only salt for condiment; he lodges to his mind in any pighutch or doghutch, roosts in outhouses; and wears a suit of tatters, the getting off and on of which is said to be a difficult operation, transacted only in festivals and the hightides of the calendar. The Saxon man if he cannot work on these terms, finds no work. He too may be ignorant; but he has not sunk from decent manhood to squalid apehood; he cannot continue there... There abides he, in his squalor and unreason, in his falsity and drunken violence, as the ready-made nucleus of degradation and disorder (1839: 182-183)

'Settled hostility'

The poverty and social conditions the Irish experienced in Scotland were very similar to those experienced by the Irish arriving in England. The experience of Irish immigrants in Scotland could not be said to be worse than that suffered in England. It was just mediated through a different lens. Scotland's reaction to the Irish immigrants was to be heavily influenced by the profound changes which the country had undergone. Scotland had over the previous three hundred years moved from being a Catholic to Protestant country and from an independent nation to one embracing the Union with England. These developments had a very profound effect on the nations psyche and the development of societal structures. In particular the Act of Union recognised the specificity of the Scottish context by allowing for the continuation of its separate legal, education and church systems.

This arrangement, what Nairn describes as a 'peculiarly patrician bargain' between the two ruling classes, effectively left the moral wellbeing and statehood of the nation in the hands of the Kirk (Nairn, 2003). So while Scotland would have no parliament the state of the nation would be annually discussed by the general assembly of the Church of Scotland. Which makes all the more remarkable the Church of Scotland's report entitled 'The Menace of the Irish race to our Scottish Nationality' (Scotland, 1923). The report outlined the perceived damage the Irish were doing to the moral fabric of Scotland. It should be noted that indigenous Scottish Catholics and Irish Protestant immigrants were excluded from criticism.

Ireland had resisted the reformation which Scotland had embraced. Thus the vast majority of the Irish arriving in Scotland at the end of the 18th century were Catholic, many only spoke their native tongue. Of this situation Scottish philosopher David Hume wrote, in Carlylean terms, in his aptly entitled *History of England* that:

> As the rudeness and ignorance of the Irish were extreme, they were sunk below the reach of that curiosity and love of novelty by which every other people in Europe had been seized at the beginning of the century and which had engaged them in innovations and religious disputes, with which they were still violently agitated. The ancient superstitions, the practices and observances of their fathers, mingled and polluted with many wild opinions, still maintained an unshakable empire over them; and the example alone of the

> English was sufficient to render the Reformation odious to the prejudices of the discontented Irish (cited in Lebow, 1973).

The attitude of the majority of Scots to the Irish has been described as one of 'settled hostility' (Handley, 1945). This hostility can be placed in three categories: economic, political and moral. Economically the native worker viewed the Irish as competition whose presence would have the effect of driving down wages, forcing native Scots to move or change job. However as Handley points out:

> It was not the case of Scots abandoning types of unskilled labour to the strangers in favour of the skilled branches, because both the unskilled and skilled forms of labour were new ones, created by the requirements of the industrial revolution that was underway. The Irish in Scotland made that revolution possible and by their labour established jobs for Scottish workers (1945: 74).

Irrespective of the contribution the Irish worker made to economic stimulation and job creation the hostility between the two sets of workers often manifested itself in outright racial conflict. During the 19th century it was not uncommon for a game of 'hunting the Barney' to take place during the Glasgow Fair; 'Barney' being the negative nickname given to Irish immigrants of the time and used in much the same way as Paddy would be today. Essentially any Irishman entering the area of the fair would be captured and subjected to abuse about the way they dressed or spoke and then beaten. The fair would often end with young men arming themselves and heading for the Irish areas around the Saltmarket to break the windows, doors or heads of any unfortunate Irish they could find (Handley, 1945). Such behaviour was by no means confined to Glasgow or west central Scotland and similar racial attacks were documented in Edinburgh, Aberdeen, Perth and Inverness (Handley, 1945).

The geographic spread of such levels of hostility had very little to do with the numbers of Irish residing in the locality. Indeed there is no need for any Irish to be present to ensure the existence of anti-Irish feelings. And while the number of English workers in Wales during this period far out stripped the Irish it was still the Irish who were the main object of hostility (Hickman, 1995). Redford points out that there were many Scottish migrants engaged in agricultural work in the first half of the 19th century however very little is known of them as they didn't receive poor relief or come before the courts in high numbers (Hickman, 1995). The reasons for this may be numerous but the point is that neither Scottish agricultural migrants in England or English works in Wales were segregated in the same way as the Irish. As Hickman (1995: 81) argues:

> Irish labour was distinguished from the rest of the seasonal workforce, not just because the Irish were an essential component of the harvest workforce, but because of the extant notions of 'the Irish'. The conjunction of migrant labour, poverty and Catholicism was recognized as Irish and as 'immigrant'. This explains why the Irish were seen, categorized and subject to the attention of the magistrates and poor law guardians to a greater degree than, for example, Scottish migrants. The latter were poor too, but they were part of a longer established and more acceptable union, and they were Protestants.

In making the case that the Irish were a racialised minority in Scotland we need to move beyond the black/white paradigm of race. The experience of the Irish in Scotland during this period can be contrasted with the experience of Irish immigrants in the United States who it has been argued would (eventually) lay claim to 'whiteness' (Theodore Allen, 1994). Knox, for example, very rarely used the terms black or white. A complex character who claimed to be related to John Knox, he was a firm opponent of organised religion and opponent of monarchy. He was also an outspoken critic of European colonialism, which he described as seizing land 'by fraud and violence' (Knox, 1850).

The views of racialists like Knox in the 19th century are not reducible to the advocacy of the superiority of 'white' over 'black'. As Gibbons (1996) has pointed out, for the imperial British nation the whiteness of the Irish served to complicate not simplify their status:

> ...a native population which happened to be white was an affront to the very idea of the 'white man's burden' and threw into disarray some of the constitutive categories of colonial discourse. The 'otherness' and alien character of Irish experience was all the more disconcerting precisely because it did not lend itself to visible racial divisions.

When exploring the connectedness between racialism and racism in the context of British colonial nationalism we are working on theoretical foundations laid by Balibar who describes the relationship between racial-ism and racism as follows:

> Racism – a true 'total social phenomenon'– inscribed itself in practices (forms of violence, contempt, intolerance, humiliation and exploitation), in discourses and representations which are so many intellectual elaborations of the phantasm of prophylaxis or segregation (the need to purify the social body, to preserve 'one's own' or 'our' identity from all forms of mixing, interbreeding or invasion) and which are articulated around stigmata of otherness (name, skin colour, religious practices). It therefore organises affects (the psychological study of these has concentrated upon describing their obsessive character and also their irrational ambivalence) by conferring upon them a stereotyped form, as regards both their 'objects' and their 'subjects'. It is this combination of practices, discourses, and representations in a network of affective stereotypes which enables us to give an account of the formation of a racist community (or a community of racists, among whom there exist bonds of 'imitation' over a distance) and also of the way in which, as a mirror image, individuals and collectives that are prey to racism (its 'objects') find themselves constrained to see themselves as a community (Balibar 1991: 17-18).

One Scotland?

Accounts of the Irish experience in Scotland traditionally focus on the process of assimilation and the role of the Catholic Church in Scotland in support-ing the Irish community while facilitating this assimilation process (Devine, 1991). Other accounts focus narrowly on the immigrant experience, some-times in specific geographical locations in Scotland (Mitchell, 1998). Less has been written about the role the presence of the Irish in Scotland played in the formation of a cross class British and Scottish national identity and state formation. In other words, on what the story of Irish immigration and the experience of the immigrants and their ancestors tells us about Scot-land and the Scots. This is particularly so in the making of working class in Scotland which was a heterogeneous and multi-racial formation from the industrial revolution onwards (Miles, 1982), and Scotland's specific role in developing discourses on race, religion and nation which placed the Catholic

Irish as a racialised Other in an effort to underpin British state formation and national identity.

Once here their relationship with the Scottish Catholic church was complex and often contradictory. On the one hand they found the solidarity and relative harmony that came from living amongst other Catholics. On the other hand while the Catholic Church was very keen to service this huge influx they were conscious of Scotland's recent history of anti-Catholic societies and riots. Indeed it has been suggested that, in the 1790s, there were 43 anti-Catholic societies in Glasgow and only 39 Catholics (Cooney, 1982). So while Scottish bishops were desperately in need of priests they were also making it clear to the Vatican that they would rather not have Irish priests (Gallagher, 2013). During this period the only Catholic seminary in Scotland was even reluctant to accept children of Irish immigrants into the fold (Gallagher, 2013). This was partly due to the fact that Scottish priests had recently began serving as British army chaplains and many Irish priests defended their flocks right to resist the same body (Cooney, 1982). It was also driven by a fear of outright colonisation by their Irish cousins, the Scottish Catholic church was after all downgraded to missionary status between 1603 and 1878 (Gallagher, 2013).

Many of the Irish arriving in Scotland did so as a consequence of various political rebellions at home, particularly 1798 and 1803 and they maintained their political views in their new home. This met with disapproval from Bishop Scott and the Scottish Catholic hierarchy. Scott himself commented of his congregation 'they are very national in their ideas and sentiments – rather too much so in some cases' (Handley, 1945). This simmering resentment between parishioners and church surfaced publicly in 1823 with the formation of the Glasgow Catholic Association whose aim was to support the work of Daniel O'Connell for Catholic emancipation. Led by an Irish teacher named William McGowan they would, over a period of time, raise various complaints against Scott and others ranging from lack of financial transparency to 'occasional display of anti-Irish feeling very nearly completed the alienation of the intelligent and sensible portion of the congregation' (Handley, 1945). The Association attempts to raise enough money to start a Catholic newspaper and open a library were thwarted when Bishop Scott condemned the group from the pulpit and had McGowan removed from his teaching position (Gallagher, 2013). As Hickman has noted, the Catholic Church played a key role in denationalising the Irish (Hickman,

1995). In Scotland this has lent added weight to the 'Scottish Catholic' construct which in turn plays into the state narrative of 'One Scotland'.

It is clear that by the middle of the 19th century Scotland was in the midst of dramatic urban expansion. As industrialisation gathered pace, people flocked to the urban centres searching for work and an escape from rural poverty. However as these fledgling cities and towns expanded the infrastructure required was absent. Inadequate housing and water supply allied with practically non-existent sanitation resulted in horrendous living conditions. In each of these over populated centres could be found Irish workers and their families. Almost always occupying the lowest paid jobs and living in the very worse conditions.

No event dominates Irish history more than *An Gorta Mor* (or The Great Hunger) beginning in 1845. In 2015 the Scottish Government's Education Scotland website was still claiming that 'before (*An Gorta Mor*) emigration from Ireland could best be described as a trickle. After the famine it became a flood'. In fact this period marked for Irish immigration to Scotland what Handley describes as 'both the end and the beginning of an epoch' (Handley, 1945), after rising steadily for half a century the number of Irish immigrants to Scotland would fall swiftly thereafter.

By the middle of the 19th century the structural requirement for Irish migrant labour was broadly accepted and the state began to focus on the settlement of the Irish workers. This was particularly the case in Scotland where Irish labour played a central role in the workforce compared to many other parts of Britain. The State's response to the issue of settlement was to attempt to address the perceived problems of Irish settlement in Scotland. As Swift has argued the Irish in Victorian society were:

> Outcast from British capitalism as the poorest of the poor, from mainstream British politics as separatist nationalists and republicans, from the 'Anglo-Saxon' race as 'Celts', and as Catholics from the dominant forms of British Protestantism, the Irish were presented as the outsiders of contemporary society on the basis of class, nationality, race, and religion, a people set apart, rejected and despised (Swift 2001).

This occurred at a time when social relations were in a state of flux and capitalism was striving to mould the working class into a viable labour force respectful of law and order and under one national banner. It is in the context of the State response to the Irish that we must view individual responses. As Balibar has pointed out, racist behaviour is never just 'a relationship to the Other' rather it is relations mediated through the State and 'lived' (Balibar and Wallerstein 1991).

Conclusion

When you consider the continuing size and profile of the Orange Order in central Scotland or the failure of the state to deal with the widespread singing of songs at football and within communities whose lyrics include the expressed desire to be 'Up to our knees in Fenian blood' or 'The famine's over, why don't you go home', indicates not just a problem with racism but a historically and politically specific racism aimed at the Irish in Scotland (MacMillan, 2011). When the Irish Consulate in Scotland raised concerns over 'The Famine Song' with the SNP Government, the response was telling. 'The Scottish Government is totally committed to combating sectarianism and bigotry' (Forsyth, 2008). In other words this was a problem of intra-Christian rivalry and not of racism. This displays a worrying misunderstanding of racism and Scotland's history.

As we have seen Irish participation in Scottish society was not without its challenges and obstacles, taking place as it did at a time when Scottish and British national identities were being constructed and class and state formations were coming to the fore. The key lesson of the Irish experience in Scotland is not that it was exceptional, because it was not, or to feed some modern craving for victimhood. Rather the key lesson is that anti-racism in Scotland cannot focus exclusively on state racism or racism associated with British nationalism. The starting point for Scottish anti-racism must be an acknowledgement of the indigenous ideology of racism developed here and enthusiastically pursued against Irish migrant labour in Scotland.

CHAPTER 4

The Contemporary Position of Irish Catholics in Scotland

Maureen McBride

Introduction

'WE DON'T HAVE ROOM FOR RACISM, we're too busy with bigotry!' This quote from *Fleshmarket Close* (2004) a popular crime novel by Scottish writer Ian Rankin, echoes the popular, academic, and political consensus at least until relatively recently: while Scotland might have a problem with sectarianism (in this case, intra-Christian sectarianism), racism was 'England's issue'. Of the many myths embedded in much of the popular discourse on Scotland, the myth of an egalitarian society – one that is more inclusive, more welcoming of migrants and with more progressive attitudes towards minorities when compared to England – is one of the most enduring and powerful. Yet in relation to Scotland, sectarianism and racism are not two separate phenomena. Indeed, Finn (1990) argues that sectarianism is the preferred term because it perpetuates the 'national myth' that Scotland is a country free from racism. This can be partly explained by the fact that Scotland's largest ethnic minority – Irish Catholics – have been largely absent in most sociological accounts of race and ethnicity. Despite historically representing Britain's biggest migrant group and a key source of labour, the Irish diaspora has been described as an 'invisible ethnic minority'; which in turn has helped to sustain the myth of cultural homogeneity in Britain prior to 1950s immigration (Mac an Ghaill, 2001: 180-190).

In this chapter I will highlight how claims of difference and of cultural exclusion are frequently dismissed by political and media commentators.

With some exceptions (cf. Solomos, 2003, Mac an Ghaill, 2001), the Irish also tend to be neglected in academic work on race and racism in Britain. The Irish experience illustrates that 'race' is not always associated with skin colour, yet Hickman (1998: 288) suggests that the 'official discourse of the state and of the 'race relations' industry does not acknowledge that Irish people in contemporary Britain might have experiences or be subject to practices which are based on ethnic differentiation or racist discrimination'. For Hickman, this is the result of the 'forced inclusion' (ibid: 30) of the Irish within the national collectivity. Regardless of how these processes of inclusion are viewed, it is reasonable to suggest that if the Irish are not included in ethnic minority socio-economic indicators, for example, residual prejudice or discrimination might be overlooked. The Irish Catholic community's experience of prejudice and discrimination in Scotland specifically has not been considered by academics to a great extent, despite Scotland being a major centre for Irish immigration. Indeed, the key sociological literature on Scottish society, such as McCrone (2001) *Understanding Scotland*, only briefly touches on issues involving Irish immigration and the subsequent integration into Scottish society. Some sociologists have conducted research on and written about Irish Catholics in the growing literature on sectarianism, however the most prominent of these (Rosie, 2004; Rosie 2015; Bruce et al, 2005; Paterson, 2000b; Walker, 2001) often reduce the debate to a narrower focus on demographic changes, such as rates of intermarriage or educational and employment indicators. These are of course important, but fail to capture more complex processes of social and cultural inclusion or exclusion, something partially addressed by Finn et al (2008) and Bradley (1995, 2000).

The aims of this chapter are two-fold. Firstly, I intend to offer the beginnings of an historical-sociological explanation of sectarianism, the term most frequently used to analyse the position and experiences of Irish Catholics in Scotland and one which elevates the religious aspect of discrimination over prejudice based on race and ethnicity. Secondly, I aim to critically explore claims of anti-Irish racism in contemporary Scotland. The fact that in the 19th century the Irish were thought of as a 'race apart' is frequently neglected by historians and sociologists alike, so the 'transition' of Irish Catholics from a racialised group to a subset of Christianity is under-explored. Moreover, the dominant sociological accounts in contemporary Scotland tend to frame the debate as 'Protestant-Catholic relations' in a way which negates power relations, despite the fact that the latter was historically the oppressed group, a point which will be illustrated in this chapter. It is contended that this is the result of insufficient attention to historical context in most analyses. Abrams (1982: 2) argues that historical sociology is 'not some special kind of sociology; rather it is the essence of the discipline'. In the firm belief that history matters to understanding the present, this chapter will contribute to debates on the question of anti-Irish racism in contemporary Scotland by placing these in a historical context which pays appropriate attention to issues of race, ethnicity, nationalism, colonialism, and social class. In doing so, I will draw on extracts from my PhD fieldwork, in which participants discuss experiences and perceptions of anti-Irishness. Historical context is crucial if we wish to engage properly with claims that anti-Irishness in Scotland is a problem that has not gone away.

Key caveats and theoretical concerns

Before beginning I need to make some important points of clarification. Firstly, it is a necessary limitation of this chapter that it focuses solely on Irish Catholics, thereby excluding Irish Protestants (around 25 per cent of Irish immigrants to Scotland) and Catholic migrants from countries such as Poland, Lithuania and Italy. Moreover, prior to large-scale arrival of the Irish, Scotland had a small Catholic population and a strong anti-Catholic narrative ran throughout the 18th century (Gallagher, 1987). It is acknowledged that the conflation of Irish and Catholic (virtually interchangeable from the mid-19th century onwards) is problematic. Despite the fact that the vast majority of Catholics in Scotland now are of Irish descent (Devine, 2008), in contemporary Scotland, most Catholics from Irish backgrounds simply consider themselves Scottish. According to the 2001 Scottish Social Attitudes Survey, just 8 per cent of Catholics opted to describe themselves as Irish. Catholicism is not always practiced, often representing a religious or even a cultural marker, and any identification with Ireland is often fluid and tenuous. However, my own fieldwork would caution against concluding that the Irish heritage of Scottish Catholics is unimportant. While most of my participants defined themselves as Scottish, many spoke of their Irish ancestry and their attachment to this. Irish Catholic identity in Scotland therefore is complex and contested: there is no unitary history or 'experience'. The term 'Irish Catholics' is used with appropriate caution in discussion of historical context, and in relation to contemporary Scotland 'people from an Irish Catholic background' fits better with how my participants describe themselves.

Finally, there is the theoretical concern regarding whether prejudice and discrimination towards Irish Catholics in Scotland should be described as racism. Sectarianism is certainly a contested term; however it is equally contentious to talk about anti-Irishness in contemporary Scotland as a type of racism. As Song (2014b: 107-108) comments, 'our understandings and conceptualizations of racism are highly imprecise, broad, and readily used to describe a wide range of racialised phenomena'. Some conceptualisations of racism distinguish between racial discrimination and racial prejudice (Miles and Brown, 2003). In the former, minorities may face barriers to certain employment, educational opportunities, or housing, for example; whereas the latter consists of more subtle forms of prejudice such as particular attitudes or negative treatment that still results in processes of othering and may affect the day-to-day lives of individuals, but without the structural barriers/ disadvantage. Song (2014b) draws on Omi and Winant's (1994) definition, which states that simply holding a prejudicial view of an individual or group based on apparent racial difference does not constitute racism; rather, there has to be evidence of structural disadvantage or domination. Song (2014b) therefore argues that there is a need to distinguish between racism – with its historical and structured system of domination – and the broader idea of racialisation. Therefore, while it is useful to note that most sociological accounts overlook the issue of unequal power relations between Irish Catholics and Protestants in Scotland, we have to be mindful of the casual use of the word 'racism' in relation to the present.

Certainly many victims of anti-Irishness perceive their treatment as a form of racism (see '"I am a victim of anti-Irish racism", says Scots writer', *The Herald*, 12 January 2014). This framing is also reflected in some of the fieldwork that I have carried out, which is discussed later in the chapter. It could be argued that claims of anti-Irish racism (both historically and today) are not taken seriously because race is still very much seen as being aligned to colour differences, despite the challenge to the black-white dichotomy for understanding racism in more recent years. According to Hickman (1998), 'anti-Semitism and anti-Irish racism reveal that there is nothing new about cultural differentiation as a basis for racist discourse in this country', however she argues that this is neglected because of the notion that 'no white group could experience the level of racism which a black group can'

(289-290). On one hand, research suggests that Irish Catholics in Scotland are highly unlikely to experience structural discrimination or widespread prejudice on account of their perceived 'race' in the way that, for example, African Americans in the United States or British Muslims still experience. There is remaining structural disadvantage mainly among older Catholics (Walls and Williams, 2003) but inequality is dying out. In this view, citing 'racism' when describing the Irish experience could be deemed an inflation of the term, and it is important to question whether we risk creating a 'culture of racial equivalence' by comparing the experiences of the Irish to, for instance, people who migrated from the Caribbean or the Indian subcontinent in the 1950s–1970s. However, if this concern leads us to neglect the lived experiences of a minority group because of their apparent 'whiteness', there is the potential that we create or reinforce 'hierarchies of oppression'. This will be reflected on throughout the chapter, by looking at the extent to which the Irish were subject to an 'historical and structured system of domination', and how processes of racialisation might impact upon Irish identity in Scotland today, considering specifically how participants in my research utilise concept of racism in relation to perceived anti-Irishness.

Historical context

In the previous chapter, Jim Slaven details the impact of 19th century migration and the racialization of the Irish in Scotland. This chapter focuses on contemporary Scotland; however it is important to ground this with some discussion of the position of Irish Catholics historically – acknowledging of course that Irish Catholics could not ever have been described as a homogenous group. This is vital not simply as scene-setting but because this neglected part of history very much matters to understanding the present. This section will illustrate how the Irish were denigrated and regarded as a 'race apart', and then discuss how the resultant unequal power relations between Irish Catholics and the dominant Protestant majority played out in economic, social and cultural life in Scotland.

In the early decades of the 19th century at least, Irish Catholics in Scotland were viewed by many as a 'root cause of many social evils' (McCrone, 2001: 13), set apart by their customs, traditions, religion, and in some cases language. They were depicted as an 'inferior race', and there is much evidence to suggest that this took the form of 'old' biological forms of racism as well as attacks on their culture (Miles, 1982: Devine, 2008). The Irish were demonised in the media, stereotyped as violent and backwards, and accused of bringing disease and spreading criminality (Curtis 1984). Thinking about the wider context of this immigration, the arrival of Irish Catholics came at a time of 'obsession' with racial classification (Virdee 2014), and the Irish were regarded in some quarters as a threat to the native Scottish 'race'. In this respect, 'racialism added a gloss of scientific respectability to nativist and sectarian opposition to Irish Catholic immigration' (Kidd, 2003: 883). The position of Irish Catholics in Britain was complicated by the colonial relationship between Britain and Ireland, and the power relations associated with this. Having already been racialised in the Irish colony, the aforementioned processes of exclusion based on supposed racial inferiority helped to place the Irish migrants as part of the 'unrespectable working class': they 'became the racialised outsider within the British nation' (Virdee, 2014: 24). The Catholic religion played a crucial role. As Colley (1996) notes, British national identity was anchored to an 'uncompromising Protestantism' by defining itself against the Catholic enemy. Religion crucially intertwined with nationalism to symbolise what it meant to be British, and the 'racialised outsider' status was exacerbated by the religion of the majority of Irish migrants. This was no less the case in Scotland. For Irish Catholics, religion and higher levels of poverty distinguished them from the Ulster Protestants, who as well as a shared religious faith were also more acquainted with Scottish values and institutions because Ulster had been largely a Scottish colony in the seventeenth century (Gallagher, 1987: 2). These factors will undoubtedly have impacted upon on Irish Catholic immigrants' feelings of inclusion and attachment to national identity – both Scottish and British.

Unequal power relations between the Irish Catholic minority and the Protestant majority in the economic sphere are well-documented. It was the already very low social class position of Irish Catholics as well as their alleged 'alien character' and values that led to them being 'despised and feared' (Gallagher, 1987: 12). This racialisation and the resultant economic exclusion and disadvantage undoubtedly hampered their ability to move themselves out of poverty. Irish Catholic workers faced discrimination in the labour market, with 'No Irish need apply' notices representing the most overt racist practices (Bradley, 1995). Economic exclusion came in more subtle forms too, as employers were known to attempt to ascertain if a prospective employee was a Catholic from an Irish background from names or schools attended for example (Walls and Williams, 2003). As well as excluding Irish Catholics from certain companies and industries, those who did find work were often denied promotion and largely confined to unskilled or low-skilled manual labour: they 'formed the marginal or unskilled proletariat' (Gallagher, 1987: 2). Irish Catholic workers also faced antagonism from trade union leaders and activists (1987: 31). Recent research urges us not to overstate the levels of unrest. Virdee (2014: 17) points out that Irish Catholics in England played a crucial role in the working class movement, and in Scotland signs of class consciousness crossing the religious divide were evident in 'Red Clydeside', for example (Gallagher, 1987: 3). Nonetheless, to an extent Irish Catholics were scapegoated and victimised as a result of economic crisis. When used as strike-breakers they 'incurred the wrath of the native workforce' (Mitchell, 2008: 18). Gallagher (1987: 100) notes that religious divisions in the labour market were compounded by the establishment of the Freemasons, which entrenched the Protestant identity of the skilled working class. Anti-Irish racism was thus interwoven with various other types of discrimination and social divisions to keep Irish Catholics in an inequitable power relationship with the dominant Protestant majority. Thus, although it is important not to overstate the level of exclusion, such factors may explain why, when compared to experiences in other countries with high levels of Irish immigration, Irish Catholics in Scotland have fared notoriously badly. Devine (2008) notes that Catholics from Irish backgrounds in Scotland achieved economic parity with non-Catholics by the 1980s, much later than was the case in the United States (1901), New Zealand (the 1920s) and Australia (the 1930s).

In the 20th century several socioeconomic changes helped to transform the lives of many Irish Catholics in Scotland. Inequality between Catholics and non-Catholics was alleviated by the Education Act of 1918 which brought Catholic schools – previously outside of the state system and therefore unfunded – under state control, with vast improvement in resources. Inequality was further addressed through the expanded public sector which arose from the rise of the Welfare State, and the educational revolution of the 1960s which, through measures such as expanding universities and providing more opportunities, helped the Scottish working class in general (Devine, 2000). Perhaps most importantly, changes in the labour market from the 1970s and 1980s removed much of the overt discrimination present in certain industries, as local family-based businesses were increasingly replaced by (or accountable to) national or multinational firms (Devine, 2000). Staff recruitment and promotion became increasingly meritocratic (Paterson and Iannelli, 2006), vastly reducing the scope for employers to discriminate based on factors such as religion or ethnic background. Some scholars suggest that progress has been overestimated, as will be discussed later in the chapter when the assumption of socio-economic equality – used by sociologists to demonstrate that prejudice against Irish Catholics is a thing of the past – is critiqued. However it is also important to note that historic structural inequalities such as economic discrimination sphere were complemented by social and cultural marginalisation and it is perhaps in these areas that the legacy of unequal power relations between Irish Catholics and the dominant Protestant majority is most evident.

For example, referring to Protestant militancy of the interwar period, as anti-Catholic sentiment was channelled into political activity, Rosie (2008: 158) acknowledges that while there may have been little success politically 'in the cultural realm they left a wealth of bitter memories'. The post-war period was also not one of gradual integration, as the 'Troubles' in Northern Ireland in the 1970s and 1980s resulted in a return to the type of 'routine criminalisation' of Irish people in Britain which had been a feature of the mid to late nineteenth century. Epitomised by the examples of the 'Birmingham Six' and the 'Guildford Four', the Irish became the 'suspect community', an enemy within (Mac an Ghaill, 2001: 192), as they had also been in the 1920s in terms of fears of Irish diaspora support for revolution in Ireland. Although this particular 'othering' based on apparent terrorist threat was temporary, it will have impacted to some extent on Irish Catholics' feelings of inclusion within the nation. The processes of cultural inclusion and exclusion are extremely complex, and evidently impacted upon by historic power relations between Britain and Ireland.

Moreover, as noted earlier, the Catholic religion was a key marker of difference and target of prejudice towards Irish migrants. It is well known that in the interwar period, the Church of Scotland (then still a powerful institution compared to the present day) regularly petitioned the government with the aim of prohibiting further immigration of Irish Catholics and even campaigned for the repatriation of some, such as those who were in prison (Devine, 2000). However this use of language referring to the Irish as a 'race apart' continued in the following decades. Devine points out that in 1952, while the Church was publicly denouncing racial discrimination and promoting the rights of Africans in colonial territories they denounced Irish Catholics for 'displacing the native Scottish Protestant population from the industrial areas of the west' (2008: 192), and encouraged employers to discriminate in favour of the Scottish 'race'.

Of course it is important to note that while structural forces certainly influenced the development of an outsider identity amongst Irish Catholics, they were not simply passive victims of social or cultural exclusion. For Mac an Ghaill (2001: 194), exclusion was not simply a result of hostility from the dominant Protestant majority in Britain. Rather, the Irish diaspora have been active agents in their cultural formation of outsiders, 'actively disidentifying' with Britishness due to historic colonial relations between Britain and Ireland, and thus choosing to retain a national and ethnic sense of belonging to Ireland. In Scotland, the Catholic Church also played a role in the 'voluntary segregation' of Irish Catholics through attempts to discourage intermarriage, for example (Mitchell, 2008). In terms of the cultural sphere, in 1875 Hibernian Football Club in Edinburgh became the first prominent Irish Catholic football club in Scotland (Kelly, 2007), closely followed in 1888 by the establishment of Celtic Football Club. Celtic in particular became an outlet for the expression of Irish Catholic identity and culture (Bradley, 2006).

Arguably it is in the realm of sport that the question of how Irish Catholic identity is most visibly expressed and reacted to. Certainly it was not always positively received. Bradley (1996: 38) states that in 1952 the Scottish Football Association demanded Celtic cease flying the Irish tricolour at their stadium or be disallowed from continuing to play in Scottish football. The fact that a national flag was the target highlights the importance of factors other than religion itself. It is impossible in the case of Irish Catholics to separate religious discrimination from prejudice based on ethnicity and nationality. Bradley notes that following Celtic's refusal to comply the Association dropped their demand as it transpired that they did not have the legal powers to enforce it. However the threat itself reveals how expressions of Irishness were still viewed by some as very problematic, including by those in influential positions. The SFA secretary who launched the campaign, George Graham, was a Freemason and a member of the Orange Order (Devine, 2008: 193). This attention on Celtic's Irish heritage was contrasted by the establishment's silence (at least at that time) on the sectarian practices of their rivals. Rangers Football Club openly pursued an anti-Catholic recruitment policy – for players and other staff – for much of the 20th century, and the first high-profile Catholic signing in 1989 resulted in fans placing a wreath outside of Ibrox stadium mourning the loss of '116 years of tradition' (Murray, 1998: 44). One participant in my research stated that he knew of several people who stopped attending Rangers matches following the first signing of a Catholic, and had not returned to Ibrox since. Again, a lack of qualitative research makes it impossible to state causal links between these examples and levels of social and cultural integration of Irish Catholics, but they are unlikely not to have had some impact.

The effects of historical discrimination and inequalities are not erased when they cease, and this chapter argues that disregarding evidence of structural inequality and social and cultural marginalisation not only trivialises the lived experiences of people from Irish Catholic backgrounds who do feel partially excluded and sometimes targets of prejudice, but also results in an explanation of 'sectarianism' which attributes blame to the 'poor values' of individuals. On the question of a 'culture of racial equivalence', where the Irish Catholic experience may be said to diverge from the experiences of other minorities is in the permeability of certain boundaries. Song's understanding of racism as 'a structured system of power and domination... which has a historical basis' (2014b: 22) notes that it is not fixed. Rather, it is changeable, and it could be argued that structural discrimination of Irish Catholics in Scotland was dismantled throughout the twentieth century in a way that might not have been possible for more visible ethnic minorities. The rest of this chapter will critically explore the question of whether Irishness in Scotland is still considered problematic today.

Contemporary Scotland

This chapter has argued that much of the academic work on the experiences of Catholics from Irish backgrounds in contemporary Scotland tends to neglect historical context and power relations, and as such has ultimately failed to deal effectively with claims that anti-Irish Catholic racism is a problem that has not gone away. Following a brief overview of the dominant scholarly work in the area, this section will explore such claims, drawing on examples highlighted in the media and some of the literature, as well as discussions with participants from my PhD research. Through interviews and focus groups with supporters of Celtic and Rangers I sought to investigate issues relating to the Offensive Behaviour at Football and Threatening Communications Act (2012), but also to gain different perspectives on sectarianism, racism (including anti-Irish racism) and how political, national and other identities are expressed and received in Scotland more generally.

A myriad of socio-economic changes in the 20th century certainly transformed the place of Irish Catholics in Scottish society. A consequence of this, however, is that overly positive claims have been made by prominent sociologists and historians that discrimination and inequality has gradually been eroded over the past century and is now a thing of the past (Devine, 2008; Bruce et al, 2005; Rosie, 2004). Yet although demographic shifts are important, they are limited in the sense that they cannot capture complex processes of inclusion and exclusion. In a small qualitative study of discrimination in the workplace in Glasgow, Finn et al (2008) found that anti-Catholic attitudes persisted in some areas, albeit in a far subtler form than the direct discrimination of previous decades. Similarly Walls and Williams (2003) note that a significant minority of Catholic participants in their research reported personal experience of discrimination at work, and that the majority of Catholics over the age of 50 in the west of Scotland 'have lived their lives at an economic disadvantage, probably now irreversible' (765). Such studies help to provide an alternative perspective on the study of sectarianism in Scotland, a field generally dominated by quantitative approaches. Yet Bruce et al's (2005) rebuttal of Walls and Williams' (2003) study largely dismissed the data as 'hearsay' and 'perception'. Indeed, the authors commented that:

> When the expert social scientists and historians who study sectarian discrimination in Scotland differ about the causes of apparent disparities, there seems no reason to assume that lay witnesses are experts in anything other than their personal experiences (and even there we must allow that people can be wrong about the causes of their experiences; see the very large number of occasions on which employment tribunals find against claimants) (Bruce et al, 2005: 155).

Without the space necessary to explore methodological debates on quantitative and qualitative approaches, it is logical to assume that the lived experiences of people – whether Catholics from Irish backgrounds or any other group previously subject to discrimination or exclusion – cannot be captured by studies that rely on surveys or census data. Even cautious acceptance of socio-economic equality leaves questions unanswered. Gallagher (1987) emphasises the fact that it was a combination of skills shortages and other social and economic shifts in the latter decades of the 20th century that were responsible for diminishing discrimination in employment, not 'affirmative action' or increased tolerance towards the minority group. It is therefore possible (and likely) that intolerance and prejudice do not disappear even if the mechanisms for preserving economic advantage are no longer there. The residual prejudice may not be sufficient to reproduce structures of domination (Song, 2014b), but may play out in other ways, affecting the everyday lives of Catholics from Irish backgrounds. The rest of this chapter will explore some examples of this.

In early 2011, a campaign of hate towards certain high-profile figures in Scotland was the subject of intense media focus. Neil Lennon, the then Celtic manager, received death threats and, along with two Celtic players (also Catholics from Northern Ireland), received bullets in the post. Attempts were also intercepted to send viable parcel bombs to Lennon, his QC Paul McBride and Labour MSP Trish Godman (both high profile Celtic-supporting Catholics), as well as to Cairde na hÉireann, an Irish Republican group based in Glasgow. Lennon was publicly attacked by an opposition supporter in May 2011 and called a 'Fenian bastard', though the 'religiously-aggravated' aspect of that charge was dropped when the case went to trial (Reid, 2013). Around the same time, what could be described as a 'moral panic' arose from a high-tension game between Celtic and Rangers, in which the latter team had three players sent off. Despite the absence of actual disorder amongst fans, the state's response to the media furore was to introduce a programme of anti-sectarianism work in schools and other community settings, and to push through a controversial piece of legislation: the Offensive Behaviour at Football and Threatening Communications Act (2012) – 'which I will return to later in the chapter'. What linked the individuals and groups targeted in the aforementioned campaign that initiated the legislation was a (real or perceived) nationality – Irishness. The Irish Republican group for instance has no connection to the Catholic Church or to Celtic Football Club, and the group's organiser highlighted the controversy over how the problem should be defined by commenting that 'we would see what happened as more about anti-Irish racism than sectarian' (*Belfast Telegraph*, 24 April 2011).

There are other high-profile instances of what has been claimed to be anti-Irish racism in contemporary Scotland. In January 2014, two young Irish-speaking brothers from Donegal were reportedly thrown out of a taxi in Glasgow because they refused to stop speaking in Irish Gaelic (*Irish Independent*, 9 January 2014). In the same month, a man was imprisoned for six months for abusing journalist Angela Haggerty in an online tirade, including calling her a 'taig' and a 'Fenian', which the sheriff described as 'racist and religious' (*The Herald*, 12 January 2014). The Irish were historically a racialised group but a key question is whether these contemporary examples are rightly described as racism. One of the victims, the journalist, defined it as such, as did media reports, but the perpetrator was convicted of 'religiously aggravated breach of the peace'. Song (2014) notes that the MacPherson report defines a racist incident as 'any incident which is perceived to be racist by the victim or other person', however she contends that perception is not enough: there has to be, as stated before, the creation or reproduction of structures of domination. The belief that the real problem in Scotland is anti-Irish racism as opposed to religious discrimination was echoed by some of my participants, although I deliberately avoided using the concept in my questions during interviews and focus groups. One interviewee commented:

> I think that there's still deep entrenchment within institutions in Scotland that are anti-Irish and anti-Catholic, I don't think there's any doubt about that. I think it's more anti-Irish to be honest (Interview with Celtic supporter, mid 40s).

Interestingly, very few of my participants identified themselves as religious, so this may have impacted on the tendency to downplay the religious aspect of the prejudice and discrimination that they felt people from Irish Catholic backgrounds in Scotland still endure. Another interviewee stated that:

> To call, to label everything sectarian which is what people generally do, is lazy, because a lot of it I don't think is sectarian, I think it's institutionalised racism, to be honest, a lot of the time. It's dressed up as sectarianism when it isn't actually (Interview with Celtic supporter, mid-20s).

Instead of religious aspects, participants emphasised other 'markers' of difference such as place of birth, having Irish-sounding names, accents or language, aspects of a person's appearance or the cultural activities that they engaged in. The difficulty associated with how exactly this apparent social problem should be defined was highlighted by other interviewees:

> I think it's probably mostly to do with religion but I do think it could be racist as well, if you're shouting something at a guy because he is from Ireland, just because it's not part of Britain, well the Republic of Ireland anyway. I think that would be seen as racist (Interview with Rangers supporter, early 20s).

> I still think in this country we've got institutional sectarianism and institutional racism. And I use the word racism deliberately because they're discriminating against the Irish, and that's racist. If you call someone a black bastard that's seen as racist, if you call me a Fenian bastard, making reference to my Irish origin, that's racism as well in my book (FG participant, Celtic supporter, mid-60s).

This of course raises questions around a culture of equivalence, which will be discussed later, but it also highlights the firm belief of some of my participants that Irish Catholics in Scotland are indeed subject to a form of racism. Speaking about the treatment of the former Celtic manager, another participant commented:

> Lennon was being demonised for being an Irish Catholic, there's nae doubt about it, if Lennon had a Glesga accent, eh... or a London accent, I don't think he'd have got the same treatment (Interview with Celtic supporter, mid 40s).

This example raises interesting questions about the role of the media in propagating negative images of particular individuals or groups. Reid (2008) has argued that media coverage of Lennon often reinforced negative stereotypes of Irish people as aggressive and fiery. For Reid, the tone and language used in some articles could be construed as a racist discourse, though in far subtler ways than the explicitly racist depiction of Irish immigrants in the press in the nineteenth century. She cites examples where derogatory humour is used to demean and even dehumanise Lennon – e.g. 'a demented animal' – and argues that in the context of historic anti-Irish and anti-Catholic bigotry, such narratives 'are therefore part of the broader discourses of discourses of otherness directed towards the social practices and cultural institutions associated with that community, including Celtic FC' (2008: 84).

Whether it is in decline or not, and regardless of how it is framed, there still appears to be a sense that Irish Catholics remain an 'outsider' group to some degree. Some of my participants noted personal experience of this, and two examples are outlined here. One interviewee, an Irish-born male who moved to Glasgow in the late 1980s, spoke of feeling like an outsider when he heard the 'Famine song', an infamous chant which includes the line 'The Famine is over, why don't you go home?' The song was previously sung by Rangers supporters until it was banned in 2009 after being declared 'racist' in a court of law.

> I listened to this, not listened to it but... it would come to me and it was jaw-dropping because for the first time I felt I was under attack in a sense. I was an Irish national and being told to fuck off home, no business here (Interview with Celtic supporter, early 70s).

The interviewee previously had little strong attachment to Irish nationalism, despite his family historically being involved in Irish nationalist activity. He had lived in various countries before settling in Glasgow. But he explained that the experience of hearing anti-Irish chants in Scotland elicited a feeling of attachment to his heritage that he would not have expected:

> It was, in fact, I realised later, a sort of tribal instinct, that for the first time in my life, in my mid-40s, I was experiencing a sort of tribal adherence.

The song was not directed at him personally, and he was not even attending a Celtic match at the time, however he felt that this was an attack on his 'group', highlighting the strength of collective identity.

Another participant, in this case a young male born in Scotland but with Irish heritage, described how he felt that his Irish name was a 'marker' of difference, one which may potentially attract negative attention. He explained that in his role as a taxi driver, norms such as his name being displayed on his taxi licence and given to customers when they order a taxi on the new booking system, took on added meaning for him:

> I still feel the need to hide my name badge in the car all the time, because I don't want them seeing my name. I would never have that on show, never ever have it on show. And now we've got, because we're on this new system, we've got an app, and apparently it tells you the driver's name. So I'm actually kind of worried, if I'm

picking up from certain pubs and they see (name). I don't know if it'll say my second name, I certainly hope it doesn't. And it'll say driver (name) and I just think, automatically in my head think they're going to be going, Fenian taxi driver here (Interview with Celtic supporter, late 20s).

This account challenges the dominant sociological explanation of the position of Irish Catholics in contemporary Scotland because while structural economic inequality may be a thing of the past, in this example there are clearly processes which impact on the behaviour of the participant while at work. His concerns may be groundless, influenced by 'stories' of economic and social exclusion that have been passed down over generations, or they may be justified. Regardless, the reliance on demographic indicators by sociologists means that the lived experiences of some individuals, who feel that particular markers of their ethnic or national backgrounds might single them out for hostility, are marginalised or dismissed.

In both of the examples cited, the participants talk of feeling 'outsiders' and not fully part of the nation that they live in. Their experiences probably do not meet the criteria of what constitutes racism in Song's (2014b) analysis because the power imbalance that existed perhaps even a generation ago between Irish Catholic minority and the dominant Protestant majority is no longer present. However, it could be argued that the 'structures of domination' are recent enough in the memory to matter. As noted earlier, it is generally accepted that there is socio-economic equality, at least for younger Catholics. Yet just because prejudiced attitudes cannot be enforced in the way that they once were, as the mechanisms for preserving economic advantage have all but disappeared in most sectors, there are arguably still spaces in Scotland where it matters. The residual culture that remains is important and helps to shape outcomes for Catholics in everyday life, something that can only be illustrated by privileging the lived experiences of such individuals.

Returning to Song's (2014b) 'culture of racial equivalence', it is notable that one of the participants compared his experience to what he imagines would be experienced by more visible minorities:

It's no right you should be made to feel uncomfortable at your place of work... but I dare say that a lot of Asian taxi drivers will find things ten times worse than I will here when they pick up drunk people (Interview with Celtic supporter, late 20s).

There is an acknowledgement that more visible minorities are more likely to receive negative treatment, supporting Song's assertion that 'not all racial essentialisms create or reproduce structures of domination, or damage and denigrate their target populations to the same degree (or in the same ways)' (2014: 121). Avoiding being marked out as different by hiding a name badge would not be sufficient for many other minorities. This also highlights the fact that victimisation of people from an Irish Catholic background in Scotland is highly contextual. The potential threat of violence or any level of harassment is greater in this case because the individual's job involves direct contact with members of the public, including picking up customers from pubs which are known to have connections not only to Rangers but also to Loyalism and in some cases Orangeism. However this would not be the norm for most people from an Irish Catholic background in Scotland in their day to day lives.

Song's 'culture of equivalence' frame is also a useful way to explore what Law (2015: 105) referred to as 'an equality of group hatred'. McBride (2013) also found in the literature and the media a persistent theme of sectarianism being portrayed as a product of the tensions between and poor behaviour of two equivalent groups of people 'despite the fact that the debate involves majority and minority communities and the historical legacy of high levels of prejudice towards the minority group' (29-30). The expression of Irish Republican identity is often discussed in very much the same way as, for example, marches by the Orange Order and associated organisations. One consequence of this dominant narrative is the recent claim from the Orange Order that they now represent an ethnic minority, and therefore should have the right to express their identity without criticism:

> We have a distinct culture stretching back hundreds of years in the city and I would class us as an ethnic minority entitled to promote ourselves the same as any other faith (Eddie Hyde, Grand Master of the County Grand Orange Lodge of Glasgow, June 2015).

According to Song (2014b: 117), one of the risks associated with the concept of racialisation is that is has 'collapsed multiple and variable forms of racial phenomena (including assertions of 'reverse racism') into an undifferentiated mass which requires more critical scrutiny'. Hyde's interpretation of the Orange Order as an ethnic minority denies historic power relations of the previously dominant Protestant majority and an oppressed

Irish Catholic minority. Of course, the Orange Order does not represent the majority of Protestants in Scotland and never has, but culturally they have been regarded as a powerful institution perhaps because of their visibility in public spaces. The constitution of the Orange Order in Scotland 'commits its members to the defence of Protestantism and the British crown' (Kauffman 2008: 159). Reilly (2000: 29) argues that 'Orangeism flourishes only where there is a strong perception of a Catholic threat and the sense of a need to resist it'. Without the space to explore in depth the impact of Orange Order marches on Scottish society, which occur regularly for several months of the year, especially in Glasgow and surrounding areas, it is likely that the inherent anti-Catholic nature of the Order will have had some impact upon Irish Catholics' sense of inclusion historically. This is particularly the case in working class areas, as the frequency of marches refutes the idea generally accepted by mainstream media and society that parades as a once a year occurrence. For many Catholics in Scotland – including some of my participants – Orange Walks are a frequent and unwelcome reminder of historic prejudice and inequalities.

Another consequence of this culture of equivalence is that the historically oppressed group are considered to be equally culpable for the continued existence of the sectarian problem in Scotland. This can be identified in debates around the controversial Offensive Behaviour at Football and Threatening Communications (2012) Act. It is important to note that despite the context of the legislation and the rhetoric surrounding its introduction, the word 'sectarianism' is entirely absent and the focus is instead on 'offensiveness'. Concerns have been raised that certain expressions of Irish identity – predominately songs, flags and banners associated with Irish Republicanism – are marked out as offensive, unfairly deemed sectarian and even criminalised. Yet failure to place certain behaviours, or the use of songs or symbols, in a historical context which highlights the struggle against British imperialism, or the negative treatment of Irish immigrants in nineteenth century Scotland and their descendants thereafter, or the historical inequalities faced by Catholics, results in an apolitical and ahistorical 'moral judgement' of poor values of individuals or social groups. As a result, the legitimacy of expressing certain Irish identities in Scotland is called into question.

This chapter argues that openly expressing an Irish identity in Scotland is sometimes considered problematic. Kelly (2010: 2) argued that, for some, 'having a stated position on Irish politics... is sufficient condition to be labelled sectarian'. This theme was echoed by some participants in my research. One stated his frustration that:

> ...people's expressions of Irishness somehow means they are about to set up an active service unit of the fucking IRA! (Interview with Celtic supporter, late 30s)

There was a sense among some participants that the notion of the Irish as a 'suspect community' has not entirely disappeared.

On the other hand, this 'cultural invisibility' also includes a denial of ethnic minority status. The difficultly for some to comprehend the Irish as a racialised or ethnic minority was recently encapsulated by the comments of former Labour MP for Paisley and Renfrewshire North, Jim Sheridan. Sheridan argued that the Irish should not be regarded as an ethnic minority and added public money must not be spent on a St Patrick's Day parades (*The Herald*, 25 February 2015). He stated:

> People need to look forward, move forward and think of a modern Scotland and stop living in the past (Jim Sheridan, Feb 2015).

This could be interpreted as an assertion that if sections of the Irish Catholic society wish to hold onto that part of their identity, their status as Scots comes into question. While again acknowledging that levels of exclusion varies greatly between different groups, there are some parallels with the increasing political and media discourse that British Muslims can only be fully accepted as British if they give up certain aspects of their identity due to the apparent incompatibility of some aspect of Islam and 'British values'. The 'denial of difference' of Irish Catholics in Scotland was echoed by other leading politicians and media figures in Scotland:

> They are an integrated, fully respected and loved members of our community, they are not different, this to me, I am afraid, I think is a little bit divisive (Mary Scanlon, Conservative MSP, March 2015).

In exploring this theme of the denial of difference, and the perceived lack of legitimacy of Irish identity, it is interesting to note that several Rangers supporters that I interviewed referred to the 'fake' or 'faux' Irishness of the Celtic support. While there is not space for a full exploration of this in this chapter, the types of sentiments expressed included an interesting perspective on the Famine Song mentioned earlier:

First time I heard it I laughed. And, the reason I laughed was because it mocks all Celtic fans, they're always 'we're Irish, we're Irish, we're Irish'. Well you know what... (gestures indicating 'go away') (Interview with Rangers supporter, late 60s).

Assuming these attitudes are not unusual amongst sections of the Rangers support, this perhaps goes some way to explain why the sense of 'outsider' is still apparent for some Irish Catholics. Claims of 'cultural invisibility' have also arisen from the current debates about an Irish famine memorial in Glasgow. Despite being one of the centres of Irish famine migration, Glasgow is not home to one of the 142 famine memorials worldwide, with perceptions (including some voiced by my participants) that such a memorial could attract trouble. Similar concerns of 'controversy' were voiced over plans for celebrations to mark the centenary of the 1916 Irish Easter Rising (*The Herald*, 5 December 2015, 'What's the problem with city council and marking the Easter Rising?'). Indeed, future reflections on the 2016 centenary are likely to provide an interesting case study on how certain Irish identities are expressed and received in contemporary Scotland, which may help to further explore the question of whether Irishness is indeed still considered by some to be problematic. A cursory look at the comments page of the *Motherwell Times'* article on 'Councillors vote to fly Irish flag' (11 February 2016) as North Lanarkshire Council respond to a request to fly the Tricolour to commemorate the centenary of the Easter Rising – with comparisons to Isis – would suggest that there is still at least a bitter minority for whom expressions of Irishness are simply not tolerated.

Conclusion

This chapter has argued that Irish Catholics historically were a racialised group which suffered structural discrimination and societal prejudice. It is acknowledged that throughout the 20th century significant socio-economic changes have removed much of the structural bigotry: in this respect, the dominant sociological explanation is valid. However, explanations which focus on structural changes do not properly take into account the legacy of past discrimination and inequality, and residual tensions which may arise from these. Devine (2008) notes that the Church of Scotland publicly repented for their actions in the early-mid 20th century but claims that there may still be residual tensions as the memory of being victimised will not disappear quickly. The common-sense explanation of sectarianism marginalises claims of the Irish as an ethnic minority and a racialised group, and the 'equivalence' frame which focuses on 'Protestant-Catholic relations' crucially neglects the historic unequal power relations touched upon in this chapter.

Research should adequately consider the historical context in terms of the role of the British state, intervention in Ireland, the impact of colonialism, and anti-Catholicism and anti-Irishness dating back to the 19th century. Returning to Song's (2014b) argument that we need to distinguish between racism – with its historical and structured system of domination – and broader process of racialisation, it is vital to be clear that there are obvious hierarchies of oppression. Expression of Irish culture in Scotland may be received negatively and there are some examples of overt anti-Irish bigotry, but the institutional and societal racism faced by more visible ethnic minorities is generally stronger and more difficult to avoid. Nonetheless, this has previously led to dismissal of people's lived experiences of oppression or prejudice as simply at best 'perceptions' based on some kind of historical story, or 'paranoia' with no real foundational basis. More qualitative research on this topic is needed in which people's experiences and claims of prejudice are not simply dismissed because there are worse forms of it elsewhere.

CHAPTER 5

The Trouble with Sectarianism

Alex Law

Each society, at each moment, elaborates a body of social problems taken to be legitimate, worthy of being debated, of being made public and sometimes officialised and, in a sense, guaranteed by the state Bourdieu and Wacquant (1992: 236).

Introduction: paradoxes and conundrums

ALMOST ALL STUDIES OF 'SECTARIANISM' in Scotland point to a central 'paradox' or a 'conundrum' – that while there are widespread *perceptions* of a serious problem of sectarianism very few people have ever had any direct *experience* of it (Ormston et al, 2015: 269). Sectarianism is not something that 'we' do but something that other people do to other people in other places (Rosie, 2015: 330). Metaphors abound to capture this elusive but apparently deep-seated social problem. It is compared to glass bottles (problem of perception), glass ceiling (problem of discrimination), and a glass curtain (problem of exclusion) (Ormston et al, 2015), or, alternatively, to a Cobweb (a problem with many gaps in-between) rather than a joined-up Patchwork (a societal-wide problem) (Goodall et al, 2015), or an Iceberg where what you see above the surface is all that exists with no hidden depths of sectarianism submerged below (Bruce, 1988; Rosie, 2015). If there is, as much research demonstrates, 'a considerable perception-reality gap when it comes to public understandings of sectarianism' then the presumed threat posed to civility and public order can only present itself as 'a subtle but intractable problem' (Ormston et al, 2015: 284).

This paradox is compounded by a conundrum – sectarian insiders and non-sectarian outsiders appear to occupy completely different perceptual worlds. 'The public', insofar as their views are known through opinion polls or attitude surveys, categorise some practices and groups as sectarian even though the groups classified in this way typically deny that their beliefs and rituals are sectarian in nature. Since some 'find it difficult to even recognise' that their attitudes are sectarian more robust research is needed so that 'this enduring problem in Scottish life' will be more widely perceived and discussed (Goodall et al, 2015: 293).

For instance, while Orange and Republican marches and parades create anxiety within communities participants themselves deny that their intentions are sectarian in the least (Hamilton-Smith et al, 2015: 325). Marches, parades or 'processions' appear provocative to the 'community' and the police, especially in areas of urban marginality and community stigmatisation. Yet, as Hamilton-Smith et al (2015) note, anxieties about sectarian processions may be related to much deeper, underlying issues. The more deprived that an area is then the greater the perception of sectarian prejudice and tensions will be. Ormston et al (2015: 277) also found that Catholics feel more harassed than other groups the more deprived the local area is, although even in the most deprived quintile only 17 per cent of respondents felt threatened by parades.

Despite these relatively low-level concerns, state authorities in Scotland nominated sectarianism as a fundamental social antagonism disfiguring the national community (Law, 2016). This was far from the opening of the process of governmental attempts to curtail sectarianism. During the 1980s through to the 2000s sectarianism had been elaborated, repeatedly and episodically, as a legitimate subject for public discourse, classification and state intervention. In 2005 a Government summit on sectarianism hailed by the Labour First Minister Jack McConnell as 'historic' led to the Scottish Executive's 2006 *Strategy on Tackling Sectarianism in Scotland,* which promoted the use of Football Banning Orders (FBOs) to exclude persistent offenders from football grounds.

By 2011 this strategy appeared ineffective and insufficient to governmental authorities. Indeed, sectarian offences were under-represented in the issuing of FBOs, and even more serious sectarian and racist offences failed to result in FBOs being issued (Scottish Government Social Research,

2011: 14). It was only following sensational media coverage of a football game between 'the Old Firm' of the Glasgow clubs Celtic and Rangers, that sectarianism was nominated as an official crime. This is despite the fact that the term 'sectarianism' itself is contested, subject to multiple interpretations and cannot be defined in Scots Law. With the passing of legislation, the Scottish Government committed a budget of £9 million to address sectarianism, about which a lot is said but not enough it seems is known.

The gap between sectarian practices and sectarian perceptions is regularly compared to the well-known paradox of rising public fears of crime at a time when many forms of violent crime are actually falling. In the case of crime, popular misperceptions are routinely explained as the result of ideological constructions by 'the media' and government that stoke exaggerated moral panics (Cohen, 2011). In contrast, the role of the media and government in the construction of sectarianism has not been to the forefront of academic studies (see Kelly, 2010, for an exception). Instead, research concentrates on the supposedly de-civilising aspects of bad behaviour around football and parades, including contentious cultural paraphernalia – flags, songs, football colours, marches – in an attempt to uncover the 'tacit nature of sectarian sentiment' (Goodall et al, 2015: 297).

Sociologically speaking, the afterlife of 'sectarianism' expresses definite social and political conditions that make possible both the lived experience of sectarianism, insofar as this can be divined, and the symbolic classification of sectarianism as an outdated mode of distinction. Sectarianism valorises symbolic distinction and separation as prohibitions against social and ideological promiscuity and contamination between established and outsider groups (Weber, 1946). As with the religious field more strictly defined, every consensus of symbolic meaning serves the simultaneous classificatory function of vision and division, inclusion and exclusion, integration and differentiation (Bourdieu, 1991). Symbolic capital that only recently sanctified a relatively privileged position in the social field, such as Protestant Unionism, can find itself devalued, despite relatively unchanged ideological content, by the valorisation of emerging and increasingly dominant forms of symbolic capital as represented by the 'civil religion' of sub-state nationalism.

This chapter attempts to situate the moral panic around sectarianism in wider relations of social power. A civilising offensive is mobilised by the legitimate sources of symbolic nomination to regulate and discipline de-civilised outsiders. This is experienced differently as resentment and *ressentiment*, depending on where groups are distributed in social space. On the one hand, the sources of legitimate symbolic power experience *ressentiment* as a chronic maladaptation of outsider groups to the civilising canopy of the national habitus. On the other hand, the de-civilised sources of illegitimate symbolic power experience resentment as relatively short-lived losses of control associated with football rivalries. Indeed, fierce sporting rivalries may provide a controlled example of how collective effervescence and cathartic release may help to lower the threat to group integrity posed by other groups and foster greater symbolic equality in a game of more or less evenly-matched sides (Elias, 2008: 231).

Dominant and dominated sectarianism

With little evidence of public disorder or inter-communal violence, the social power of media and political nomination classify football, flags, songs, parades and marches as contentious, provocative and a grave sectarian threat to the social fabric. Such powers of nomination and classification rest on the accumulated force of a centralised apparatus able to separate legitimate from illegitimate forms of symbolic capital (Bourdieu, 2014: 273).

Naming processes are always prescriptive and descriptive, bringing into the field of perception what it asserts already exists objectively in any case. Processes of legitimate nomination, such as that concerning sectarianism, often reify and enclose groups as self-contained phenomenon with little connection to wider processes of nation and state formation. As Bourdieu (1991: 122) argued, 'All social destinies, positive or negative, by concentration or stigma, are equally *fatal* – by which I mean mortal – because they enclose those whom they characterise within the limits that are assigned to them and that they are made to recognise'. By enclosing groups into determinate categories of legitimate-civilised and illegitimate-de-civilised, authorised nomination reifies the symbolic conditions for a double-bind cycle of de-civilised sectarian violence.

Against the prevailing academic consensus that sectarianism was only ever a marginal problem and that football provides a safety valve for social tensions, Gallagher (1987: 1) warned in the 1980s that football rivalry acts as an incubator of religio-political bigotry that threatens to expose the fragile nature of the civilising process: 'The enmity and hysteria sometimes on display at Old Firm matches can serve as a timely reminder of just how thin the crust of civilisation is'. Indeed, football-related sectarianism expresses what is repressed routinely. As such, pleasure can be taken from group transgressions, forever threatening a return of the repressed. As Billig (2002: 185) argued about bigotry more generally:

> What is socially forbidden can become an object of desire and pleasure. If there are taboos on the expression of bigotry in contemporary society, outward prejudice may take the form of a forbidden pleasure. Bigotry, then, becomes a temptation.

This was evident when the transformation of moral values which began in the 1960s coincided with the escalation of state and paramilitary violence in Northern Ireland. Sections of the Rangers' support succumbed to the sectarian temptation, taking pleasure in virulent anti-Catholic denigration and indulged in a culture of alcohol-fuelled fan violence leading to major crowd disorders throughout the late 1960s to the 1980s. Scotland remains one of the few countries where public declarations of Irish heritage, such as St Patrick's Day, the anniversary of the 1916 Easter Rising, or the flying of the Irish tricolour on a public building, can result in intimidation and threats from small groups of Loyalist fundamentalists.

Yet the sectarianism of the dominated waxes and wanes in emotional intensity, physical threat and ideological rancour: by the 1980s anti-Catholic bigotry was already in slow decline. This centrifugal process has been assisted by the development of a national habitus in Scotland that has shed much of the Unionist ideological legacy. The more insecure that an established group like Protestant Unionism feels, the more that they tend to be unrelenting and dogmatic about the inferiority of the outsider group and the supreme value of the established group (Elias, 2008: 230). Conversely, the more secure that a group feels of its own value the more that they can afford to adopt a more detached and accommodating relationship to outsiders.

Although sectarianism is often treated as if it represented an unchanging symbolic monolithic, it operated as a mode of justification in different ways at different times and places. On one side, the 'dominant sectarianism' of the dominant classes in Scotland asserted their right to dominate through the ideological privileges conferred by sectarian exclusions and superiority over groups classified as 'Irish Roman Catholic'. On the other side, the 'dominated sectarianism' of the dominated classes tended, as Bourdieu (1991: 19) notes of the religious field more generally, 'to impose on the dominated a recognition of the legitimacy of the domination and of the symbolic modes of expression of this domination (that is, the lifestyle and religiosity of the dominant classes)'. The same symbolic content of sectarianism therefore must perform different functions if it is to mediate quite distinct, even contrary social conditions.

What is classified from above as 'sectarian' refers to beliefs and practices that once functioned as symbolic justification for reproducing unequal relations of power between supposedly cohesive 'communities'. Yet the material and ideological sources of sectarianism in 19th century Scotland has been continually modified as a mode of justification as the social structure itself changed historically. Its residue functions today as an unwanted reminder of the accumulated history in the development of the national habitus in Scotland.

Moral indignation and sectarianism

In 2011 the legitimate forms of symbolic domination in the political field in Scotland – journalists, police, politicians and academics – converged at a single point: something needed to be done about sectarianism. This concentration of symbolic power produced a self-sustaining escalation process of symbolic amplification often associated with moral panics (Cohen, 2011). Even before the controversial Old Firm game took place in early March 2011 the Scottish Police Federation had called for a ban on the fixture. On the day after the game Strathclyde Police Chief Stephen House called on the First Minister Alex Salmond and the Scottish government to organise a Summit between the police, the Scottish Football Association and the Old Firm to address violent disorder at and around the Glasgow football rivalry. Football-related disorder was debated in the Scottish Parliament. In the end, a six-point plan was agreed at the Summit to control the fixture. This was envisaged by the SNP First Minister Alex Salmond as 'not the end of a process but very much the beginning of a series of actions'. Legislation was hastily enacted in 2012, the Offensive Behaviour at Football and Threatening Communications (Scotland) Act, specifically targeting football rivalries as the source of de-civilised attitudes, symbols and conduct afflicting Scottish society. Subsequently, academic research was commissioned and experts appointed to provide the legitimate authority of scholarly capital for the new regime of punishment and reform.

Such concentrations of symbolic domination demonstrate that a simple opposition between the devolved state and Scottish civil society is untenable. Instead, as Bourdieu (2014: 36) argues, there is 'a continuous distribution of access to the collective, public, material or symbolic resources with which the term 'state' is associated with'. One of the functions of the symbolic continuum is to perform the alchemy of transforming particular interests into universal disinterest. In this case, the classification and punishment of subjects as sectarian must appear as an act of universal disinterest, in the name of the public good, above all particular points in social space.

Performing the alchemy of disinterested punishment is a central feature of what sociologists and philosophers have called '*ressentiment*'. *Ressentiment* can be distinguished from the English word 'resentment'. Resentment refers to a transitory emotional response to symbolic insult, offence, humiliation, and frustration in a situation of social interaction (Meltzer and Musolf, 2002). By outwardly displaying resentful displeasure, resentment is an active form of retaliation, as in fierce sports rivalries, at least for a time until the emotional injury passes, in football rivalries typically in the hours after the end of the contest. *Ressentiment*, on the other hand, refers to a generalised, long drawn out and passive desire for retribution against a perceived, often abstract moral injury to the social body that resists redress. Revenge in such cases is constantly postponed since it is checked or restrained on a more or less permanent basis by external social constraints, leading to a feeling of powerlessness that can only be addressed by imaginary or symbolic violence.

Nietzsche (1996) attributed the social sources of *ressentiment* to the sublimated emotions of 'slave morality' found in Judeo-Christianity and socialism. Unable to strike at the oppressor, Nietzsche argued, the slave morality transformed objective powerlessness into subjective strength by valorising humility, patience, empathy, restraint and mercy. Nietzsche's anthropological speculations were given some sociological foundation by Max Scheler (1972) and Svend Ranulf (1964). In contrast to Nietzsche, Scheler (1972: 50) located *ressentiment* processes within the structure of a society where 'equal rights (political and otherwise) or formal social equality, publicly recognised, go hand in hand with wide factual differences in power, property and education'. An unrelieved tension between formal equality and power inequalities characterises the devalued position felt by the dominated fractions of the dominant class. Such tensions may be released through illusory valuations and 'an urge to scold' that is both attracted to and repelled by the denigrated object. 'In *ressentiment* one condemns what one secretly craves; in rebellion one condemns the craving itself' (Merton, 1968: 210). Yet the repressed always manages to return to the field of perception of the *ressentiment* attitude, whose re-appearance discloses 'a silent, unadmitted 'reproach" (Scheler, 1972: 76). Only an inversion of values, turning pleasure into restraint and punishment into reform, delivers *ressentiment* from the desire for an impossible revenge.

> When the reversal of values comes to dominate accepted morality and is invested with the power of the ruling ethos, it is transmitted by tradition, suggestion and education to those that are endowed with the seemingly devalued qualities (Scheler, 1972: 77).

Ranulf (1964) further argues that *ressentiment* restructures what are specifically middle class dispositions and perceptions. A disposition for moral indignation and disinterested punishment, Ranulf argues, exists for middle class groups compelled to exercise a high degree of self-control and outward restraint in contrast to outsider groups relieved of the same need to constantly sublimate the emotions. Outsider groups that enjoy the freedom to transgress the symbolic order invite the 'repressed desires' of a hostile middle class compelled to serve. Only those aspects of middle class experience are selected that justify imposing the *ressentiment* pattern of feeling onto the world as a disinterested form of punishment.

Moral indignation is 'the emotion behind the disinterested tendency to inflict punishment', a pattern of punishment that has no direct benefit or gratification for the moraliser (Ranulf, 1964: 1). Official *ressentiment* over sectarianism is strikingly evident in the moral indignation displayed by politicians, police, jurists and journalists, even academics. Such groups exercise the monopoly power of nomination and classification that separates legitimate from illegitimate forms of symbolic capital as part of what might be termed 'a civilising offensive'.

As we have already seen, it is not difficult to come across the moral indignation of journalists, senior police officers and politicians. Even disinterested legal opinion is required to give expression to *ressentiment*. Moral indignation finds support for its transvaluation of values in a vague and elastic conception of offensiveness. As the Lord Advocate's (2012) guidelines on the Offensive Behaviour at Football And Threatening Communications (Scotland) Act note, the offence refers to behaviour motivated by religious or other hatred, including behaviour that any *'reasonable person* would be likely to find offensive' or could incite public disorder. As Ranulf argued, the disinterested right to punish depends on moral indignation of an injured but reasonable person or group offended by symbolic violence. In this case, disinterested punishment relies on the judgement of a police officer as 'the reasonable person' present at the time of the offence. Here the context needs to be perceived as 'threatening' or 'offensive' and songs and chants interpreted as motivated by hatred on racial, religious, cultural or social grounds, or by hatred of a group, support for terrorist organisations, or the mocking or celebration of 'the loss of life or serious injury'.

Within the symbolic continuum, the least dominated fraction exercise more autonomy than more dominated fractions, enabling politicians to draw selectively on the rigorous findings of scholarly research produced to inform criminal justice policies. Government-funded research into sectarianism has amply demonstrated the absence of bounded sectarian communities or the religious basis of sectarianism, yet politicians and media persist in mobilising such discredited formulae.

As part of the dominant fraction of the governing class, the Minister for Community Safety and Legal Affairs, Paul Wheelhouse, claimed in his foreword to the Scottish Government 2015 report on the effectiveness of the Offensive Behaviour at Football And Threatening Communications Act that it is 'a step on Scotland's journey to building a better nation':

> ...singing, chanting and shouting of racial and sectarian comments acts as a way of normalising derogatory attitudes and souring relationships or inflaming existing, strained relationships within or between Scotland's communities... [The Act] was designed to send out a clear message to those who let their passion and pride become violent and offensive (Scottish Government, 2015a: 3).

Here the danger to Scotland as a civilised nation is one of (legitimate) sporting passions getting out of control and inciting widespread social disorder and physical violence. While there is evidence of episodic drink-fuelled, physical violence associated with football rivalries, its relatively rare occurrence compels moral indignation into a fascination with symbolic violence.

Symbolic violence is a problem for disinterested punishment, the Minister claims, because it risks escalating conflict between Scotland's 'communities', supposedly already under strain. Here, as elsewhere, 'community' functions as a magical word, implying self-contained, discrete boundaries between rival groups that endanger the overriding unity of the national community. Disinterested punishment is therefore necessary to avenge unnecessary offence to disinterested reasonableness.

Finally, moral indignation conflates racism with sectarianism in a charged semantic slippage. Since racism is officially illegitimate, the coupling extends the elastic semantics of sectarianism. This includes outlawing symbolic support for 'terrorists' and political anti-state violence, which has no necessary relationship to racism. A further claim is made for the transvaluation of values that turns punishment into reform. Here it is claimed that the Act has had a 'positive impact' and made 'real improvements', even though the academic evaluation of the effectiveness of the Act was much more circumspect and noted the difficulty of disentangling secular trends towards self-restraint from any specific improvement arising from the implementation of the legislation.

Sectarianism therefore becomes an all-encompassing term that includes any political, religious or cultural symbols or conduct that may be found offensive from the point of view of disinterested, self-restrained servants of the public. Academics share the moral indignation of governmental authority – indeed praise it where it furthers the needs of scholarship. As one government-funded study argued, a clear need was identified for 'nuanced scholarship that assists the Scottish Government ambitions of eradicating sectarianism in Scottish society. We note also the positive benefits of the recent Scottish Government programme of publicly-funded research' (Goodall et al, 2015: 302).

Without increased public discourse around sectarianism academics warn that the negative impact on individuals 'may be more severe' (Goodall et al, 2015: 299). Public policy and criminal justice approaches to sectarianism need to be 'informed by an accurate understanding of the attitudes of the Scottish public as a whole, as well as those of key sub-sections of society' (Ormston et al, 2015: 268). Similarly, and despite the paltry evidence of sectarian practices beyond low-level disruptive and derogatory conduct, a leading expert on sectarianism mobilises the *ressentiment* conviction that there needs to be 'a sea-change in attitudes on what is and what is not acceptable in everyday Scottish life' (Rosie, 2015: 334). In such cases, the normative stipulations of disinterested academic research run the risk of functioning as an echo chamber to legitimate political and media demands for a civilising offensive.

A further example of moral indignation emerges from the restrained discursive style adopted by the Scottish Government's Advisory Group of academic experts. Sectarianism is defined by the government experts in the catch-all terms of religion, nationalism, politics and football:

> Sectarianism in Scotland is a complex of perceptions, attitudes, beliefs, actions and structures, at personal and communal levels, which originate in religious difference and can involve *a negative mixing of religion with politics, sporting allegiance and national identifications*. It arises from a *distorted expression* of identity and belonging. It is expressed in *destructive patterns of relating* which segregate, exclude, discriminate against or are violent towards a specified religious other with significant personal and social consequences (Advisory Group, 2013: 3.9, emphasis added).

For disinterested nomination sectarianism is the 'distorted' and 'destructive' expression of hostile relations in a violent segregation of 'them' and 'us'. This cannot be reduced to anti-Catholic or anti-Irish discrimination alone since the Catholic or Irish 'us' may feel 'destructive' enmity to the Protestant or British 'them'. By enshrining an equality of group prejudice each side is able to claim to be victims of sectarianism in the face of real or imagined humiliation by an apparently more privileged outsider group. In the process, power imbalances are overlooked. For instance, despite an extremely unequal public presence of Loyalist marches (773) compared to Republican ones (41) in 2012 (Hamilton-Smith et al, 2015: 310), both were seen as problems of equal magnitude and lumped together under the common nomination 'sectarian'. Research also reports a higher, though not by a great deal, incidence of perceived anti-Catholic prejudice and discrimination than anti-Protestant prejudice in Scotland (Ormston et al, 2015).

Such prejudice as exists tends to register as a more general cultural feeling than taking a more concrete form like employment discrimination or harassment. A spectrum of sectarian attitudes can be plotted on both sides of the divide from 'hard-bitter' to 'soft-banter' on an ascending scale of prejudice, bigotry and hatred, making the classification of behaviour as sectarian dependent on the context of communication regardless of historical and ideological content. Therefore, despite its historical roots in anti-Irish Catholic hostility and discrimination, sectarianism in this definition persists in Scotland as an equality of group hatred requiring disinterested punishment. No distinction need be made between the historically formed position of a formerly dominated outsider group and a formerly dominant established group. Disinterested experts appear indifferent to the ideological meaning of symbols, only that they give illegitimate offence to the national habitus.

The uses of sectarianism

A governmental nexus of legitimate nomination and classification imposes moral indignation and disinterested reform and punishment on devalued 'sectarian' symbols and subjects. Illegitimate physical and symbolic violence are bundled together by governmental authorities as part of what has been termed a civilising offensive. The idea of a civilising *offensive* is indebted to Norbert Elias' (2012) theory of civilising *processes*. As public space is pacified by the state monopoly of violence and taxation, personal and inter-personal life becomes more interdependent, less violent, more restrained and predictable within an unplanned and *long-term* process. With the loosening obligations of family and occupational bonds group relations increasingly take on the character of voluntary forms of association rather than an inescapable fate. This gives rise to a more self-conscious, less emotionally-charged and less spontaneous form of social habitus.

The conceptual development of a civilising offensive was shaped initially by Dutch sociologists to refer to self-conscious, planned and short-term reforms that aim to improve what powerful groups see as 'barbaric practices' of lower classes (Powell, 2013). As Kitty Verrips (1987: 3) put it:

> The term 'civilising offensive' is used by Dutch sociologists and historians to refer to a wide range of phenomena, from nineteenth-century bourgeois efforts to elevate the lower classes out of their poverty and ignorance and convince them of the importance of domesticity and a life of virtue, to the oppression of popular culture in early modern times and, in general, 'the attack on behaviour presumed to be immoral or uncivilised'.

Civilising offensives are closely related to the *ressentiment* attitude produced by the unrelieved tensions of middle class restraint. In his survey of the concept, Ryan Powell (2013) argues that civilising offensives seem to succeed in modifying group conduct and perceptions when they are pushing at an open door, that is when they function as part of a process where the pattern of relations are already moving in the desired direction, which the civilising offensive merely makes more explicit and intelligible.

With increasingly non-violent social relations and increased pressures of self-restraint *ressentiment* is also able to fester over protracted periods of time as the unreason of reasonable people. *Ressentiment* fears of sectarian violence demand recourse to the disinterested punishment of football supporters in a context where rates of non-sexual violent crime fell to their lowest level for 40 years (Scottish Government, 2015b: 19). Violent crime rates in Scotland had been increasing for a long period from the 1970s to 1980s, plateaued during the 1990s, before entering a downward trend in the early 2000s, since when it decreased sharply by around 60 per cent. Little of the remaining violence in society is classified as sectarian, despite the semantic elasticity of the term and the perpetual cycle of media publicity, political campaigns and supportive scholarship. In the Scottish Crime and Justice Survey of 2012/13 (Scottish Government, 2014b: 68), of the intimidation and harassment reported by respondents less than 5 per cent was said to be motivated by 'sectarianism', and even fewer were worried about the threat of sectarianism compared to the chances of random assault or gang-related violence.

It appears that as the real risk of physical violence declines, sensitivity increases towards other, more symbolic 'crimes' requiring the disinterested punishment demanded by a renewed civilising offensive. In a Scottish context, Flint and Powell (2013) situate governmental attempts to curb sectarianism as a civilising offensive within the wider context of the 'civilising' of football spectatorship in the UK in order to address perceived crises of incivility and urban disorder within disorderly public spaces. Largely symbolic rivalries of football offer a convenient displacement activity to legitimate governmental civilising offensives (Waiton, 2013). Civilising offensives open with moral panics shaped by a governmental media offensive to shift illegitimate violence, physical and symbolic, behind the scenes of social life.

Public alarm over sectarianism, insofar as it is uncovered by social attitude surveys, responds to journalistic coverage of and political comment on football rivalry rather than a simple reflection of pre-existing structural or institutional processes. Football is therefore typically seen as the main source of sectarianism, especially among younger people, with Orange Order marches a distant second as a contributing factor. Moreover, survey respondents who perceive sectarianism to be widespread put its causes down to a broader range of factors than football alone, including social media and the politics of Ireland (Ormston et al, 2015: 281-4).

Football affiliations crystallise long-run historical processes in Scotland, particularly the rivalry between the Glasgow clubs, Celtic and Rangers. One team, Celtic, is associated with a historically suspect, outsider minority religion, Roman Catholicism, and a despised foreign nationality, Irish. Glasgow Rangers, on the other hand, for a long time represented the establishment group in Scotland. As a symbol of Protestantism and Scottish Unionism Rangers refused to employ Roman Catholics, a sectarian practice that was abandoned in the 1980s. Celtic traditionally signed players of all denominations. From the 1890s, middle class directors of the club pursued sporting success at all costs. Modernisers put the club on a professional basis and established a profit-driven, private limited company, something that traditionalists saw as a betrayal of Celtic's founding community-based, charitable ideals. Modernisation of the club also enabled middle class leaders of the Irish Catholic community to integrate into the wider sports, legal and business establishment in Scotland, even as they remained committed to a distinctive Glasgow Irish politics (McCallum, 2013).

'Sectarianism' became a public order matter limited to and given expression by football tribalism. Yet the tensions excited by intense club rivalries provide football with its specific function as a temporary rupture with the mundane routines and constraints of daily life. Elias and Dunning (2008) describe public rehearsals of symbolic rivalries and the oscillating tension-balance of football as a 'controlled de-controlling of emotions'. Football has a cathartic effect that permits under controlled conditions what the dull routines of everyday life forbid.

Moral indignation over football hostilities is merely one aspect of a broader governmental-media civilising offensive to legitimate welfare and criminal justice policies in the UK, with particular symbolic and material denigration reserved for sections of the dispossessed working class under conditions of urban marginality (Rodger, 2008). Media representations of poverty in Scotland wed neighbourhood decay and poor cultural taste to bestial gangs, knife crime and territorial violence in disdainful discourses about 'Neds' and urban working class areas in contrast to the civilised national habitus routinely affirmed by all reasonable people (Law and Mooney, 2011).

As such, the civilising offensive follows a general pattern of media escalation and de-intensification over time. Before the 1990s newspaper reports about 'Neds' were almost non-existent and only began to increase in frequency after 1999, spiked in the early 2000s, followed by a rather erratic decline, albeit without returning to its pre-1990s level (Law and Mooney,

2011: 118). 'Sectarianism' shares a similar pattern of media escalation and de-intensification. In his analysis of major national newspaper titles in Scotland, Waiton (2016) demonstrates that there was a gradual but limited increase in the frequency of the use of the term 'sectarianism' during the 1990s, from an almost complete absence in 1992, peaking ten years later with the public debate about 'Scotland's shame' (almost 300 references to sectarianism), falling away again by 2009, before re-emerging with a vengeance as a heightened national discourse in 2011 (350 references).

With the cyclical emergence of sectarianism as simultaneously a media, legal and political narrative, fears of an urban underclass of gangs and Neds were overlaid with the resurrection of another time-honoured bogeyman: the fear of wider quasi-religious conflict between Protestants and Catholics in Scotland. Yet much research demonstrates a weak or non-existent relationship between religious belief and structural discrimination in Scotland. Moreover, religious observance and church attendance are in terminal decline. Data shows that young people are less and less religious than previous generations, resulting in a calamitous decline in Church of Scotland attendance since 1999 from 35 per cent to 18 per cent (2013) – 'nothing short of a collapse amongst all but the oldest category' (Rosie, 2015: 338).

Despite the chasm between religious practice and sectarian relationships they continue to be treated as synonymous or inter-related categories that rise and fall together. Religion is now often seen as a matter of the private beliefs of individuals rather than a shared ethos structuring an entire way of life for the community. Protestantism had of course been central to the development of the national habitus in Scotland – from the Protestant Unionism of the Reformation in 1560, the Union of the Crowns of 1603, and the Union of Parliaments if 1707. While the process of British state formation preserved the position of the Kirk, since the 1970s the established power advantage conferred by Protestant Unionism has dissolved in the acid of a specifically secular Scottish national habitus.

Traditionally, sectarianism referred to exclusionary relations between relatively coherent social groups defined by religion and ethnicity (Weber, 1946). Such dense moral cohesion of self-regulating sectarian groups no longer characterises contemporary Scotland. More than 80 per cent of Catholics claim one or more close Protestant friends while 76 per cent of Protestants claim close Catholic friends. Only a tiny per cent from each category do not know anyone from the other group (Ormston et al, 2015: 279-80).

Social proximity also results in a stronger perception among non-Catholics that Catholics are more likely to experience direct forms of discrimination. The material and moral universe that once gave meaning to sectarianism as a practice to maintain group 'purity' against outsider contamination has all but disappeared in Scotland. Long-run processes of secularisation have weakened the moral authority of religious sects and churches as markers of group cohesion. As a result, intra-Christian religious antagonism is nowhere as virulent or widespread as it was once assumed to be.

A slow accumulation of economic, cultural and social capital prepared the conditions for the colonisation of middle class professions by upwardly-mobile sons and daughters of Catholic manual workers (Paterson, 2000a). As Boyle (2011: 213) argues 'there is a significant body of evidence that the Irish Catholic community has enjoyed an intergenerational rise to promi-nence, wealth, and economic parity. In many respects, many migrants and descendants have risen to form part of a confident and assertive Irish Cath-olic middle-class community in Scotland'. Publicly-funded Catholic schools appear to have played a key role in mitigating occupational exclusion, par-ticularly since the 1960s as employment in Scotland increasingly relied on credentials rather than less formal familial or associational structures. The social alchemy of turning socio-economic dispossession into one of cultural possession is ambiguously experienced as one of social integration and group difference within the national habitus.

While much of the research on life chances for Catholics show that Scot-land has become increasingly meritocratic over the past half century, they are still more likely than their Protestant counterparts to live in deprived areas, to rent their homes, to suffer poorer health, to be the victims of crime, and to experience imprisonment, and exhibit significantly lower than average men-tal and physical wellbeing. Around 60 per cent of Roman Catholics live in Glasgow and Clyde valley area, which also contains 70 per cent of the 15 per cent most deprived areas in Scotland. Partly, this is explicable in terms of the legacy of the historic multiple disadvantages and discrimination towards Irish Catholic descendants from 19th century waves of immigration to the erosion of the industrial base and the rise of the welfare state after 1945.

What this points to is a change in the power-balance between previously dominant and dominated groups in a situation of increasingly fluid group boundaries (Elias and Scotston, 2008). Roman Catholics in Scotland were viewed as a suspect community by the established Protestant group through the construction of negative images of the Roman Catholic Church or the paramilitary politics of Irish republicanism, as well as all sorts of imagined barbarous group practices such as idleness, ignorance, criminality, alcoholism, promiscuity, and so on. Immigrants excluded in such ways from the we-relation of the established national group may look to the state as a survival unit for protection and shelter. In the case of Catholics in Scotland, the right to publicly-funded denominational schools was granted by the Education Act of 1918, in the process helping consolidate the we-feeling of group difference, not only as a bulwark against collective inferiority but also as a mechanism of social integration into the wider British state-society (Finn, 2003), a process consolidated a generation later with the setting up of the welfare state.

On the other hand, the long-established social habitus of Protestant Unionism no longer maps effortlessly to the post-imperial national habitus of modern Scotland. Identifying with the trappings of an imperialist British ruling class and the Orange Order meant that even poor Protestants could feel themselves emotionally superior to Catholics in Scotland. Protestant workers may therefore have felt 'compensated in part by a sort of public and psychological wage', as WEB du Bois (1992: 700) said of poor whites in the South, while Catholics were despised as social inferiors. However, the sectarian separation between established Protestants and Catholic outsiders in 19th and 20th century Scotland was never as absolute, systematic or murderous as the inter-racial system in the US. The prospects for a rigid sectarian divide akin to the deadly racist divide between poor whites and poor blacks in the southern states of the US was tempered by complex social inter-dependencies and struggles for working class solidarity in the industrial centres of Scotland.

Changing power balances in context

It is insufficient to plot an ascending continuum between all forms of antagonistic established-outsider relations as the eternal underlying conditions that make mass violence possible. Instead, it is necessary to locate the power ratio between groups within the specific character of the state formation process, conditions of crisis, and the national habitus. In its most extreme forms, feelings of group humiliation, decline, and victimhood can in conditions of state crisis give rise to mass redemptive violence and fascist movements (Paxton, 2005). An essential precondition for mass violence is a thoroughgoing process of ideological compartmentalisation of social, spatial, institutional and psychological group isolation and dis-identification (de Swaan, 2015). Alongside this, the state formation process plays a vital role in the escalation of violence. So while all states contain political, ethnic or religious categories that do not fit seamlessly into the dominant self-images of the nation, they only lead to mass violence in conditions where the state monopoly of violence is suspended or becomes instrumental in turning dormant identifications into deadly 'killing compartments'.

Moreover, the de-civilising process depended on the permissive conditions of struggles for the state monopoly of violence. *Ressentiment* against European Jewry found its murderous expression in the Holocaust of Nazi mass killing and extermination camps only after Jews were constructed as complete outsiders defiling the purity of the national *Kultur*. In this case the dispersed means of violence of the failed Weimar state was replaced by the concentrated mobilisation of the means of violence by the Nazi state (Elias, 2013). The physical annihilation of outsider ethnic and national groups took place in particular 'enclaves of atrocity' where the target group could be isolated and concentrated and all self-restraint suspended as the killers underwent what de Swaan (2015: 125) calls 'a regression in the service of the regime'.

In the USA, as Elias (2008: 215) notes, the state formation process placed significant means of violence under the control of a sub-group of the population, the white citizenry, and, except for wartime emergencies, systematically excluded another sub-group, the black citizenry, from a defensive share in the means of violence. One sub-group exercised life and death power over the other sub-group. To demonstrate the nature of the extreme power imbalance, Elias (2008) used Lee Harper's novel *To Kill A Mockingbird* as a local case study of 1930s Alabama. Although the black character Tom Robinson accused of raping a white woman, Mayella Ewell, is patently innocent the white mob is nevertheless required to kill him. In their eyes Robinson is guilty of symbolically offending white privilege: 'the killing of a black man suspected of a sexual crime against a white woman was closely connected with the loss of value felt by white men if they were unable to avenge the crime, real or imagined, by killing the person whom they held responsible for the deed' (Elias, 2008: 227).

Although the Robinson family represented the highest stratum of the black community while the Ewells were at the bottom of the white community, the social distance between them loomed like an abyss into which a black man could fall at any time. There was not even a pretence that the law would even-handedly treat as a crime the murder of a black man since that would injure the self-worth of the established group and threaten to uncover the arbitrariness of symbolic privilege.

Nor was the sectarian operation in Scotland as punitive, degrading, violent and systematic as the Penal Laws imposed on Ireland by the British state. Theodore Allen (2012) contends that the invention of 'whiteness' can be traced to the Protestant ascendency in post-1689 Ireland, a judgement already corroborated in 1792 by Edmund Burke. Burke called the systematic exclusion of Catholics from the privileges of state an 'unparalleled code of oppression... manifestly the effects of national hatred and scorn towards a conquered people' (Burke, 1792: 341). Burke was concerned that failures of British statecraft in Ireland, while subjugating the Catholic majority of the 'plebeian class' under the 'exclusive power' of the Protestant minority, exercised 'daily and hourly, an insulting and vexatious superiority' in a 'state of humiliating vassalage (often inverting the nature of things and relations)' (1792: 334).

By creating a sectarian form of Protestant rule, Britain therefore deprived itself of Catholics who might become members of the Irish landowning class and mobilise the authority of property to restrain the mass of dispossessed Catholics from violent resistance, as threatened by the Protestant-led United Irishmen. Instead, Burke (1792: 332) worried that Ireland was 'divided into two distinct bodies, without common interest, sympathy or connexion; one of which bodies was to possess *all* the franchises, *all* the property, *all* the education: The others were to be drawers of water and cutters of turf for them'. By using excessive violence over a long period to enforce Catholic oppression, Burke concluded, British rule had itself created the conditions for 'a mob' to emerge that would resist the humiliation of dispossession using violent means 'without temper, measure, or foresight'. When it finally came, the republican rebellion of 1798 was put down with savage state repression amidst civil war atrocities, while the British rulers manipulated a sectarian counter-revolution of the recently-formed Orange Order to divide Loyalist Protestants from Republican Presbyterians (Smyth, 2000).

The increased integration into a national habitus of Catholics in Scotland may be more usefully compared to the situation of the Protestant minority in the Republic of Ireland. Protestants in the 26 counties were transformed from a formerly powerful established group into an outsider group in the midst of the vast Catholic majority. In this case, a former outsider group became the established national group: 'To this day, in the Republic, both the minority Protestant community and the majority Catholic community are very conscious of the Protestants' former status as a powerful established group' (Mennell et al, 2000: 76). As they exchanged positions, however, both sides absorbed attributes of the other group. Protestants became increasingly restrained about any lingering sense of moral superiority and even adopted some of the negative perceptions of the Protestant ascendancy long felt by Catholics, in part as cultural guilt for the past oppression of the majority by their ancestors.

While bourgeois Protestants continue to enjoy economic power they suffered a grievous loss of social and political power as outsiders to the new power elite of the Irish state. A profound sense of ambivalence is experienced by the small Protestant minority seeking a public role in a state conditioned for much of its history by the influence of the Catholic Church. As Protestants decline numerically and proportionately as 'mixed marriages' become more prevalent, community reproduction through endogamy becomes increasingly difficult to sustain. On the other hand, Catholics have become far more self-critical of their own church and cultivate some of the civilising restraints exemplified by the Protestant minority.

Clearly, the situation of the formerly dominant Protestant minority under the Irish state represents an inverse example to the formerly dominated Catholic minority in Scotland. More closer to the established-outsider relations in Scotland perhaps are the processes examined by Elias and Scotson (2008) by which two groups that resembled each other in almost all respects – white, working class, English, Christian – were nevertheless still divided into hostile groups on the arbitrary basis of how long they had lived in the area. Social images of other groups are formed by 'an optical illusion', Elias argues:

> the images which the 'established', which powerful sections of a society have of themselves and communicate to others, tends to be modelled on 'the minority of the best'; it inclines towards idealisation. The image of 'outsiders', of groups who have in relation to the established relatively little power, tends to be modelled on 'the minority of the worst', it inclines towards denigration (Elias and Scotston, 2008: 7).

A sense of superiority is defended all the more vehemently the longer it has been established as an inter-generational tradition using 'almost everywhere the same weapons, among them humiliating gossip, stigmatising beliefs about the whole group modelled on observations of its worst section, degrading code words and, as far as possible, exclusion from all chances of power' (Elias and Scotston, 2008: 158).

In the case of a long, drawn-out group decline, however, temporary triumphs and a certain continuity in collective rituals, for instance around sport, parades or religion, allow the reality of the changing power-balance to be obscured or denied, despite the dwindling social stock of the group. This is not a linear process but a dynamic and uneven one. In the long-run the personal and group habitus is reformed by uneven and independent developments of locality, work, religion, family, education, politics, and nation. In such ways irrational bigotry has been compelled to recognise and trail the emerging but obdurate realities of modern Scottish society. Fantasy we-images – expressed as triumphalist chants by Rangers fans in the manner of 'We are the People' and 'Simply the Best' – merely heighten the seething but temporary resentments of football rivalries.

On the other hand, the *ressentiment* expressed by official moral indignation for disinterested punishment is functionally reproduced by the established professional middle class in Scotland. Not only the fans but the club itself misrecognises its own changed position in the cultural field as a dominated institution, as when club resentments led to the banning of a BBC journalist for alleged biased reporting, inviting a boycott of the club's ground in retaliation by the BBC, a more dominant institution. On the other hand, the declining institutional power of newspapers in west central Scotland finds it more difficult to protect the professional autonomy of journalists. In early 2016, the respected journalist Graham Spiers resigned from *The Herald* while columnist Angela Haggerty was fired from the *Sunday Herald* after the club complained to the newspaper management about the legality of reports of continuing bigotry among Rangers fans. Supported by the National Union of Journalists Haggerty was reinstated weeks later. Haggerty had been subject to what was described as a four-year long online campaign of anti-Irish racism after editing a book charting Ranger's financial woes, leading to a conviction for religiously aggravated breach of the peace (*Sunday Herald*, 12 January 2014).

Wide variations in social distance and emotional intensity between established and outsider groups permitted by the state formation process indicates some of the difficulties associated with uniformly applying a 'wages of whiteness' approach from its original context to another one where it is has, at best, limited explanatory value. It also highlights the analytical value of the dynamic nature of the established-outsider model developed by Elias to account for the arbitrary valuations of group power imbalances at particular stages in the state formation process.

Whither sectarianism?

A linear model of escalating violence that informs so much of the justification for criminalising offensive conduct at football matches does not bear scrutiny. It is not the case that what Hannah Arendt called the 'banality of evil' festers at football grounds in Scotland among anonymous nobodies ever ready to engage in sectarian violence. Alongside Northern Ireland, Scotland is one of the few nations where the term 'sectarianism' is officially nominated as a fundamental social problem. Yet unlike Northern Ireland, Scotland has not experienced systematic discrimination against the democratic, civil and social rights of a minority religion or nationality, their forced territorial segregation, the formation of paramilitary groups, and decades of anti-state and sectarian violence. Despite the absence of systematic inter-communal segregation, however, public concern about 'sectarianism' has not faded away as might be expected but has instead become a leading political, legal and academic discourse (Law, 2016).

Given the gap between the limited experience and widespread perceptions of 'sectarianism', the term itself does not merely describe some pre-existing phenomenon (Kelly, 2010). Legitimate processes of nomination and classification by governmental authority help to construct what it aims to punish and reform. Institutional and legal measures were introduced to target sectarianism as a failure to adapt to the civilising national habitus. 'Sectarianism' carries an emotional and ideological charge that labels some social relations as irrational and 'mindless' implying that others are civilised and 'mindful' or reasonable. Populist terminology like 'sectarianism' needs to be submitted to the critical analysis of long-run changes in social relations between groups, including the interest in disinterest of governmental power to name, classify and punish.

Rather than reify groups as things in themselves a more adequate socio-logical approach concentrates on the changing power dynamics of social relations. A shift in the power-balance has occurred such that any continuing sense of polar opposition between singular Protestant and Catholic 'communities' as the cultural basis of sectarianism fails to register the reality of long-run sociological processes, the role of governmental nomination, and the moral indignation of disinterested, self-restrained middle class professionals. When a phenomenon such as sectarianism is nominated officially as a 'problem' and neither governmental regulation nor self-regulation are perceived to be able to exercise control or restraint over recalcitrant subjects, a sociology of *ressentiment* compels the state to assume external powers to address the situation. The legitimate nomination of illegitimate names requires the force of a moral indignation that operates under the guise of disinterested punishment.

Uncovering the social sources of sectarianism therefore depends on establishing the relational processes of symbolic communication that constructs sectarianism as a phenomenon that so alarms 'the public'. Unfortunately, the focus has been less on media, legal and political constructions and omissions of sectarianism as moral indignation demanding disinterested punishment. Instead, the central focus has been on the de-civilised outsiders of male working class football fans and the threat that they present to the symbolic and physical integrity of 'the community'. In this sense, sectarianism has been described as a 'social anxiety' that arises from the disjuncture between general perception and individual experience (Rosie, 2015: 330). However, sociology needs to identify the changing power dynamic that names and classifies the unfounded perceptions of the public and understand the social and political function of moral indignation.

Part III:

Contemporary Racisms, Anti-racism and the Policy Field

CHAPTER 6

What do we know about BAME Self-reported Racial Discrimination in Scotland?

Nasar Meer

Introduction

THE CONTRIBUTIONS IN this wide-ranging collection have done at least three things. Firstly, they have drawn our attention to competing histories of modern Scotland and how these reflect dynamics of the 'core' and 'periphery'. Secondly, they have explained how race-making is stitched into the fabric of national identities in Scotland (and why this is important in raising contemporary constitutional questions). And thirdly, against this background, the contributors have assessed the success and failure of race equality strategies as a matter of public administration. In this chapter I wish to add a further set of considerations by more narrowly focusing on two concerns. The first and main activity is to provide an overview and interpretation of a cross-sectional survey of 502 Black and Minority Ethnic (BAME) people in Scotland – the first survey of its kind to focus exclusively on BAME experiences of discrimination. The second is to dwell a little on the policy process in Scotland, and specifically consider the prospects, and capacity, of a much vaunted 'Scottish approach' to pursue race equality.

Surveying BAME Scotland

We should begin by registering that the way we quantitatively measure experiences of discrimination on the grounds of race and ethnicity very much varies from one survey to another. For example, the British Social Attitudes (BSA)

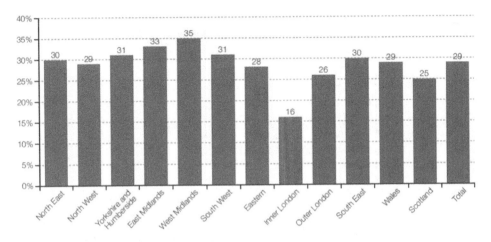

Figure 1 Aggregated Self-Reported Prejudice in the UK

survey asks people the following: 'Would you describe yourself as prejudiced against people of other races?' [10] Using the same question between 1983-2013 they report that in eight of the ten years following 2001, levels of a self-reported affirmative to this question were at 30 per cent or higher, compared with the low point of 25 per cent in 2000-2001 (the 'rolling average' moves from 28 per cent to 34 per cent). They interpret this as a trend that was falling during the 1990s but which 'ticked up' in the first decade of this century. What is especially interesting for our purposes is that this data reports that Scotland has the lowest level of reported prejudice in the UK outside London (figure 1).

One of the obvious flaws with this approach is that 'prejudice' is a notoriously problematic term through which to gauge racial and ethnic discrimination, focusing as it does on individual attitudes and dispositions rather than social systems (Meer, 2014). In a more practice based study which tested for racial discrimination in recruitment processes in British cities, including Glasgow (see figure 2), it has been shown that BAME groups were much less likely to be successful with their applications, even discounting differences such as age and education (Wood et al., 2009).

While this relates only to the early stage of the recruitment process, the shortlisting, to secure a job interview the researchers had to send out 74 per cent more applications for ethnic minority candidates compared to white candidates. When they controlled for other factors the researchers attributed

---

[10] http://www.natcen.ac.uk/blog/is-racial-prejudice-on-the-rise

	All sets of applications (%)	Positive response among set of three (%)
London	40	35
Manchester	17	20
Bradford and Leeds	10	15
Birmingham	16	12
Glasgow	6	8
Bristol	8	7
Other areas	3	3
Base (n)	987	155

Figure 2 Discrimination in practice based recruitment in the UK

this to having a name associated with an ethnic minority background. Unfortunately the numbers of applications sent to employers are too small for differences between the cities to be statistically significant, but the authors conclude there was little to suggest that racial discrimination was a problem confined to particular cities in Great Britain for the results suggest high levels of discrimination in recruitment practices across the board (Wood et al., 2009: 41). In another study, Nicholls et al., (2010: 5) use the concept of 'unfair treatment' to take in questions of discrimination and prejudice as encountered across the equality 'strands' of gender, ethnicity, sexual orientation, disability, religion and belief, and age. Rather than a study of the scale and frequency of discrimination per se, however, these authors showed that 'discrimination was a term that the participants were familiar with', and that respondent provided a clear account of how discrimination 'was directly linked to difference and people being treated differently because of their characteristics'.

This is especially relevant for our purposes because this chapter argues that BAME groups have a familiarity with the concept of racial discrimination, to the extent that they can answer direct questions on this. This has long been supported by qualitative findings, but is also expressed in the largest study of BAME groups ever undertaken in Britain. While some years out of date, the *Fourth National Survey of Ethnic Minorities* (Modood et al., 1997: 131) asked direct questions about the perception of discrimination in the course of reporting, for example, a significant increase since the previous survey [1984] in the belief that employers discriminate on the grounds of race and ethnicity. In the following survey data I tackle racial discrimination and directly ask BAME groups about their experiences, and here there is both good and bad news to report. The survey[11] findings confirm that BAME groups in Scotland have firmly established themselves in Scottish society; feel a strong attachment to it, and like all groups hold diverse sets of views on what they think Scottish society should be like. The experience of discrimination however is one that cuts across BAME experiences and appears to be under-reported and tackling this should be of central importance to policy makers.

As figure 3 below illustrates, this includes the findings that 31 per cent of the aggregated sample 'Agreed' with the statement 'I have experienced discrimination in Scotland in the last 5 years'. This is however varied amongst different groups. For example nearly 45 per cent of respondents with a Black African Caribbean heritage, compared with 29 per cent of Asian heritage and 23 per cent of the Mixed heritage respondents, agreed with the statement that they had 'experienced discrimination in Scotland in the last five years'. Within this slightly more men (33.7 per cent) than women (28.4 per cent) agreed with the statement, and while 18-34 yr olds (30.8 per cent) and 35-54 yr olds (29.7 per cent) were similar there was an increase for those aged 55+ (35.5 per cent).

When asked similar but intentionally less personalised questions, nearly 35 per cent agreed with the statement 'discrimination is a widespread problem in Scotland' and 42 per cent agreed with the statement that 'other people would perceive discrimination to be a problem in Scotland'. As figure 4

---

[11] Undertaken during the summer of 2015, data were made representative by being weighted by sex, age, ethnic group and region of Scotland. Targets were derived from the 2011 Scottish Census regarding the demographics of different ethnic groups in Scotland. Respondents were recorded at the local authority level but grouped into three large regions for weighting purposes (North East and Highlands, Eastern Scotland and South Western Scotland). Those giving an ethnic group of 'Other' were not weighted up or down by ethnic group but were held constant on that aspect of their weighting, as we considered that there was room for ambiguity in the definition of an 'other' ethnic group and were concerned that people who gave this answer by phone might differ from those who gave this answer to the paper census questionnaire, on which it was clear that 'other ethnic group' was mostly for those who considered themselves to belong to the "Arab" ethnic group. In terms of geography, this was recorded at the local authority level but grouped these into three large regions for weighting purposes, as the bulk of the BAME population in Scotland are concentrated in the Greater Glasgow urban area (broadly analogous to the South Western Scotland region in the regions cross-break).The survey achieved a rim weighting efficiency of 91.4 per cent. The maximum respondent rim weight was 2.471 whilst the minimum respondent rim weight was 0.556 (these weights are well within acceptable quality bounds and reflect the good quality sampling during the fieldwork stage).

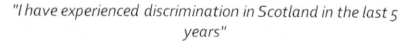

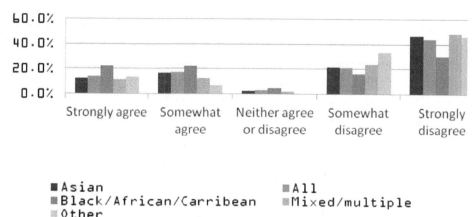

Figure 3 Self-reported experiences of discrimination in Scotland

illustrates, of those who reported experiencing discrimination, more than four-fifths (82 per cent), felt this was due to their real or perceived ethnicity, and a further 42 per cent felt it was due to their real or perceived religion.

There was a slightly increased tendency for Muslim respondents to self-report experiences of discrimination, and this is consistent not only with

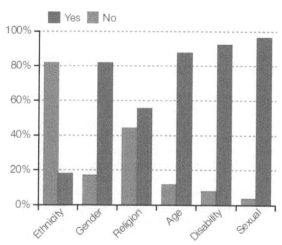

Figure 4 Perceived sources of self-reported experiences of discrimination in Scotland

UK wide research (IHRC, 2015) but is also linked to a marked difference in Scottish attitudes to the public visibility of non-Christian difference, and Islam in particular. For example, Ormston *et al.*, (2011) have shown that Christian and Muslim symbols enjoy a different status in terms of public attitudes of acceptability, noting in particular the prevalence of the view that employers should be allowed to request the removal of Muslim religious symbols but not that of Christians. In more qualitative work, Hopkins et al (2015) too have charted the self-reporting of the racialisation of Muslims in their sample of Scottish schools.

In our survey all BAME groups who reported facing discrimination did not restrict it to a single area, but identified instead perceived discriminatory experiences in employment – either 'in getting a job' (36 per cent) or 'in being promoted' (31 per cent) – as well as 'in education' (35 per cent) and in the use of transport services (35 per cent). Smaller proportions, though still around a fifth of the representative sample, said they experienced discrimination in 'achieving equal pay' (22 per cent) and in 'using health services' (18 per cent). As figure 5 details, over half of the sample (52 per cent) also said they had experienced discrimination 'in other areas' in the last 5 years.

If we dwell on the sector of employment for a moment, beginning with the first, and as touched upon above, the vignette by Wood et al., (2009) has shown that BAME candidates in Scotland do indeed pay an ethnic penalty in terms of employment opportunities throughout the application process. In

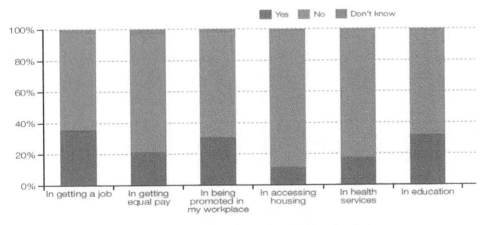

Figure 5 Experiences of Discrimination by Sector

a quite comprehensive report the Scottish Parliament's Equal Opportunities Committee (2016) registered these disparities, noting that despite equivalent education and skills BAME Scots were more likely to be unemployed or in low-paid work than White people. This was especially highlighted in the written submission from the Coalition of Racial Equality and Rights (CRER), which stated that *17.7 per cent of BAME people interviewed for local authority jobs were appointed, compared to a figure of 31.9 per cent for white interviewees (2016: para 15).*

It is a finding that sits in a broader employment gap between BAME and white people in Scotland, and which Scottish Government (2015a) data has shown to be significant: in 2013, 57.4 per cent BAME groups were in employment compared with 73.8 per cent of non-BAME groups. This discrepancy can be seen to permeate efforts to redress inequalities too, with the Modern Apprenticeships being the most prominent example, and where the proportion of people from BAME groups numbering 2.1 per cent against 5.2 per cent of those possibly qualified to be in receipt of one (Skills Development Scotland, 2016).

Interestingly, my survey found that 60 per cent of respondents who had experienced discrimination in the last five years did not report it to any kind of authority. This was despite 82 per cent of the entire sample insisting they would encourage a friend or family to make a formal complaint if they thought they had experienced discrimination.

This suggests that perceptions of both low-level and more obvious experiences of racial discrimination in Scotland go under-reported. What this

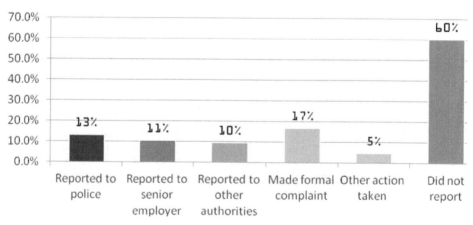

Figure 6 Action as a result of discrimination

needs to set against is the seemingly paradoxical finding that 65 per cent of the entire sample 'Strongly' or 'Somewhat Agreeing' with the statement 'I have confidence in the laws against discrimination' (with 20 per cent disagreeing), and 64 per cent agreeing that they had confidence in the authorities and other organisations to pursue discrimination cases (25 per cent disagreeing). How should we understand this? I would suggest that one way is to think about this is the way in which race functions as an absent-present. By this I mean that the nature of race as a social phenomenon is such that it spans the micro-, miso-, and macro-, in a manner that makes is simultaneously absent and present across what, following Bourdieu, we have come to call the social field.

This sounds like a contradictory statement unless we grasp that the social and political history of Scotland, no less than that the rest of the UK, means that it has come to think of itself in racial terms without necessarily intending too (or at least not being conscious of itself as doing so). How could it not? While some maintain that historical disadvantage (not least at the hands of the English) has meant race is less present in people's sense of what Scotland is, the attitudinal survey data does not bear this out (Bechhofer and McCrone, 2012). Perhaps more profoundly, any serious record of Scotland cannot ignore the place of race within it, in so far as the Scottish story, just as the British one, is 'Bursting with Skeletons' (Marquand, 2009). Throughout various cycles of British expansionism and colonial settlement, the sons and daughters of Scotland made up its military and civilian ranks in copious numbers (Stenhouse 2004). In the most profitable parts of the East Indian Trading Company, roughly half of the accountants and officer cadets were Scottish (Devine, 2003: 251). In the words of the third Earl of Rosebery, this relationship 'Scotticised India and Orientalised Scotland' (quoted in Devine 2003, 126). Indeed, from the middle of the 19th century, the British Raj system was created under a Scottish governor (General James Dalhousie), while elsewhere the Scot Charles James Napier effectively annexed the Sind province (a large part of modern Pakistan). Hence, by the mid-19th century, when one in ten of the British population was Scottish, one third to a quarter of the civil service elite grade of the East India Company was Scottish. So 'as late as 1928, the Chief of the Imperial and Indian General Staffs were both Scots' (Pittock, 2008, 9), while the hymns of war 'Scotland the Brave' and later 'Flower of Scotland' were appropriated as popular national anthems (McCrone, 2001: 158).

The legacy of this is perhaps what Goldberg (2006: 339) means when he characterises race as disappearing 'into the seams of sociality, invisibly holding the social fabric together even as it tears apart'. As is illustrated in the chapters throughout this collection, there are a variety of different conceptual repertoires for conceptualising this incubation and diffusion of race, how it is sustained in structures and felt by people.

I have tried to systematically summarise these elsewhere and so do not need to repeat here (e.g. Meer, 2014), but suffice to say that different concepts concerned with race-making can bear a family resemblance whether or not their proponents emphasise this. For example, the literatures on 'Critical Race Theory' (Delgado and Stafancic, 1993), 'Everyday Racism' (Essed, 1991) and 'Racial Formation' (Omi and Winnant, 1986) all share in common the view that racial inequalities are a normalised feature of the social field – how and why this has become so is probably more disputed. My preference is the racialisation thesis, because it sets out to span micro-, miso- and macro- in interrogating the processes of race making throughout (Meer, 2013).

If we focus on everyday practice, another helpful lens is that of 'racial microaggressions' which has come to describe a variation of everyday racism. With a provenance in critical race theory research, and so a further illustration of the connections across different repertoires, Sue (2007: 271) characterised racial microaggressions as the 'brief and common place daily verbal, behavioural, or environmental indignities, whether intentional or unintentional, that communicates hostile, derogatory or negative racial slights and insults'. If we accept that the understanding of race and racism cannot be reduced to a microaggressions approach, we can use it with caution to explore some of the survey findings under discussion. Specifically, we might rely on a reading of racial microaggressions not so much to explore the acts themselves, but the manner in which they are negotiated by BAME Scots who, in our findings it would appear, compartmentalise or bracket off microaggressions in their wider negotiation of social life. This is of course a complex practice and the claims in favour of it as an explanation are limited without qualitative data, but this reading would also appear to be supported by the secondary literatures too (e.g., Hopkins et al., 2015).

Equally however we should not ignore the reports that BAME Scots do make, which also tell us as much as their absences, and in obvious respects point to a clear pattern of tendencies. This includes the finding that for the year 2015–2016 race-motivated hate crimes were also the most common hate crimes (3,712 reports) (Crown Office and Procurator Fiscal Service (COPFS) 2016). The Scottish Household Survey (2015) meanwhile reported that of the 9 per cent of people in Scotland who had experienced some form of harassment during the previous 12 months, at least 10 per cent attributed this to race or ethnicity. When respondents in my survey were asked if they felt incidents of racial discrimination were increasing or decreasing, 21 per cent stated they have become 'more frequent', 22 per cent 'less frequent', and 43 per cent that they had 'stayed the same' over the last five years. Over half (54 per cent) agreed and nearly a quarter (24 per cent) disagreed with the statement 'the Scottish government is doing enough to tackle discrimination in Scotland'.

The study also asked respondents about national identities, and found more than a third of the entire sample (35 per cent) described themselves 'equally Scottish and British', with Scottish Muslims notably more likely to do so at over 42 per cent. Precisely *both* 38 per cent of respondents voted in favour and against Independence in the 2014 referendum respectively. When asked whether an Independent Scotland 'would be better or worse placed to tackle discrimination in Scotland', 22 per cent said it would be 'better placed' and 17 per cent said it would be 'worse placed', and 47 per cent said it would 'make no difference' (12 per cent answered 'Don't Know' and 2 per cent refused to answer). As has already been established in the literature, in this collection and elsewhere, the in-group status of BAME Scots has implications for the claims they might make upon the nation.

A 'Scottish approach' to race equality?

We certainly know from other fieldwork that racial discrimination occurs across the UK – for example, that BAME applicants are less likely to be successful in applying for a job even discounting differences such as age and education. As this survey shows, we cannot assume this is not an issue in Scotland too, and the findings are presented in the context of a much vaunted distinction in Scottish policy-making, including that focusing on race equality.

Scottish approaches to Race Equality have come a long way since Martin MacEwen (1980) wondered if 'race-relations' in Scotland were best characterised by 'ignorance or apathy'. This complaint looks firmly out of place today even though matters of equality are formally reserved to Westminster in the Scotland Act (1998). Scotland, as the UK, has broadly understood tackling discrimination as something active in seeking to treat people equally rather than resting on a benign ideal of equal treatment. In theory at least, this reaches beyond how different groups might blend into society, and relies on group-specific instruments to outlaw discrimination based on gender, disability, age, sexual orientation and so forth, as well as monitoring the institutional under-representation among such groups (Meer 2010). Amongst this increasingly intersectional configuration, approaches to race equality have developed what Hepple (2011) calls an 'unsettled apparatus' that is also reflected in Schedule 5 of the Scotland Act 1998 (c46), which incorporated the functions of the third Race-Relations Act (1976). Other developments however can be traced to a distinctively Scottish, rather than UK, experience.

Firstly, in terms of *categories*, successive Scottish Acts tackling religious bigotry and incitement to religious hatred have adopted tariffs and sanctions that make the treatment of religious discrimination more symmetrical to racial discrimination than is the case in England and Wales. Other chapters in this book will demonstrate the lively debate over the form and scale of sectarianism in Scotland (see also Raab and Holligan 2012). Government initiatives, through legislation such as the Offensive Behaviour at Football and Threatening Communications (Scotland) Act 2012, make special mention of religious discrimination, and offer equivalent protection on the grounds of race, colour, nationality, ethnicity, sexual orientation, gender identity and disability. It is also worth remembering that Scotland also recognised Gypsy/Traveler communities as racial and ethnic groups sooner than elsewhere in the rest of the UK.

Secondly, as the new Race Equality Framework (2016) illustrates, Scotland has retained a public commitment to race equality and explicitly sought to entrench its mainstreaming. During the UK wide consultation on harmonising different equality bodies and different equality legislation, one repeated concern was the risk of rolling back equality achievements. Where there was no immediate 'dilution' and settlements were 'levelled up' across different grounds, a concern remained that separate commissions would no longer be able to agitate for equality on specific grounds. With more streamlined legislation, it was feared, a less favourable political administration in more cash-strapped times would encounter less resistance if they moved to undermine existing settlements.

Craig and O'Neil (2013) point to these developments in England, noting the budget of the harmonised Equality and Human Rights Commission

(EHRC) was reduced by the Coalition government (2010–2015) to the equivalent of less than one of its constituent bodies (from £70m when it started in 2007 to £17m presently). While this affects Scotland, too, the EHRC in Scotland and the Scottish Government has tried to mitigate this by bolstering its commitment to equality. Thus, in May 2012, the Scottish government placed specific duties on public authorities, also known as the Scottish Specific Duties, which requiring a listed authority to publish a mainstreaming report on the progress it has made in integrating the three needs of the General Equality Duty (GED) to: (i) Eliminate unlawful discrimination, harassment and victimisation; (ii) Advance equality of opportunity, and (iii) Foster good relations. This is in contrast to the discontinuation of statutory equality impact assessments in England, and possibly marks a divergence from understanding race equality instruments as an administrative burden, signalled by placing the public sector equality duty in the government's 'red tape reduction challenge'. Some observers have characterised these developments as forming part of a wider 'Scottish approach' that traverses a number of policy domains, but which is underwritten by a distinctive 'style' of government (Keating, 2005). Cairney (2016: 339) offers a useful description of the provenance and different possible iterations, at least in the policy studies literature, as something which began with devolution:

> [A]s a broad idea about how to govern by consensus in an era of 'new politics'; developed from 2007 as a way to pursue a 'single vision', cross-cutting government aims, and an outcomes-based measure of success, developed in cooperation with the public sector; and became, from 2013, a way to articulate, and measure the impact of, key governing principles ('assets-based', 'co-production', 'improvement methodology') and address specific issues such as inequality. In other words, when articulated by the Scottish Government, 'Scottish approach' describes, increasingly, a large number and mix of specific reforms, aims and principles – and is distinct from the more general academic notion of 'policy style'.

While there is some ongoing work in this area[12] the study of race within this approach remains largely overlooked, and which is why this collection is so important. One of the ways in which we might explore whether we have the burgeoning features of a Scottish approach in this area is to consult the

[12] See www.raceequalityscotland.com

new Race Equality Framework Scotland (2016). This was brought together by the Coalition for Race Equality and Rights (CRER) and Scottish Government's Equality Unit. In addition to a wide range of stakeholders it reflected a broad consultation with strategic partners including the Council for Ethnic Minority Voluntary Organisations (CEMVO), the Back and Ethnic Minority Infrastructure in Scotland (BEMIS), the Scottish Refugee Council (SRC), and the Equality and Human Rights Commission (EHRC), and so reflects a collective commitment to this issue from a range of colleagues. The Framework document itself shows that there has been a sincere effort to reflect on the successes and limitations of prevailing race equality approaches in Scotland, and an attempt to identify gaps in data and other kinds of practice based knowledge that might hinder the delivery of effective race equality strategies. Given the proposed period of the new Framework it is reasonable to expect that if there is more formal commitment to race equality in Scotland, then greater divergence is plausible. Does this point to evidence of a distinctive 'Scottish Approach' to race equality?

There are areas where I think the new Framework has the potential to mark a real advance. The first is on embedding race equality effectively into the induction and continuing professional development (CPD) for public sector staff, and doing this not only for national level actors, but taking it to Scottish Local Authorities where much of the race equality strategy has to be delivered. I think this is crucial when we consider the 2012 Scottish Duties. Amongst other things these require Local Authorities to generate work force data. Given we know race inequality is partly sustained by the status quo in such things as occupational location and hierarchy, not least in the recruitment of new workers and the departure of existing workers, this data is crucial – precisely because it provides local authorities with insights as to where in their cultures of practice and institutions, discrimination can be found.

Over a quarter of Scotland's Local Authorities have not generated workforce data, and so are not compliant with the Scottish Duties 2012; that is the aggregate and the figures are much higher for some local authorities. So the new Framework marks an important commitment to ensure that national strategies do not stay at the national level, nor see the national as an endpoint in a way that misses the importance of implementation. There are of course a set of policy logics that ought to draw our attention to the local. Chief amongst these is that local authorities are key actors, and understanding the choices they make about what to implement and how to implement it are crucial. So it is very prescient and heartening to see the Framework committed to what is happening on the ground and why.

The second is reporting. This is not just a data management issue but is about fostering the confidence amongst BME groups to deem it worthwhile to speak up. And the commitments in the Framework to develop progress reporting mechanisms that are transparent and accountable are so very necessary. It is important however not to trade a focus on outcomes for processes. As the authors in this collection show, ethnic penalties continue to permeate life chances in education and employment. Moreover it is not yet clear how successfully, from a race equality perspective, the new Public Sector Equality Duty that accompanied the Equality Act 2010 has been embedded in Scotland. So whilst Scotland has much that is distinctive, it is uncertain how the various initiatives and policies intended to promote race equality are being delivered or indeed the nature of the overall national trajectory.

Where then does this leave us?

The survey discussed here suggests that Scotland has more of a problem with racial discrimination than some UK data would have us believe – to the extent that UK wide surveys can be misleading in telling a story about Scotland. The areas in which BAME groups are reporting experiencing discrimination is not restricted to a single area: e.g., the labour market, but includes the use of public transport and health care. There is clearly a significant problem of under-reporting, yet the striking finding is that this is not about alienation but instead more about BAME groups in Scotland living with and negotiating race across the social field. If a Scottish approach is to develop beyond progressive political rhetoric (which is not without value), then it should begin with ensuring that existing statutory commitments are more consistently put into practice, especially in terms of the Equality Duty, not least by making full operational use of existing instruments.

CHAPTER 7

Cultural Racism and Islamophobia in Glasgow

Paul Goldie

Introduction

THE APPOINTMENT OF Humza Yousaf as Minister for Europe and International Affairs in the Scottish Parliament gives the appearance that the Scottish National Party is unlike other nationalist formations. Indeed, with the SNP's openly declared position of 'civic nationalism' a message is sent out that ethnic minorities are treated favourably in Scotland. Achievements in representation are important; however, this does not mean that anti-Muslim racism is not a problem in Scotland, only that a career in politics is a viable option for Scottish Muslims. This qualifying statement is necessary because that same MSP received a tirade of racist abuse whilst selling *The Big Issue* at Glasgow Queen Street station (BBC News, 2015a). Furthermore, recent research has demonstrated that the ethnic group most likely to be victims of racist incidents in Scotland are Pakistanis (Scottish Government, 2015b). This chapter explores the issue of anti-Muslim racism against the backdrop of the prevailing myth that Scotland has no issue with racism.

The first section will explore the multifaceted migration process that has resulted in the establishment of a Scottish Muslim community. The second section of this essay will examine the idea of 'race' and the concept of racism in a bid to demonstrate how Scottish Muslims have undergone a process of racialisation over the past few decades. The third section will focus on the theoretical relationship between racism and nationalism and demonstrate how the idea of national belonging resulted in the formation of an inclusive/exclusive discourse (Malik, 1996). The fourth section will examine the existing literature on the Muslim experience in Scotland. In doing so, it will highlight the scant attention that this subject has received within academia. The penultimate section will draw upon empirical work that I undertook a number of years ago into the presence or absence of cultural racism, involving structured interviews with 'white' Scottish residents of the east-end of Glasgow, looked at issues of Scottish culture and belonging. The final section will provide a discussion on: anti-Muslim racism in Scotland; how it 'operates' and what the consequences are for future research.

Migration to the UK

The majority of Scotland's 77,000 Muslims are descended from migrants from the Indian sub-continent – most of who came from Pakistan and Bangladesh (Census, 2011; Visram, 1995). The socio-economic conditions that brought these 'new Scots' to Scotland's shores are worth exploring because understanding people's past can help us better understand their present circumstances. As Miles (1993: 9) argues history is important because 'it permits an assessment of the extent to which contemporary realties may be specific to the contemporary conjuncture, or to a particular epoch... or alternatively are universal attributes of all social relations'.

Migration from India dates back to the 1600s where capitalist elites sought to expand their operation and exploit India's rich spice trade (Mann, 1992). During this period those same elites employed Asian seaman known as Lascars to meet the demand for labour on the ships that operated between the two nations. Over time this source of labour would be central in the crewing of ships that fed the arteries of empire. The significance and enduring nature of this migration is demonstrable in that lodging houses for Lascars were still being built in Glasgow as late as the 1930s (Garret, 2015).

Colonial relations also resulted in many wealthy capitalists commonly referred to as Nabobs employ Asian nannies or Ayahs, to look after their families whilst in India and on the long journey home to Britain. Gratitude for their services was often in scant supply, and many had their employment cruelly terminated on arrival in port. In sum, much of early Asian migration into Britain was from poor working-class Indians who sought to make a living through a connection with the Empire (Visram, 1995).

The largest flow of migration from the Indian sub-continent into Britain occurred after ww2. The violent and bloody separation of India and Pakistan

resulted in many fleeing for a better life in Britain. In particular, many Indians came to Britain to escape the unrest in the Punjab; a substantial number
of which settled in England and more latterly Scotland (Edward, 1993). On
arrival, many were welcomed by a British capitalist class whose business
benefited from a cheap exploitable labour force. Also, state elites were for-
tunate as the migration rovided the skilled and unskilled labour needed to
implement the post-war settlement. Consequently, many doctors, nurses and
labourers came to settle and work in Britain (Mann, 1992). Finally, during
the post-war period, migration also occurred from African countries such as
Kenya where many south Asians, who settled there through their connection
with the British Empire, were expelled due to the unrest caused by a further
phase of de-colonisation (Edwards, 1993).

Asian migration from Africa caused particular concern amongst political
leaders of the time who feared that up to 200,000 potential migrants could
exercise their right to settle in Britain as Commonwealth citizens (Visram,
1995). So acute were these fears amongst politicians that the 1962 Commonwealth Immigration Act was introduced to curb 'black migration' from
the colonies. It is at this point that it could be argued that the boundary of
'race' and 'nation' mesh in an attempt to construct Scotland (and Britain) as
a 'white' nation. Virdee (2014: 112) argues that the following decades saw
sustained levels of discrimination so much so that 'Asian migrant labour and
their British-born children had come to occupy a distinctive position in class
relations – as a racialised fraction of the working class'.

The most recent policy which contributed to the establishment and
growth of the Scottish Muslim community is that of dispersal. In 1999
Glasgow City Council volunteered to become a dispersal site for asylum
applicants. This policy was carried out clumsily and with very little thought
for the communities they were to join. Housing estates in Sighthill and Car-
donald were expected to accept significant amounts of asylum seekers against
a backdrop whereby the media and certain UK politicians were stigmatising
them as scroungers (Scottish Government, 2003). During this period there
were claims that asylum seekers were receiving preferential treatment in
terms of access to housing and social services. Therefore, many residents
of the communities earmarked as dispersal sites felt that their social-class
position was on a precarious footing.

This section has sought to demonstrate that over the past few hundred
years a significant heterogeneous group of migrants has entered the UK and,

through a process of signification (which will be discussed later), has come to what might be described as a Scottish Muslim community. The countries where many Scottish Muslims have ancestral connections are as diverse as Pakistan, Bangladesh, Kenya, Eritrea, Afghanistan, and more recently Syria (Scottish Refugee Council, 2012; Guardian, 2015).

The idea of 'race' and the concept of racism

Before discussing anti-Muslim racism in Scotland it is worth exploring the idea of 'race' and the concept of racism. The idea of 'race' entered into scientific discursive practice during the enlightenment. It is throughout this period that 'race' came to 'refer to a biological type of human being and science purported to demonstrate the number of characteristics of each 'race', and the hierarchical relationship between them' (Miles, 1989: 39). A number of key proponents of scientific 'race' theory were Scottish. For example, Edinburgh born phrenologist George Combe (1788 –1858) used his scientific method of skull measurement to claim that Indians were savages and, when questioned about slavery in America, Combe stated that African Americans were inferior to 'whites' (Gosset, 1997: 73). It is not coincidental that the idea of 'race' gained such a favourable reception amongst certain elites during a time when western European nations sought to colonise, subjugate, and eliminate populations throughout the world.

Scientific 'race' theory endured throughout the 19th and early into the 20th century and formed the corner-stone of many economic, social and political projects. However, after the horrors of the holocaust were revealed the idea of 'race' was successfully challenged (Banton, 2000; Miles, 1993). Although 'race' thinking was discredited as a category of scientific analysis it could not be so readily challenged as a category of social and political practice (Brubaker, 2000). Therefore, the idea of 'race' would continue to shape social relations between peoples long after its scientific usefulness had been called into question.

Many argue that the idea of 'race' still 'operates' through an articulation in discourses surrounding culture (Balibar and Wallerstein, 1991; Barker, 1981). Taguieff (2001) states one of the reasons for this transmutation is because anthropologists have made the argument that it is culture not biology that determines the essence of who we are and how we behave. For Taguieff this leaves the 'intellectual space' for racist elites to deploy the argument: if indeed culture is the true essence of who we are – and that all cultures are equal and essential to the progression of the singular human race – then arguments can be made against intercultural contact, cultural mixing and the maintenance of separate development. Therefore arguments originally used to challenge racists doctrines have been 'turned about' to justify racist conduct (Taguieff, 2001).

In approaching the legacy of what Montagu (1998) fittingly terms *Man's Most Dangerous Myth,* Miles (1989) has sought to approach the 'problem of race' through using the analytical concept of racism produced through a process of racialisation. In referring to racialisation Miles (1989: 79) talks of the 'signification of some biological characteristic(s) as the criterion by which a collectivity may be identified as having a natural, unchanging origin and status, and therefore as being inherently different'. Alongside this process of significa-tion is the negative attribution of a particular characteristic; examples could be lazy, criminally inclined or barbarous savage. If we couple Miles's definition of racialisation with the cultural absolutist position that emerged after the WW2, we can see that any signification of 'culture' can act in a similar way that 'race' has done: culture can act as a homologue of 'race' (Malik, 1996).

Shifting identities: the 'creation' of the Muslim in Britain

The primacy of a Muslim identity amongst British Asians is in many ways a recent occurrence. Previously those who are now viewed as/or self-identify as, Muslim would have been recognised by a range of national, and ethnic identities. Malik (2009) talks of growing up in a 'community that never thought of themselves as Muslim and of which religion expressed a relation-ship with God not a sacrosanct public identity'. He cites factors such as The Rushdie affair, 9/11, 7/7, the collapse of the left, and rise of identity poli-tics as being central to the formation of the Muslim community in Britain (Malik, 2009: 4-5). Malik also highlights how the policy of multiculturalism facilitated the 'space' for religious leaders to posit the primacy of a Muslim identity. It is not within the scope of this essay to further explore the geo-po-litical causes of the rise in prominence of the religious identity Muslim over other possible national-ethnic identities. However, Malik does successively highlight the processes whereby: global events shape local identities; govern-ment policies affect how groups seek recognition; a shift in political align-ment creates the space for new political identities to emerge.

The relationship between racism and nationalism

The relationship between racism and nationalism is no easy thing to disentangle. Mosse (1994) argues that racism and right wing nationalism became identical in the later part of the 19th century. Barker (1981) argues that the notion of a *homogenous way of life* acts to create the perception of a nation that shares a common culture that binds people together. Therefore, 'the danger from immigration is that the 'alienness' of the outsider cracks the homogeneity of the insider' (Barker, 1981: 20). Malik (1996) drawing on the work of 19th century philosophers, has shown how the changing 'nature' of nation states has resulted in an emergence of a concept of 'national culture' that can exclude just effectively as ideas of 'race'.

The Scottish National Party's position with regards to immigration cannot be considered right-wing. Recent press releases demonstrate the favourable position the government takes on the issues (BBC, 2015b). In terms of promulgating a myth of a homogenous way of life the Scottish government again appears to do well. In 2008 they have been responsible for running awareness raising campaigns and initiatives such as 'One Scotland, Many Cultures' – or 'One Scotland' as it is now called. However, in Chapter 1 of this volume, Liinpää has successfully demonstrated contradictions within the government's own stance on this issue. In examining the Homecoming event which spanned 2008–2014 Liinpää's contribution focused on how Scottish culture is largely framed through highland culture. Therefore, the SNP, like many others appropriate highland culture idioms as part of a wider reification of Scottish cultural identity. Furthermore during these same celebrations a selective definition of the Scottish diaspora was deployed in marketing to avoid attention being drawn to Scotland's imperial past. In particular its slave trade. Regions such as the Caribbean were avoided in favour of North America and Australia. Therefore, a critical eye is needed when checking for congruence in government rhetoric and action. A further factor that would shape the relationship between 'race' and 'nation' in Scotland is its status as a nation within a multinational state formation. It is arguable that people's attitudes surrounding 'who belongs' will be influenced by UK politicians who constantly talk down the benefits of migration and talk up the corrosive affects it has on 'national unity'.

What now follows is an examination of the studies that have been conducted into the Muslim community in Scotland. What is noticeable in completing this exercise is the dearth of material there is on the subject. This is followed by the findings of my own research into cultural racism in Glasgow.

Research focusing on Scotland

As previously stated, the volume of research into Muslim lives in Scotland is dwarfed by the amount of material available in England. However, Peter Hopkins (2010) conducted a study into the lives of young Muslim men in Scotland – during which, he looked at factors that contribute to inclusion and exclusion within Scottish society. Many who were interviewed stated that being born in Scotland, upbringing, accent, and education could act to increase claims to Scottishness. This confirms a broader finding of Kiely et al's (2005) work that birth claims to Scottishness resonate strongly amongst Scots. Furthermore, it shows that a process of cultural syncretism goes some-way to making boundaries between communities permeable.

However, Hopkins (2010) goes on to argue that factors such as a percep-tion of the prevalence of a pub and club culture often marked young Muslim men out as different; therefore, acting to exclude many from an imagined view of Scottish life. Hopkins further argues that in a post 9-11 environ-ment those who display their '"Muslimness", whether this be through dress, through having a beard or simply through skin colour, are more likely to be marginalised through everyday racism' (Hopkins, 2010: 269). This research speaks to a racialisation of Muslim culture and the lingering presence of biological racism. Finally, Hopkins's work also points to a prevailing notion of Scottish culture as being hermetically sealed by some; thus, acting as the basis to exclude cultural minorities.

Kyriakides et al (2009) conducted a study into the relationship between racism and nationalism in the south-side of Glasgow and came up with findings that both conform and challenge aspects of Hopkins's work. Using Back's (1996) concept of neighbourhood nationalism they sought to inves-tigate 'the Muslim' as a racialised role sign, and to what extent this has been deemed an oppositional identity in the construction of Scottish codes of cultural belonging. The findings showed that the demonisation of the Muslim as not belonging within the imagined national body is challenged at the multi-ethnic neighbourhood level. Further, factors such as accent, dress, and behaviours disrupt the linkage between somatic features and national belonging. As such: "whiteness" has become an unstable identifier of Scottishness... [and that a]...processes of cultural syncretism which previously included blacks whilst excluding people of Asian descent are fragmenting' (Kyriakides et al 2009: 290).

Siriaj (2011) conducted a study of the meanings that Glasgow Muslim women attach to modesty and the hijab. Of those who wore the hijab in Glasgow many felt that it was a way in which to access public spaces whilst managing people's perceptions of them. Conversely, there were those who felt that wearing the hijab in Glasgow located women in a secondary position. Siriaj's (2011) findings highlight the tensions that can exist between western liberal ideas of equality and those wanting to practice modesty as part of their faith in Scotland.

Finally, Hussain and Miller (2006) conducted a wide ranging study into the effects of the intersection between multiculturalism and multinationalism. They similarly argue that much of the literature on ethnic minorities in Britain focuses on England and is transposed onto the wider United Kingdom. The study looks at both 'visible' and 'invisible' minorities and concluded using a range of measures, 'that the Majority of Scots are less Islamophobic than the English' (Hussain and Miller 2006).[13]

Empirical findings of my own Glasgow-based study

The following research was conducted in 2013 with a small scale sample, and sought to 'test' for the presence or absence of cultural forms of racism in the east-end of Glasgow. The east-end was selected because it was an area undergoing transition. That is to say, it was an area that was undergoing significant changes in the demographic make-up of the area. This state of flux was attributable to the policy of dispersal and a process of EU expansion. I thought that if there was going to be evidence of hate-speech amongst residents it would be directed towards asylum seekers and recent EU migrants. What I never expected was the prejudice which emerged against Scotland's Muslim community.

The research began by looking at how participants self-identified. This is significant because looking at tensions between self-identification and ascription of identity can shed light on discourses of belonging (Balibar, 1991). Initially all participants were asked: Do they see themselves as Scottish? All participants with the exception of one strongly identified themselves as

---

[13] Hussain and Miller (2006) looked at attitudes to Pakistani Scots and the English in Scotland.

Scottish. John, a 35-year-old resident of Glasgow stated that: 'I do see myself as Scottish although I do have a British passport, if asked; I always say that my nationality is Scottish. I was born in Scotland therefore I am Scottish.' John shows a clear preference for the identity Scottish over British. It shows the tensions that exist between the ascription of a nationality, in this case British in legal documents such as passports, and his preferred identity Scottish. Therefore, in this instance, the participant chooses to align themselves with a distinct national identity within a supra-national body. Further, this extract supports Kiely et al's (2005) assertion that 'birth claims' strongly influence claims to Scottishness. Other potential reasons for this rejection of Britishness as a primary carrier of identity could be the historical dominance of Englishness in the construction of Britishness; whereby, many Scots felt the former defined the latter. Further, it is possible that an Anglophobic mind-set may play out in the process of self-identification due to the historic relationships between the two nations.

When participants were probed regarding their strong sense of Scottishness many reflected on this and began to problematise this in their minds. Mary, a 30-year-old woman from the Baillieston area of the city, was one such participant:

> I do feel particularly Scottish, but funny enough if you go back in my family it's Irish. But that's that thing with the west of Scotland and Ireland and I have always tried to avoid that part of it by saying I'm Scottish rather than that sort of Irish heritage. I was born here and that is why I have sympathy with Pakistanis and Asians, cause they were born here just as I am. Therefore they are as Scottish as I am – although my parents are Irish.

This extract shows how competing discourses on nationalism can create confusion in the minds of those wishing to self-identify. Mary has internalised a notion of 'ethnic nationalism' whereby blood and family lineage play a key part in defining who can belong to the nation. However, Mary chooses to justify her choice of national belonging under a 'civic' paradigm: those who are born in a country and adopt the culture can become part of the nation. The tension is evident in her final sentence where she states that she identifies as Scottish 'although her parents are from Ireland'. The decision to deploy a particular conception of national belonging appears to stem from Marys Irish heritage which she openly says she has 'tried to avoid'. This latter point is of interest as it points to a problematic relationship between being considered of Irish descent and claims to Scottishness.

The next question sought to explore how national culture was constructed in the minds of those taking part in the study. The question would explore the relationship between nation and culture. More specifically, the aim was to understand what people felt were central aspects to being Scottish and if 'national culture' was viewed as hermetically sealed and thus could act with inclusive and exclusive tendencies. This formula follows Anderson's (1991) notion of imagined communities; therefore, it is conceivable that individuals in imagining the nation can imagine a unitary national culture. This question is also important because it was through the 'process which national culture, history, and identity were created was also the process through which the relationship between citizen and foreigner was transformed (Malik 1996: 140). The question was asked: what does it mean to be Scottish? Respondents found this difficult to answer and took a considerable amount of probing. Jim, a 25-year-old resident of the Parkhead, area stated: 'To me it means to belong, and I think it's a very identifiable country, erm and we have wonderful traditions, and I think they are very well upheld.' Jim continues:

> You just look as was in Oban the other day, and there was this tradition of an event that's been going on for 18 years to try and bring people together, aw wearing tartan, to dae a real Scottish dance in the main street, and its been running for 18 years and it's based on tradition. Also there's the Glasgow show the World Pipe Band Show [Championships] you know they are all very, erm, set in stone. So that, to me, we are a very traditional country. And I like that. You know, I think we are an open responsive nation, I think that when you are abroad the Scottish people are the first people to engage in conversation. I think we are very warm that way, I don't think that there aren't any inhibitions with us.

These extracts are of interest as they highlight a number of aspects surrounding the 'imagining' of a Scottish culture. Firstly, Jim believes that Scottishness is upheld and maintained by traditions that have a long history, and that the nations 'culture' is recognisable and distinct from other national cultures. He feels that sartorial choices and cultural practices such as dancing are important signifiers of Scottishness. Secondly, the text testifies to the formulation of a cultural absolutism in the minds of citizens, and such a process can be internalised and creates a clear distinction between who belongs and who are 'aliens' within the national boundary. Finally, the extract from Jim demonstrates ideas about the 'national character'. He feels that Scots are warm, friendly approachable and straight-talking. These personal characteristics were repeated by all participants during the research. Mosse (1995) argues that any a process that looks for the 'national character' inevitably creates an ideal type and can often lead to the creation of the countertype.

Not all of those who participated in the research articulated a unitary notion of national culture; two participants identified geographical variations of the 'Scottish character' and 'culture'. Suzie, when asked the question says:

> Not everyone is the same, if you look at Edinburgh and Glasgow these can be seen as two totally different cities. I mean we are friendly and helpful, but they are standoffish and snobby. I think it's cause they have the Capital there or something. So I suppose within Scotland there are different cultures. [...] I wouldn't dress in a kilt and start speaking Gaelic or things like that but I am Scottish.

This extract is a good example of what Baumann (1992) calls the incredible incongruence of nations. This instability results in elites engaging in polemical language regarding homogeneity in a bid to maintain the integrity of the nation; however, this language crumbles under scrutiny from its citizens. Similarly, this extract illustrates how Back's (1996) concept of neighbourhood nationalisms can be used to show how local populations do not uncritically absorb notions of a racialised national identity.

The next section sought to explore the Scottish Government's aspiration of 'One Scotland: Many Cultures'. Also the aim of this line of questioning was to see if culture within national boundaries can act as a homologue of race (Malik, 1996). Questions focused on whether certain cultural minorities were viewed as incompatible with a 'true Scottish identity'. The significance of this line of questioning is drawn from the work of Taguieff (2001) who argues that the most dominant form of racism today is a relentless fear of mixing fused with a racialised nationalism. With this in mind the question was asked: Were there any groups within Scotland who participants felt were incompatible with a Scottish Identity? In response seven of the participants cited South Asian Muslims as a group that were viewed as a 'problem group' not able to be 'truly' Scottish. One participant stated that:

> I was gonnae say, I had to work in the past with Indian and Pakistani people who in many ways were born here but they still remain themselves as being Pakistani or Indian, they stick to their own culture they don't really [participant pauses] They mibay skim the surface of the Scottish culture but they seem to think more of their own.

Jamie was then asked could they give an example of what they meant about 'sticking to their own culture' he responded by saying:

> Now I worked with the husband, now he was like yourself – dressed in western gear. His wife came in dressed in the sari. Every time now I felt that she stood out, because of how she dressed, if she were dressed the way we were. I felt that she would have got on better with society.

At this point, clarification was sought on which item of clothing Jamie was referring to. After a discussion it became clear that they were talking about the hijab. I then asked if Jamie felt that dress was important in conveying who we are:

> Yes dress definitely makes a difference because erm, if they stick to that traditional dress it makes them stand out, whereas I think if they have been born an brought up in Scotland they should wear what we wear and not stand out because of what they are wearing.

Jamie's response to this questioning sheds light on the relationship between national culture and belonging. Firstly, it appears that the racialised group – the Scots Asian Muslims – are at odds with a 'true' Scottish identity. The participant is conflicted by birth and cultural claims of belonging. This is the case because he talks of how although Scottish Asians were born here yet they 'remain themselves'. Therefore, it would appear that birth claims to Scottishness are only deemed 'valid' if they are backed up by adherence to perceived cultural norms. As such, although Scottish Muslims are born in Scotland they 'remain themselves' as being 'Pakistani or Indians' because they maintain traditional dress. Jamie goes on to say how the wearing of other clothes such as the Burka is a conscious expression of a desire not to 'fit in'.

> I find the [Burka] very intimidating. I must say because I was in a shop recently and behind me I saw a black apparition. I got the fright of my life because I am not expecting to see something like that. And I feel that if you go to a country that you should accept that country's culture.

Raymond, a 19-year-old shop fitter from Glasgow, exhibited much of the same language as Jamie. His perception was that Scottish Muslims exhibit high levels of insular behaviour and reject assimilatory demands. Raymond believes that cultural mixing in the Asian community more generally is forbidden and can blight the lives of families. Further, he feels that practices such as arranged marriages make cultural mixing undesirable as a 'white' Scottish person. Raymond when asked the question talks of why he feels a cultural divide has emerged he says:

> Fear, because they are afraid, and feel that it is safe to keep together. And ourselves perhaps we are afraid of their culture as well as it is entirely different to ours, like arranged marriages and to marry outside of their own culture is unacceptable whereas Scots are fine with that. Going to other countries and marrying people is fine. But them [Scots Asians] they believe that to cross that cultural barrier can be devastating for families.

Raymond goes on to discuss Islam:

> Thinking about Muslims. I mean everyone is entitled to their own religion but it's what we don't know about it. We tend to think about Muslims in that things are going on in the world [James gesticulates] things about terror. And I suppose it's the same as Protestants and Catholics. But with them you don't really know them. It's the fear of the unknown. I mean the media says that all Muslims are terrorists that is silly 'cause it's like saying that all Scots are mean.

Here Raymond problematises the highly prevalent discourse which equates a Muslim identity with terrorism. The discourse is challenged by drawing on the historic tensions that has existed within the Christian faith. As such Raymond feels that both Christianity and Islam can be equally associated with terrorism; however, the point of departure is familiarity. This is evident where Raymond talks of 'not knowing them'. Therefore, for this participant, the absence of interaction with Scottish Muslims marks them out as a possible threat.

Not all participants viewed Asian Muslims as 'insular' and rejecting of 'assimilatory' demands. Ben, a 25-year-old brewery worker, talks of the role of fear on group formation. When asked the question if he felt that there were any groups that he felt were incompatible with a Scottish identity he states:

> Probably people from Asia, I think it's because they feel intimidated. They tend to go in to groups rather than try to merge, which I don't think is a good thing. It's a shame they feel that way.

However, Ben goes on to problematise this position in his own mind – drawing on the recurring theme of cultural absolutism. He states that 'however, culture has got a part to play in it; you got to understand that theirs is really different from ours. So that's difficult to merge'.

The final response to this question shows the conflict in the mind of white Scottish residents wishing to comprehend the situation of Scots Asians. He recognises that racist prejudice can cause groups to come together and seek security. He recognises that this has detrimental effects for people and indeed feels empathy for them. However at the last minute Ben talks of the distinctiveness of Scottish Muslim Culture and how this is difficult to 'merge' with 'our' own Scottish Culture.

Racialised nationalism

The final question asked whether participants felt that the identity 'black' and Scottish were identities that mesh neatly or if they are considered by participants as oppositional. The reason for asking this question was to explore the issue of racialised nationalism, and whether differing modalities of racism gain traction in different space-time configurations. Essentially has there been a shift of prejudice based on biology to culture; therefore allowing the space for a cultural racism to flourish. Participants were asked do they think whether one could be Black and Scottish. One participant, Nick a glass maker from Cranhill, stated that:

> I think if you asked that question ten years ago, it would have been separate, but know times have moved on and I think we are moving on with generation so I mean some black people are as Glaswegian or more so than some other Glaswegians are. Or Scottish people are. You know a lot of people in Scotland want to associate their selves with Ireland or the States, 'oh my Granny

came from America, or my Granny is Irish'. But we have moved
on now so that blacks can be just as Glaswegian as anybody else.

Nick states that he feels that historically Scottishness has been constructed
as a white identity; however, for him the past decade has saw a shift whereby
being Scottish and Black have come to be compatible identities. This extract
is interesting as it destabilises ideas around anti-black nationalism outlined
in Paul Gilroy's *There Ain't no Black in the Union Jack* (1987). Therefore for
this participant whiteness has become an unstable identifier of Scottishness.
What is also of interest here is that the change in attitudes that Nick mentions correlates with the implementation of the policy of dispersal which
saw significant levels of 'black' migration into parts of Glasgow. Therefore,
it could be an indication that such a policy went a large way to challenging racialised nationalism. Finally, this participant held strong views on the
incompatibility of Scottish Muslims on cultural grounds; therefore, it would
appear that culture rather than perceived biological differences can operate
with greater exclusionary function.

A further participant Elaine was also asked the same question and
stated that:

> That's a kind of tricky one really. I think if initially I came across
> someone who was black, and they had been born and bred in
> Scotland you just don't probably because we consider ourselves
> as a white country. You would think that, oh, am Scottish and
> am white – but you are black. I think that the fact that they were
> Scottish would be more prominent than if they were Black. I don't
> think that their colour would come into it.

This statement also shows that Scottishness has been historically constructed as a white identity; however, this is currently being challenged. As such
whiteness can no longer be considered as a stable identifier of Scottishness
and the identity Black cannot be considered antithetic or oppositional to
a Scottish identity. The extract could also suggest that a shift from prejudice based on phenotype is on the wane and such prejudicial attitudes find
articulation in discourse surrounding culture. However a note of caution
should be stated here as the relatively positive response given here could be
as the result of the success in problematising colour coded forms of racism
by anti-racist elites.

Conclusion

This chapter has sought to explore the issue of anti-Muslim racism. The section on migration has shown the heterogeneous make-up of what may be termed the Muslim community in Scotland. Awareness of this diversity is important if we are to fully understand anti-Muslim racism. For example Kyriakides, Virdee and Modood (2009) research shows how Muslims born out-with the UK are viewed as distinct and different from those born within Scotland. Also, it is fair to say that those arriving in Glasgow from Syria will experience life in Scotland far differently than the well-established Pakistani community of the south side of Glasgow.

Focusing on the dynamics of the idea of 'race' and concept of racism has helped gain a deeper understanding of how Scottish Muslims are racialised through signification of their culture: culture can act just as affectively as race in looking people in an identity which is immutable. It is through a discourse of cultural incompatibility that many Muslims in Scotland experience racism; therefore, we need to be aware of how this 'operates' in contemporary Scotland. Fekete (2004) argues that this process has been intensified due to new anti-terror laws marking Muslims out as the 'enemy within'. Such a successful process of 'othering' has acted as a basis on which to promote policies opposing multiculturalism and enforced assimilation. This is exemplified in David Cameron's recent proclamation that Muslim women who do not improve their fluency in English could have their right to stay in the United Kingdom called into question (*Independent*, 2016). It is likely that the ongoing threat of terrorism will accelerate this process as western European states struggle to grapple with terrorism at home and overseas.

The relationship between racism and nationalism is an important variable one must consider when discussing anti-Muslim racism. This is so because any appeal to the nation that involves invoking notions of common or shared culture can easily exclude minorities and sow the seeds of division. The hegemony of the SNP in Scottish politics should be a call for deeper scrutiny of the party's policy on race equality. This is so because there is no affective opposition to ensure that it is living up to its proclamation of One Scotland: Many Cultures. As such it is incumbent on us all to look beyond the rhetoric and scrutinise the reality of government practices. Research by Liinpää and others provides a necessary critique at a time of political dominance of the Nationalist Government. On balance, however, it would appear that the SNP government is committed to discussing immigration in a positive light and dealing with racism where it rears its head.

Given the limited academic publications on the Scottish Muslim experience; it is clear that more research into this group is required. It is surprising that a group which feature so highly on hate-crime figures and in media coverage of racist incidents has received such little attention in the academy. This limited focus on Scotland creates a vacuum whereby much of the understanding surrounding the issue of Muslim lives and anti-Muslim racism is transposed from England to Scotland. This has the effect of occluding any differences there may be in the day to day lives of Scottish Muslims.

My own research shows the presence of a continuing disdain for a Muslim identity among some Scots. But there are also encouraging findings within the research such as recognition of how fear plays its part in marginalising this ethnic minority. Overall, however, it appears that there is a successful 'othering' process taking part in Scotland which constitutes Islamaphobia. However, the research does not produce evidence of racism per se, as one can hold prejudicial attitudes but not necessarily act to discriminate against Muslims. Therefore, it tells us much about questions of culture, belonging and national identity but not how this plays out on the streets of Parkhead. As such, this chapter can be seen as a preliminary statement that hopefully encourages others to conduct more work that will allow us to acquire a deeper understanding of the racism faced by Scottish Muslims.

CHAPTER 8

Sites, Welfare and 'Barefoot Begging': Roma and Gypsy/Traveller Experiences of Racism in Scotland

Colin Clark

Introduction

THE SPECIFIC FOCUS for this chapter is a range of population groups who are living and working in Scotland – Roma, Gypsies and Travellers – who are not usually considered when discussing racism, at least not until quite recently (Law, 2009). Even today, it appears to still be quite acceptable to be openly racist towards such groups, whether in the letters pages of national and local newspapers or in Parliament. A consideration of this chapter will be some *reflection* of why this might be the case, as well as then looking at the *experiences, representations* and *consequences* of such racism. In this way we can possibly trace the development and enactment of racism against such communities and tentatively suggest some measures to prevent what are, in effect, forms of hate crime. For, to be clear, this is what it often is: crimes of hate based on assumptions of identity, ways and means of living and just 'being'. To be marked out as 'Roma' or 'Gypsy' or 'Traveller' is to be a *moving target*, quite literally in the case of many Scottish Gypsy/Traveller families who continue to be commercially nomadic and thus travel regularly. This chapter will attempt to not fall into a common trap, whereby quite different groups are routinely lumped together and a 'one size fits all' approach is deemed unproblematic. Instead, the difference and diversity between and within the Roma, Gypsy and Traveller communities shall be explored and accounted for. Having said this, experiences of racism and discrimination appear to be an almost universal truth. Issues of language, accommodation, education, employment and the like may be quite varied but a common experience does appear to be dealing with the impact of racism.

Who are the communities?

To begin, we should probably reflect on exactly *who* we are talking about in this chapter. For reasons of space, an entirely pragmatic decision was arrived at to confine discussion to Scottish Gypsy/Traveller communities as well as Roma who have arrived in Scotland from across central and Eastern Europe, mainly the Czech Republic, Slovakia, Bulgaria, Poland and Romania. This is not ideal, given, for example, the presence of commercially nomadic Irish Traveller families in Scotland at various points of the calendar year, as well as Travelling Showpeople who have been long-established in certain parts of the country (e.g. Govan, Glasgow). There are also, to this day, small pockets of 'New Age' Travellers dotted across the North of the country as well as families dwelling in boats across the canal networks of central Scotland and beyond. However, to keep the chapter reasonably focused such restrictions were deemed necessary. Further, in *not* discussing in any significant depth such communities, it is certainly not being suggested here that they are not susceptible to the experiences and consequences of racism. Indeed, some of the most problematic reporting in local and national newspapers typically involves reactions to Irish Traveller families arriving in a local town or village and establishing what is often referred to by journalists and local counsellors as an 'illegal camp' or, from another perspective entirely, a 'roadside encampment' (Urquhart, 2013). Similarly, Travelling Showpeople in Scotland, although tending to be quite well integrated into local communities around their sites, are nonetheless subjected to issues of discrimination, especially in cases of urban regeneration and planning laws as well as health and safety matters (Bruce, 2010; Ross, 2011).

Scottish Gypsy/Traveller communities, as I have discussed in detail elsewhere, have had a presence across urban and rural Scotland for many centuries and continue, to this day, to hold onto their own identity, language, culture and traditions (Clark, 2006; Clark and Greenfields, 2006). This is not to suggest that modernity has passed such families by, far from it, but at heart there is a profound sense of 'self' and importance attached to being part of a community that knows itself, and *flatties* (non-Travellers), very well. In a real sense, to rather invert Simone de Beauvoir's famous words, you *are* born a Traveller, not made (De Beauvoir, 1956). This sense of self and others ('outsiders') is reflected across culture, especially in music, arts, as well as the Cant language which is an important marker of difference, or boundary preservation in the language of the late social anthropologist Fredrik Barth (1969). Living in trailers and the practice of nomadism, in contrast to largely settled Romanies who have arrived in Scotland from central and Eastern Europe and tend to rent private flats, is a distinct feature of Scottish Gypsy/Traveller identity and this pragmatic mobility is often connected to commercial activities as well as family visits and the like. It is movement with *purpose and meaning*, in that sense, something the writer Bruce Chatwin (1987) understood so well in his work with nomads, especially indigenous Aboriginal communities in Australia. For other Gypsy/Traveller families, who may be settled in bricks and mortar accommodation, nomadism often remains *a state of mind* if not a current state of fact or action (Liégeois, 1994: 161). Other families, to be sure, will travel part of the year, usually the summer months, and then settle in housing or on a pitch on a private or Local Authority site for the winter months. In truth, experiences of racism, as we shall see, can equally be experienced in housing, on sites or on the road. It is not nomadism in and of itself that *triggers* or *enacts* racism; it is being identified by *flatties* as a 'Gypsy/Traveller'.

In terms of population numbers and the law in Scotland, a number of points are important to recognise and take account of. For example, according to the 2011 Census, there are just over 4,000 people in the country who self-identified as 'White: Gypsy/Traveller'. This was the first time such a 'tick-box' category appeared in a Census form and the Scottish Government have, to their credit, recognised that this 'could be an undercount' (Scottish Government, 2015b). Indeed, as I have discussed elsewhere, there are many reasons why members of Roma, Gypsy and Traveller communities would not want to self-identify as being from those communities in official forms, Census paperwork and the like (Clark, 1998). What is clear, however, from the 2011 Census data is that across a number of social indicators Scottish Gypsies and Travellers faced a number of barriers to social inclusion, including in the areas of accommodation, employment, education and access to health services etc. More recently, two further Scottish Government Equal Opportunities Committee enquiries – *Gypsy/Travellers and Care* (Scottish

Parliament, 2012) and *Where Gypsy/Travellers Live* (Scottish Parliament, 2013) – have again underlined the exclusion the communities face in these specific areas. The legal situation in Scotland, in a sense, is actually quite clear. Formally, the Scottish Government recognises Gypsy/Travellers as an ethnic minority group. However, it took an employment tribunal case in Aberdeen, *MacLennan vs Gypsy Traveller Education and Information Project* (2008), to clarify this position with Judge Nicol Hosie ruling that Scottish Gypsy/Travellers are a group that can be defined by reference to their ethnic origins and are therefore afforded legal protection under the terms of the then Race Relations Act, 1976 (now superseded by The Equality Act, 2010). Indeed, this was a tribunal case the current author was involved in and presented at, via an expert witness report based on a previously published article (Clark, 2006).

Again, as I have written elsewhere, Central and Eastern European (CEE) Romani Communities have had a presence in Scotland long before European Union accession in 2004 (A8) and in 2007 (A2) (Clark, 2014; Clark, 2015). Prior to this time, routes into Scotland and the rest of the UK tended to be via asylum and refugee movements, with Roma families in particular being subjected to a hostile reception from local and national newspapers and politicians (Clark and Campbell, 2000). After the two EU accession periods there was a recognised shift in mobility from East to West and, like the rest of the UK, some Roma families – and it was usually family and extended family migration patterns being witnessed here – made Scotland their new home ('despite the weather', as is sometimes ruefully said by CEE Roma interviewees and friends). Not unlike previous migrant groups arriving in Scotland, it was the major towns and cities that were the ports of first call and to this day Govanhill, on the Southside of Glasgow, remains a central area of residence for many CEE Romani families (but not the only one, this is important to note). Indeed, according to one report the vast majority of Roma in Scotland, some 90 per cent plus, live in and around this relatively small area of Glasgow (Social Marketing Gateway, 2013: 14). The same report gives a maximum figure of around 5,000 Roma individuals in Scotland and it is important to note this includes people from several CEE states, such as Romania, Slovakia, the Czech Republic, Bulgaria and Poland. This movement of Roma to Scotland needs to be viewed within a much wider 'push' and 'pull' context; it is both a failure of CEE states to offer safety and security, human rights and work to their Roma citizens, as well as the attraction of a 'better life' for families in Western Europe (Guy, 2015).

It is an unfortunate fact, perhaps, but the history, legacy and continuation of anti-Roma prejudice and discrimination across CEE ensures that many Roma families will keep leaving their home countries for better prospects abroad. National and local integration strategies, largely directed (imposed?) by European Union agencies, have thus far not worked to persuade many families to remain in CEE. Indeed, it must seem like shifting between a rock and hard place for those who are caught up in the wider, transnational politics of migration – for example, it is apparent that the reception many families have received in Western countries, such as France and Italy, have been hostile to say the least. Indeed, the ongoing (illegal) deportations of Roma from France to Romania, and the issue of so-called 'nomad camps' in Italy, have been front page news across EU states (Astier, 2014; Kirchgaessner, 2015). It is both cruel and ironic that such racist hostilities and aggressions in the West, more than matched by State ineptitude and indifference in the East, has been occurring during the much-lauded 'Decade of Roma Inclusion'. There are real and burning questions about what this George Soros-fronted initiative has actually achieved and changed on the ground for the majority of Roma families who are struggling with material, everyday issues of poverty, discrimination and far-right racist violence (Jovanovic, 2015).

Reflection

Before we proceed to examine some of the contemporary experiences of anti-Roma, Gypsy and Traveller racism in Scotland it is perhaps worthwhile to pause for just a moment, following the overview of who the communities actually are, to think about the *why* question. That is: *why* do such communities attract the attention of individual racists as well as fall foul of *Gadjo* (non-Gypsy) institutions that are racist in their attitudes, manner and approaches to dealing with Roma, Gypsies and Travellers? Unfortunately, it is not a straight forward answer or response; there is a deep, rich and complex history to explore in tracing the emergence of what we might term 'anti-Gypsyism'.

The Romani academic and activist, Ian Hancock (University of Texas), has perhaps done more than most to explore and try to comprehend this tradition/behaviour. Hancock suggests that at heart it is a form of exclusion that is quite deliberate and highly structured in its enactment and operation (Hancock, 2000). Indeed, it is the *embedded* nature of anti-Gypyism – how it is weaved into the very fabric of our societies and structures – that makes it all the harder to directly challenge. Anti-Gypsyism, Hancock suggests, features in our schools, social security offices, employment agencies, hospitals, letting agents, newspapers, elections and many other environments. It is not, to be sure, the actions of a few 'suspect' racists but rather the operation of a *system* that is, to draw on McVeigh's work, highly anti-nomadic and based on an exclusionary sedentarist ideology (McVeigh, 1997). Appreciated in this manner, as McVeigh argues, anti-Gypsyism can be thought of as a form of exploitation, of power-politics – this is in fact a point further developed by Romani activist Zelijko Jovanovic (2015). He has recently argued that anti-Gypsy and anti-Roma sentiments can attract votes and garner political muscle, in addition to bringing economic revenues to institutions. Jovanovic refers here to an example, widespread across CEE, of Roma children being inappropriately placed in schools for children with physical and learning disabilities just because they are of Roma ethnicity – and the fact there are often financial and racist motivations behind such placements (ERRC, 2014). As a pattern of deliberate exclusion, anti-Gypsyism is perhaps best thought of in similar ways to how the Social Psychologist Michael Billig (1995) has discussed 'banal' nationalism. That is, anti-Gypsyism needs to be understood not just in the 'extreme forms' we read about in Hungary or in Romania, where groups of far-right skinheads murder Roma men and set fire to Roma settlements (Amnesty International, 2013; European Network Against Racism, 2014). Rather, it also needs to be seen and understood in its 'banal' forms where everyday practices serve to exclude, isolate and render 'other'. A contemporary example, to illustrate, is perhaps the reporting of the 'folk devils' who dare to commit begging in Glasgow whilst not wearing a pair of shoes. This will be discussed in a later section of the chapter.

Of course, in reflecting on such themes, it is clear that European anti-Gypsyism is not a unique or isolated instrument. A range of 'others', whether they are young, disabled, poor, female, Jewish, Muslim, LGBT et al are equally restricted, exploited and cast aside via systems of oppression based on the domination of patriarchy, capitalism, homophobia, anti-Semitism and Islamphobia etc. There are subtle differences, of course, there are ebbs and flows across time/place, but underlying such 'anti-' sentiments is a neoliberal fear, a suspicion and hatred. As a strategy, to challenge such elite interests and power, alliances and coalitions across such groups must form to campaign for equality and change across our institutions. What is required is an 'opening-up', to ensure such bodies and agencies have a respect for difference, in a truthful and meaningful fashion. However, as we shall see, it still appears to be the case that Roma, Gypsies and Travellers are the neighbours that few people want, even within equality groups that claim to represent them. And it is here that a forceful truth must speak to vested power.

Experiences and representations

In this section of the chapter, specific examples will be drawn upon to illustrate the scale of the problem at hand when it comes to the 'everyday' racism directed against Roma, Gypsies and Travellers. In relation to the Scottish Gypsy-Traveller population, the example of sites and accommodation options/preferences will be examined to note the racism directed against these communities when roadside encampments (often referred to as 'illegal sites' by misinformed journalists and councillors) appear on the edges of towns and cities, such as Aberdeen and Dundee. In this type of scenario, which is of much attraction to local newspapers in particular, Gypsies and Travellers fit into a type of 'othered' 'stranger' figure that was perhaps best discussed by the sociologist Georg Simmel (1908) over one hundred years ago; they are the projected, feared 'stranger' who comes today and *might* stay tomorrow. With regard to Roma from CEE, the example of racist discrimination in terms of welfare and social security provision will be examined, drawing upon work conducted by Govanhill Law Centre and other partner organisations (Paterson et al, 2011). Here it will be shown that deliberate misinformation and racist practices are evident as Roma claimants are actively dissuaded from a system designed to offer a 'safety-net' in troubled times. Additionally, a recent 'moral panic' regarding so-called 'barefoot' begging in town centres such as Glasgow will be examined to problematise the racist claims of 'scams' and their association with 'mafia gangs' of Romanian Roma (Leask, 2014). Together, these examples illustrate the actual scale of the challenge in combating racist attitudes in public service and elsewhere; the air and climate hangs heavy with the fog of racism. We will now look at the case of Scottish Gypsy-Travellers and their struggle

regarding nomadism and preserving what is still for many families a traditional and economically important and viable way of life.

A place to stay?

> In the past when illegal Travellers have congregated they have left
> behind a hell of a mess and the taxpayers foot the bill. – Ian Watson
> (Arbroath Community Council, quoted in Strachan, 2013).

The above comment, from then Chairperson of Arbroath Community Council, Mr Watson, to a journalist from *The Courier* newspaper in June 2013,
is not an unusual response from someone in his position to the arrival of a
group of caravans onto public land (which will be almost always referred
to as a 'local beauty spot' even if in reality it is a piece of waste ground next
to a railway track or a Council recycling facility). In this instance, we are
informed by the newspaper that there is 'anger' at the 'illegal Travellers'
– although the notion is bizarre, of course, as no one is 'illegal', although
this can also be witnessed with regard to the way some commentators have
recently discussed 'illegal migrants' or 'illegal refugees', including even liberal newspapers such as *The Guardian* (Watt, 2015). The point is this is not
just semantics. Describing a population as 'illegal' sets a dangerous tone for
any discussion of an *issue* or *action* which may or may not in itself be 'illegal'. Later in this same *Courier* article, the readership is informed that any
'debris or damage' would 'hurt the economy' – an implicit suggestion that it
is only Gypsies and Travellers who are responsible for 'fly-tipping' and it is
'law-abiding taxpayers' who need to pay for the 'clean-up' after the group
moves on, a lively debate that is discussed in some depth elsewhere (Clark
and Taylor, 2014). Later in the same article, Mr Watson is again quoted: '*Vic-
toria Park is a magnet for families on a sunny day like today and this is going
to deter a lot of people from going down there.*' What is in evidence here
is another very popular trope in reporting and discussions about Gypsies
and Travellers, nomads generally in fact, that there are 'security' concerns
regarding such sites and people are advised to stay away due to 'dangers'.
What is interesting here is that this story revolves around just four caravans,
three cars and a van: this hardly constitutes an invasion of rural Angus by
the transient hordes. Yet Mr Watson is quick to point out to the journalist:
'*These camps usually get bigger if they are not moved on immediately so the
council must act quickly.*' Again, this is a very popular and often-repeated

stereotype in terms of roadside encampments; if 'something is not done' the 'problem' will be all the greater very quickly. What is deeply frustrating in such reporting as this is that rarely is the lack of pitches on nearby Local Authority sites mentioned, or the fact that transit sites (that is, temporary 'stopping places' – *'Atchin Tans* in AngloRomani – with limited facilities such as toilets and skips etc.) are generally not provided for by Councils.

Such reporting, and implicit racism, is not isolated or unique. The nature of everyday discussions and conservations about Gypsy and Traveller sites play out in very similar ways across the country as a whole. As another contemporary example, there is an ongoing debate between the Scottish Government and Aberdeenshire Council regarding a so-called 'controversial' private site development in St. Cyrus, Aberdeenshire called North Esk Park managed by Traveller, William Docherty. This is a development that has attracted much interest from *The Courier* since 2013 and multiple articles over this period, both from this newspaper and also Aberdeen-based newspapers *The Press and Journal* and *The Evening Express*. However, in one of *The Courier's* latest reports it outdone itself with the deliberately provocative headline: 'Travellers site in St Cyrus branded a risk to life' (McClaren, 2016). When examined more closely, what lies behind this headline is a rather insipid story regarding the Scottish Environmental Protection Agency (SEPA) rejection of a new report that argues the North Esk Park site is not located on a flood plain. In other words, the 'risk to life' aspect is somewhat disingenuous, to say the least, on both the part of *The Courier* and SEPA. What lies at the heart of this, of course, is not a humane concern for the lives and livelihoods of Gypsies and Travellers on the site but rather a desire to see the North Esk park development bulldozed and the families rendered homeless; it is arguably the worst example of 'Nimbyism' in relation to Traveller sites that Scotland has ever seen.

This is evidenced by the fact that another, more local, newspaper, *The Mearns Leader*, acknowledges somewhat reluctantly in a recent article that *'...some St Cyrus residents report[ed] that there have been few problems with the Travellers'* (*The Mearns Leader*, 2015). Indeed, earlier research by Tom Duncan, funded by the Joseph Rowntree Foundation, has indicated that although local residents in housing are usually concerned with the establishment of new Gypsy and Traveller sites these concerns are usually not in evidence once the sites are established and running effectively (Duncan, 1996). In other words, *flattie* fears based on myths and stereotypes disappear with experience of living next to sites. This innovative JRF research study is still unique and an updated research project on this topic would be very helpful as a means to calm fears that are being stoked by local newspapers and councillors with vested interests. Further, as Mr Docherty mentions himself in *The Mearns Leader* article, 'At the end of the day it'll be for Aberdeen-shire Council to decide. I just hope they see sense and realise we are saving taxpayers' money by putting up our own site.' Indeed, this fact, that the site is provided for and paid for by the Gypsies and Travellers staying on the site themselves and is not Council or Government funded, seems to have been curiously overlooked by all the objectors. The newspaper is also to be congratulated for actually bothering to interview and quote a Gypsy/Traveller 'voice', something that rarely happens in print media in Scotland.

What can be seen from these two examples are a few of the common, everyday themes and patterns that emerge when examining the reporting of Gypsy and Traveller sites in the local and national press in Scotland. It is telling that racialised stereotypes/tropes/fears appear in these reports that feed into and reinforce pre-existing displays of 'banal' anti-Gypyism that run through our society. Gypsies and Travellers are 'othered', deemed to be 'illegal' by daring to exist and wanting to stay in a trailer, constantly pulled apart and contrasted with 'law-abiding taxpayers' who 'fear' for their safety when a small number of trailers pull-up beside their 'local beauty spot.'

Unequal and unlawful treatment?

The next section shifts the discussion to the heterogeneous and diverse Roma communities from Central and Eastern Europe staying in and around the Govanhill area of Glasgow and an examination of their varied experiences of accessing social security and different forms of welfare provision. As noted by Poole and Adamson (2008), nearly a decade ago now, several issues emerge in the UK from what is, at source, endemic and deep-rooted racist exclusion from substantive citizenship rights in the EU countries once called 'home' by these communities. Having migrated to the UK, to escape such racialised and institutionalised discrimination, it seems that the issue of *take-up, access and delivery* of public goods and services is a 'live' one in the UK as much as it is across CEE. However, here the focus is on the substantive findings of a report by Govanhill Law Centre (GLC) as well as some critical analysis of the current situation (Paterson, Simpson, Barrie and Perinova, 2011). The research report from GLC found that Roma claimants, of various nationalities, were routinely denied their rights under EU law in terms of interactions with various public bodies, in this case, principally, the Department of Work and Pensions, HMRC and local government. The researchers found that unnecessary administrative delays in payments being issued led to situations of poverty and deprivation and several Roma families in the Govanhill area being reliant instead on emergency provisions from charities, food banks and faith groups (a finding also noted earlier by Poole, 2010). Such inefficiencies, barriers and inequalities were often caused by a refusal of benefit based upon erroneous decisions made by officials of a public authority and when complaints were made responses were either delayed or did not emerge. As noted by Duffy (2013), such treatment by public services leads to a life, effectively, on the 'edge of society' for the various Roma communities living within Govanhill.

Similarly, in cases involving the HMRC, the GLC (2011) study found that cases were often referred to their 'Compliance Team' and not informed as to what was causing the delay whilst the passports of Roma individuals and other documentation, such as child birth certificates, were held onto for disproportionate amounts of time. Further, the study found that officers of public authorities sometimes wrongly stated the law, for example the HMRC advising clients that they could call at the client's home without any notice and seize all of his possessions for a disputed overpayment (Paterson, Simpson, Barrie and Perinova, 2011: 26). The study did report that services provided by Glasgow City Council were generally well regarded and the majority of GLC's Roma clients reported their interactions with the Council as being productive and helpful, although they were still, even here, subject to differential treatment based on racialised assumptions.

As a specific example, it is productive to shine a light on the work of the Department for Work and Pensions (Jobcentre Plus). It is here that a number of pressing examples illustrate the nature of racism at the 'frontline'; how it is felt and experienced as well as the results. It is worth being mindful of the fact that under the terms of the public sector equality duty, bodies such as DWP/Jobcentre Plus should be aiming to *eliminate discrimination, harassment, victimisation and any other conduct that is prohibited by or under the Act.*' (Section 149 of the Equality Act, 2010). The GLC report, and subsequent fieldwork undertaken by the current author (Clark, 2014), showed that several Roma claimants and welfare rights advisors felt that discrimination was apparent in terms of the application process as well as decisions and outcomes at Jobcentre Plus. Often such treatment was a failing at a quite basic level; staff being 'rude' and not assisting claimants with job searches and other perfectly legitimate enquiries. Language support and communication issues are central to the dynamics between claimants/staff and a lack of interpreters a real concern in terms of trying to improve the situation. Some claimants have been told, in a rather matter of fact way, that they 'did not want to work'. Behind such contemporary treatment lies a historical culture of racism that has been prevalent in British social security systems for many years, including racism directed towards Roma, Gypsies and Travellers (Clark, 1999; Gordon and Newnham, 1985).

Aside from issues of initial reception and showing courtesy to claimants, a number of issues were raised in the GLC report regarding the receipt of correct and timely information on making claims, and the processing of claims, at Jobcentre Plus. Reports surfaced of several Roma claimants being told, incorrectly, that they were not able to register a new claim due to their nationality (Paterson, Simpson, Barrie and Perinova, 2011: 32-33). Now, whether by lack of understanding of the legislation relating to the habitual residency and right to reside tests, or a more wilful and discriminatory ignorance, this runs counter to the provision of a professional and accurate service that follows the stipulations of the public sector equality duty. Being charitable, it would seem at the very least that further training should be provided to 'street-level bureaucrats' (Lipsky, 1980) on such matters as well as sessions relating to what is now termed, in a rather asinine way, 'unconscious bias'. To be sure, it would seem that this is a breach of the public sector equality duty: staff not being trained in the relevant legislation that applies to Roma claimants who are directed to their local offices (Glasgow Southside). Looking at the GLC report, and subsequent work, there does appear to be a growing collection of data that indicates that discrimination, harassment and victimisation is happening at Jobcentre Plus offices and it is being directed disproportionately at claimants from a Roma background/heritage (Briggs, 2012).

Given the fact 'race' is a 'protected characteristic' via the terms of The Equality Act, 2010, and it is built into the public sector equality duty, it is disheartening to read in the GLC report of such systematic behaviours that disadvantage claimants attending Jobcentre Plus and attempting to claim entitlements. A further duty states that there is a need to *advance equality of opportunity between persons who share a relevant protected characteristic and persons who do not share it*. Again, relating to the above descriptions, it is noted that repeat issues of poor/difficult communication issues are still too common and the lack of provision of interpreting services to those claimants, such as Roma from CEE, who have difficulty with limited English and cannot keep pace with what is often very technical and procedural enquiries/discourses within social security. The lack of interpreters has been well-documented, in part related to cuts across the public sector in recent years (McCall, 2015). Indeed, it is rather depressing that a recommendation presented nearly a decade ago still needs to be repeated today:

> There is also a clear need for this to be supplemented by the longer-term provision of bilingual support workers and advocates who can support and assist Roma in finding suitable employment and bridge the language gap that is likely to persist for many (Adamson and Poole, 2008: 37).

On one level, Jobcentre Plus is a key facilitator in the entry of Roma into the local labour market; that is, increasing participation in public life and assisting with greater social and economic integration. However, this does not seem to be occurring as it should be due to the structural/individual issues mentioned above. Similarly, a further public sector equality duty mentions the need to 'foster good relations between people who share a protected characteristic and those who do not'. Again, Jobcentre Plus should be playing a key role here given its central role and importance in the lives and livelihoods of those claimants who register with them from a Roma background. The fact that many staff within this service are catering for such claimants differently from other groups of claimants – and are compounding mythology and stereotypes regarding inability and/or unwillingness to actively seek work – is a serious impediment to meaningful integration and social inclusion. Indeed, aside from the broader public sector equality duty, the DWP's (Jobcentre Plus) own equality strategies on 'race' appear to be failing, not least with regards to increasing minority ethnic employment rates, improving claimant experiences of services and ensuring diversity and equality training is given to all staff (Jobcentre Plus, 2008; Jobcentre Plus, 2010).

'Barefoot beggars'

This section briefly examines a 'moral panic' emerging in Glasgow around street begging, and, in particular, such 'gathering of resources' activities (in the anthropological sense) conducted by individuals from the Roma communities in and around the city centre. Although begging has been a 'public issue', in the CW Mills (1959) sense, for many years in the city, in more recent times it has been a response to benefit changes, the imposition of sanctions and a tightening of public sector welfare provision more generally (Duffy, 2015). It is also, of course, a very real and material outcome of the negative and discriminatory experiences noted above in relation to interactions with the DWP (Jobcentre Plus).

Early in the new year of 2014, Chief Reporter David Leask, from the Glasgow-based newspaper *The Evening Times*, authored a front-page feature entitled 'Warning: Scam of barefoot begging' (Leask, 2014a). In the article, Leask quotes Alan Porte, then Chief Inspector in charge of city centre policing in Glasgow as saying that such 'barefoot begging' was 'very likely to be a scam'. The commentary around the article, written by Leask, speaks of those conducting the 'scam' as returning to the city to 'lure cash from New Year shoppers.' Further, it mentions how such groups, who we are told are 'typically Roma', are on 'tour' and are 'looking for alms'. The feature then goes on to quote one individual, David MacLean (26), who says that he finds the barefoot begging situation 'a disgrace' and that it 'annoys' him. MacLean continues with the view that people who give money are 'being conned'. The presentation and framing of the article is entirely negative although there is one sentence which seeks to provide at least some context for why such activities might be occurring in Glasgow city centre: '*Roma are among the most excluded and vulnerable people in Europe – victims of institutionalised prejudice and economic discrimination – but only a few resort to 'professional' begging'* (Leask, 2014a). The article also (correctly) states that such street-work is *not* illegal. Nonetheless, the interesting notion here is the idea of 'professional' begging; we are not told what this might be or what it might look like other than it might be 'organised'. The associations here are, perhaps implicitly if not explicitly, of Romanian Roma 'mafia' criminal gangs out to deceive and to cheat: it is worth noting that these are (racist) charges and accusations that have been unfairly levelled at Roma communities for centuries now (Anstead, 2013; Jinga, 2013).

The unfortunate aspect to this initial feature was that a subsequent report was filed by the same Chief Reporter to the same newspaper just eight days later, on 10 January (Leask, 2014b). This 'review' piece was a summary of responses from members of the public to the initial article that merely underlined and reaffirmed notions of alleged Roma criminality in Glasgow's city centre (even though, as mentioned above, begging is not in itself illegal – this is only the case where it is 'aggressive' or 'causing nuisance', rather grey areas in themselves). Indeed, the follow-up piece went further by talking about 'a scam run by gangs' (as a point of fact) that then gave licence to racists to vent their feelings in print: comments ranged from concerns regarding 'immigration' and 'public nuisance' as well as 'scamming'. Two individuals are quoted, however, that does indicate a display of solidarity with the Roma community and a defence of anti-racism: Iain Findlay-Walsh suggests that: 'If people feel they have to endure sitting on the street with no shoes on in order to get cash in the winter, they probably need my change more than I do.' Similarly, Andrew Carnegie is quoted as saying: 'I am upset by the hatred... there is real bigotry against the Roma.' However, such anti-racist voices do tend to be the exception rather than the norm. It is likely such 'moral panics' around Roma begging will emerge again, as they tend to be cyclical in nature and responsive to external pressures, such as, for example, benefit sanctions (Clark, 2015).

Consequences

Having reviewed some of the *experiences* and *representations* of racism that are all too often directed towards persons of Roma, Gypsy and Traveller heritage living in Scotland, it is important to briefly look at the *consequences* of such practices on the communities themselves and how they help us understand what must be done to *challenge* such racism. On one level the impact and effects of racism on various minority ethnic communities has been well-documented and the research literature refers to issues of self-confidence, educational attainment, esteem, health and employment statuses etc. (Paradies et al, 2013; Rosenblatt, 2014). The point is that such *consequences* are real, material and felt. When shining the spotlight on Roma, Gypsy and Traveller communities the consequences are all too clear, across a range of indicators, including those mentioned above. Indeed, according to the Scottish Government (2015), in its own breakdown of Census 2011 data, Gypsy/Travellers in Scotland were *more likely* than the general population of Scotland to have no qualifications, to work in elementary positions or not work at all, to not own their own home and to be self-employed and live in a caravan. Across the four elements of the Gypsy/Traveller chapter in this Census 2011 analysis report – the labour market, education, housing and transport – the patterns and themes of exclusion and discrimination are depressingly clear and transparent. And yet this situation and grinding reality continues, day after day for the communities, despite Government report after report and consultation after consultation.

Similarly, with regard to the various Roma communities from CEE living in Scotland, the situation and consequences are also stark. With such groups, as with Scottish Gypsy/Travellers, evictions are also very common – but from insecure flat tenancies in Govanhill rather than roadside encampments in the North of the country. Language issues, as witnessed above, are more pressing for the Roma communities and the cuts in interpreter services and English as an additional language classes are having a profound impact on the inclusion of Roma into Scottish society. As discussed elsewhere, stigma remains a traumatic consequence of 'everyday racism' for Roma migrants in Scotland, especially when amorphous factors such as 'behaviour' and 'culture' are used as sticks to beat the Roma with by opportunistic politicians and journalists (Clark, 2014). The consequences of racism have a profound impact on the communities effected and there is a need for an action plan to combat such destructive behaviours and actions, possibly similar to Scottish Government and NGO work undertaken as part of the very successful 'Zero Tolerance' campaigns against gendered domestic violence.

Conclusion

Brian Niro (2003) has argued that 'race' is a 'monster'; a monster due to its resilience and its tenacity to survive both as an abstract concept and as a horrific, divisive practice. He has suggested that what has been carried out in the name of 'race', in both a historical and contemporary sense, should have consigned it to the vaults of history many years ago. And yet it persists; it twists, turns and alters, changing its form to new realities; most recently evidenced in the Mediterranean 'refugee crisis' where European fears over immigration and the resulting political squabbling over border control cost the lives of so many, men, women and children deemed somehow less worthy of life because of where they came from. This chapter has explored, to some extent, how this 'race monster' enacts its horrors against communities identified, usually by *Gadjos* and *flatties*, as Roma, and Gypsy/Travellers in Scotland. As a result, the chapter has probably not made for very pleasant reading. However, in tackling some of these thorny issues mentioned previously – sites, welfare, begging and so on – it is hoped that a greater awareness is appreciated regarding the similarities and differences within and across the populations. To be sure, there are as many differences as commonalities but at source there is a shared experience of *racism*; to be cast aside, to be pointed at, to be excluded, to be denied service just because of perceived 'difference' and 'otherness'. This external, societal rejection, whether based on a preferred mode of accommodation or based on language issues, has devastating consequences for Roma, Gypsy and Traveller communities themselves as well as Scottish society more broadly. It is clear that in the search of the Galbraithian 'good society' in Scotland, effective communication is vital in addressing anti-Gypsyism, as is supporting and nurturing people to have the confidence to speak out and challenge such prejudice and discrimination when it is witnessed, whether occurring in an urban social security office or a rural roadside encampment. This is what we must do, together.

CHAPTER 9

Racism and Housing in Scotland

Gina Netto

Introduction

EXPLORING THE EXTENT to which housing policy and the housing system is racialised is important because not only does housing provide shelter and security to individuals; it also has strong links to opportunities for employment, education and health, in part due to its close relationship with neighbourhoods. Further, housing provides the physical space for human interaction, relationships and development within the home, and the surrounding neighbourhood. Housing is thus connected with a major component of the spatial dimension of individuals' experience – the feelings, memories and experiences associated with certain geographical areas – referred to in the human geography literature as 'place' (Agnew, 1987). Housing and the surrounding neighbourhood are key sites for individual negotiation of identity with others who live in the neighbourhood and can profoundly impact on a sense of belonging (Netto, 2011a). Housing and homelessness are also key policy areas where responsibility has been devolved to Scottish Government, providing an opportunity to examine how local authorities and other housing organisations have responded to increasing ethnic diversity. Within the wider UK context, including Scotland, a housing shortage is now widely acknowledged. Housing – in particular, affordable housing – has to be viewed as an increasingly scarce resource. Indeed the chronic shortage of affordable housing, particularly in London and other major UK cities has now come to be viewed among many as constituting 'a housing crisis'.

This chapter is concerned with exploring the impact of racism within aspects of the housing system that are of major relevance to people on low incomes, including certain ethnic minority groups. The higher levels of poverty among certain ethnic minority groups compared to the white majority is well-established (Netto et al, 2011; Platt, 2007).This has continued through the current climate of recession and austerity, as evidenced through a recent study which has shown that Pakistani and Bangladeshi groups, followed by Black African and Black Caribbean groups are most likely to be experiencing persistent poverty (Fisher and Nandi, 2015). It is thus not surprising that a close relationship between ethnicity and housing disadvantage is well-established, although the forms of disadvantage have varied between ethnic groups. Common manifestations are higher levels of overcrowding, poor housing conditions and disproportionately high levels of homelessness among certain ethnic groups (Lakey, 1997; Netto et al, 2011). For instance, Lakey's study in England and Wales (1997) found that housing and neighbourhood disadvantage were compounded by a history of settlement in poor areas. In Scotland, recent evidence of housing disadvantage among ethnic minorities can be found in the analysis of the 2011 Census data which shows that they were more likely to be living in 'flats or temporary structure compared to the population as a whole and more likely to be paying higher rents by renting from a private landlord than a social landlord. White: Polish' (30 per cent), 'Bangladeshi' and 'African' (both 28 per cent) households were also reported to have the highest rates of over-crowding.

Evidence of housing disadvantage among some ethnic minority groups provides a compelling case for examining how and to what extent racism operates in key components of the housing system in Scotland. The ethnic minority communities considered in this study are wide-ranging including established communities, recent migrants, refugees and Gypsy Travellers. Manifestations of institutional and personal racism and direct and indirect discrimination will be revealed in order to highlight the impact of racism in various forms. Exposing these forms of racism is an important step in dealing with the phenomenon. It will be argued that while some progress has been achieved, much work remains to be done to achieve racial equality in housing in Scotland. Previous studies have noted the role of state institutions in maintaining racialised structures within a number of societies (Solomos and Back, 1999); this chapter extends this examination to include institutions in the voluntary sector, including housing associations. Along with local authorities, housing associations are revealed to be sites for the reproduction of racially structured social relations.

This chapter will first examine the extent to which access to the social rented sector – one of the main 'planks' of the housing safety net that provides a level of protection for poor and vulnerable UK nationals – is racialised. Then we will turn to an examination of the extent to which institutional racism operates within the provision of homelessness services, of major relevance to those excluded from the housing system. Access to and use of homelessness services are an important route into the social rented sector, and are also a form of welfare provision. Next, the chapter discusses the vulnerability of ethnic minorities living in social housing to racial harassment and the responses of housing associations to this phenomenon. Finally, the chapter concludes by drawing together the main findings relating to the nature and form of racism within the housing system in Scotland, and the extent to which progress in countering this phenomenon has been achieved.

Access to the social rented sector

Although Scotland has a large social rented sector compared with many other Western European countries, (Netto et al, 2015), it has shrunk considerably since the post-war period and the proportion of households renting their accommodation from a council or housing association has continued to fall from 29 per cent in 2001 to 24 per cent in 2011. This is due to a number of reasons, including the lack of investment in local authority or council housing, the sale of council properties to tenants at discounted prices through the Right-to-Buy scheme and cuts in new build. This has led to what is termed the 'residualisation' of social housing, and to such housing becoming the tenure of 'last resort,' rather than the tenure of choice for working class families as had been the case previously. This is borne out by evidence that the composition of people living in social housing has significantly changed to those who are most in need (Office of National Statistics, 2011). They tend to have low employment rates and to be at high risk of poverty. The majority of people now live in their own homes (62 per cent according to the 2011 Census), and the number of people living in the private rented sector has continued to increase (from 8 per cent to 14 per cent of all households). The persistent trend of high levels of overcrowding among ethnic minorities is indicative both of limited housing options and a demand for social housing, if it was appropriate and accessible.

According to the analysis of the census data, 'White: Polish', 'Bangladeshi' and 'African' households continue to have the highest rates of over-crowding (Scottish Government, 2015c).

The high demand for social housing in relation to supply thus makes it a useful site for studying the extent to which ethnic minorities have equal access to the sector. From the outset, it is worth noting that access to permanent accommodation in the social rented sector – as in many other Western European countries – is conditional on citizenship status (Netto et al, 2015). Undocumented migrants, asylum seekers, students and work visa holders and are not eligible for social housing. In general terms, in order to be recognised as eligible for social housing, migrants need settled status or to be a European Economic Area (EEA) worker which gives them the right to stay in the UK. However, the current renegotiation of the right to free movement which is currently been undertaken by the UK government could impact upon EEA nationals' eligibility to apply for social housing in England; this would depend on the terms of the renegotiation (House of Commons, 2015). As recently as two decades ago, a review of literature on race and housing in Scotland (MacEwen et al, 1994) highlighted the extent of continuing disadvantage in access and allocation to social housing and the need for greater awareness of the impact of racism, the monitoring of housing allocations and management policy. The study cited research which indicated that housing officials' notions of 'class', 'suitability' and 'deserving' proved to be key determinants of outcome, and were 'significantly and proportionately' detrimental to 'black applicants'. The findings of the review are sobering given that it was undertaken eighteen years after the Race Relations Amendment Act (1976), which extended the prohibition of racial discrimination to include indirect as well as direct discrimination.

Direct discrimination in the provision of public services, including housing, occurs when a person or groups of people are treated less favourably than others on racial grounds. In contrast to this, indirect discrimination is defined as the imposition of conditions or requirements that, while not apparently discriminatory in themselves, have the effect of lowering the proportion of people from certain ethnic groups able to benefit from access to public services, including housing. An example of such discrimination is the lack of availability of larger-sized accommodation in the social rented sector, which is significant given the larger family sizes and households in certain ethnic minority groups.

Here, it is worth making reference to the definition of institutional racism to add to understanding of how racism operates within public organisations. Institutional racism has been defined as:

> ...the collective failure of an organisation to provide an appropriate and professional service to people because of their colour, culture and ethnic background. It can be seen or detected in the processes, attitudes and behaviour which amount to discrimination through unwitting prejudice, ignorance, thoughtlessness and racist stereotyping which disadvantages minority ethnic people (Macpherson, 1999, para 6.34).

At its simplest, the phenomenon is said to occur when overt or covert policies of an institution lead to discriminatory outcomes for people from ethnic minority communities, irrespective of the motives of the individual employees of that institution (Chattoo and Atkin, 2012).

Several areas of institutional racism against ethnic minority applicants in the housing policy and practice of local authorities were identified in a further review of studies relating to ethnic minority issues in Scotland, commissioned by the then Scottish Executive (Netto et al, 2001). This included the identification of discretionary allocation procedures, an example of which included waiting times and points for 'local connection.' Local connection is defined in section 27(1) of the 1987 Housing Act as a connection which a person has with the area i) Because he or she is or was in the past normally resident in it, and this residence was of his or her own choice or ii) Because he or she is employed in it. The allocation criteria of waiting time and local connection clearly disadvantages recent migrants and certain ethnic groups in accessing social housing, indicating the racialised nature of housing policies.

Additionally, the failure among housing organisations to publicise the housing opportunities available to all sections of the population compounded the barriers to accessing social rented housing. The lack of appropriately-sized (larger) housing in the social rented sector was also highlighted as a problem in both housing associations (Dalton and Daglian, 1994; Dowie, 1996) and local authority housing (Bowes et al, 1997; Littlewood and Kearns, 1998). A number of studies have noted that the under-representation of ethnic minority people in the local authority sector led to a low take-up of Right to Buy by this section of the population (Pieda, 1995;

Third et al, 1997)). This group therefore missed out on the opportunity to enhance capital gain through the purchase of heavily discounted council homes. These studies note that the effect of this is particularly striking in Scotland given that one third of owner occupiers here became owner-occupiers through Right to Buy. As MacEwen et al (1994) noted, policies affecting the supply of housing initially determine how effective current allocation policies can be in providing access to more desirable housing. Low rates of new building by local authorities and new towns in Scotland coincided with the effects of the sale of dwellings in determining the pattern of relets. Public sector landlords had fewer new dwellings to let and the profile of their stock and relets was affected by the differential rates of sale of different dwelling types. An increasing proportion of stock consisted of tenements and flats and the more popular house types and locations were likely to have been sold. Thus, by the time households from ethnic minority groups gained eligibility and priority for social housing, the quantity and quality of the dwellings for which they qualified had declined.

Since then, some progress has been made, including increased awareness of the potential for discrimination through discretionary allocation processes and the need to counter this through ethnicity monitoring and reviewing of applicants and lets (Beider and Netto, 2012). More specifically, the Race Relations Amendment (2000) placed a positive, enforceable duty on local authorities and registered social landlords to promote racial equality, and to produce and report on annual race equality schemes, including in housing Although practice in this area is far from even, blatant racial discrimination is less likely to be evident (Beider and Netto, 2012) and has resulted in greater access to the social rented sector. However, in a review of literature and statistical datasets on poverty and ethnicity in Scotland, Netto et al (2011) revealed that non-white groups continue to be under-represented in the social rented sector, despite the importance of this sector for low income groups. They were more likely to be in the private rented sector, with a rate of four and half times that of the white households (25 per cent versus 5.6 per cent). This was partly explained by their younger age, and in some cases, more recent arrival and student occupation. Nevertheless, the study served to once again raise the question of access to social housing.

The *2013–2014 SCORE (Scottish Continuous Recording system)* Report, which collects information from Registered Social Landlords (RSLs) about the new lets they make in a given year, reported that in 2013/14, 84.3 per cent new housing associations lets were to White-Scottish tenants, 5.1 per cent White – Other British, 3.7 per cent White Polish, 1.5 per cent White – Other and 1.4 per cent African. All other groups combined made up 4.2 per cent of lets (Scottish Government, 2014a). It is difficult to assess the level of representation of the ethnic minority population in the sector due to possible changes in the size of the population since the 2011 census as well the changes in the ethnic group classification used in SCORE in 2013-2014 to match the question recommended for use in the Scottish Official Statistics. Neither is it possible to clearly discern whether any changes in representation of ethnic minorities is due to racial discrimination in the allocations process of housing authorities or racial disadvantage on the part of ethnic minorities. Examples of the latter may be found in studies of the housing needs of ethnic minority communities in the Grampian region (Netto et al, 2003a and 2003b) which found that language differences, varying levels of education and literacy, isolation and lack of knowledge of the council's allocation policies acted as barriers to accessing social housing. Other studies have noted both a preference for owner occupation among ethnic minorities as well as the phenomenon of what Third et al (1997) termed as 'reluctant owner-occupiers', that is, ethnic minorities who felt forced to buy their own homes because of the lack of appropriate housing in the social rented sector. A key factor which contributed to this reluctance was the fear of being racially harassed in certain areas, which severely constrained the choices available to them (Netto and Fraser, 2011).

It is obviously important for local authorities and housing associations to ethnically monitor applications, offers and lets and for these figures to be published. Annual reporting and review of these figures would increase transparency relating to the extent organisations were making progress in responding to demand from ethnic minorities. Practitioners with an interest in advancing racial equality in the sector have also commented that it would be a step forward for information to be published on the geographical areas where offers were made and on changes in the performance of individual housing associations over time. The implication here is that currently it is often not possible to discern the extent to which social landlords are allocating 'difficult to let' stock to ethnic minorities. In terms of reducing racial disadvantage, a variety of other approaches to facilitating greater ethnic minority access to the sector have also been recommended, including increasing the supply of housing, more effective communication between social housing providers and ethnic minority communities, the use of community languages, outreach work and active engagement with voluntary organisations that work with these communities (Netto et al, 2003a and Netto et al, 2003b). Clearly, it is also important for allocation policies and practices to continue to be monitored to reduce or eliminate the possibility of racial discrimination and to ensure equal outcomes for ethnic minority communities.

Access and use of homelessness services

Homelessness is a complex phenomenon, often arising from a combination of factors that contribute to exclusion from the housing system. Common factors include loss of employment, relationship breakdown, domestic abuse, mental health problems, substance addiction and discharge from institutional care or from the army. Among ethnic minorities, Netto et al's Scottish Government commissioned study (2004) found that some of the main factors were changes in household formation (for example, being asked to leave overcrowded housing), financial difficulties and lack of access to affordable housing, loss of independent tenancies and policies and legislation relating to asylum seekers and refugees and women escaping domestic violence. Homelessness services play a crucial role in supporting people who have lost their homes, and have few or no options in seeking alternative housing.

Netto et al (2004) found that 'visible' ethnic minorities were over-represented in the homelessness monitoring data held by Scottish Local Authorities (LAS). Of the 36,898 homeless applications fully recorded by LAS in 2002/03, the number of applicants coded as Indian, Pakistani/Bangladeshi etc, Chinese, Black or Other totalled 896 – or 2.4 per cent.[14] Quantitative analysis of this data revealed that the incidence of *recorded* homelessness affecting households from ethnic minority communities for the period 2002–2003 (that is, among those who presented as homeless) was 75 per cent higher than the population as a whole. The degree of over-representation varied considerably between ethnic minority groups, with the 'black and non-white' groups being most highly represented and the Chinese group being under-represented.

[14] It should be borne in noted that an additional 304 applicants were classed as 'White Other' (i.e. other than White Scottish, White Other British and White Irish) in 2002/03, and that 189 were classed as 'White Irish'. These households are not, however, included within the 'BME' cohort analysed above

More recent analysis by the Scottish Government separates the analysis of ethnicity within the homelessness data into two main groups: i) UK and EU nationals and ii) those granted leave to remain or refugee status. It found that the ethnic composition of this first group which amounted to 24,000 cases assessed as homeless in 2013/14 broadly reflects that of the Scottish population, although the proportion of cases from a 'White Scottish' background is higher than the population as a whole (93 per cent in the homelessness data compared to 96 per cent for Scotland as a whole. It also found that the proportion of 'White Other British' (6 per cent compared to 12 per cent for Scotland) and Asian (0.9 per cent compared to 2 per cent for Scotland) is also less than in the population as a whole. In the latter group, of the 1100 cases assessed as homeless in the same period after being granted leave to remain or refugee status, 11 per cent self-identified as White: Other (outside of the EU), 14 per cent as Asian, 21 per cent as Black and 47 per cent as Other. Neither set of figures take into account an appreciable degree of 'hidden homelessness' in certain ethnic minority communities as evidenced through reports on-over-crowding (Netto et al, 2011).

It is thus important to examine the extent to which racism impacts on access and use of homelessness services. Analysis of data from 298 agencies which returned a postal questionnaire in the Netto et al (2004) study revealed that less than half completed questions relating to service use. Less than a third reported employing any means of reaching ethnic minority households. Only a fifth reported offering some sort of specialist provision for ethnic minority users, with advice sessions and outreach work being the most common forms. Overall, these findings indicate the highly racialised practices of the majority of mainstream homelessness agencies. The lack of access of these services to ethnic minority individuals is concerning given the limited number of ethnic minority agencies operating outside of the Central Belt, including in the large rural and remote areas of Scotland.

Gaps in service provision

Not surprisingly, mainstream agencies were also less likely to offer services which took into account the needs of ethnic minority communities. Such services included interpreting and translating services, support with literacy, advocacy services, specialised legal advice, information about the availability of culturally appropriate accommodation and specialist supported accommodation projects, and responsiveness to cultural needs, including dietary needs and religious and gender preferences. Some of the mainstream agencies involved in a qualitative review of homelessness services (Netto et al, 2004) appeared uncertain about the appropriateness of their services for ethnic minority communities. In the words of one agency, 'it's hard to know because we have so few... it's hard to answer that really.' At least one agency representative was of the view that offering the same service to everyone, 'regardless of who they are,' without taking into account the specificity of their needs was offering an appropriate service. These qualitative insights support the view that institutional racism in the form of a lack of sensitivity to cultural and other differences was part of the culture of a number of mainstream homelessness agencies and manifested in their lack of efforts to respond to the specific needs of individuals from ethnic minority communities.

Perhaps one of the most important gaps in service provision by mainstream agencies was the lack of interpreting and translation services and the lack of advocacy services, which is especially significant within the context of complaints about discriminatory treatment in housing offices. Among the Gypsy Travellers who participated in the study, a recurrent theme was discrimination on the part of service providers made it difficult for them to obtain the level of service provision that they were entitled to. In the words of one individual:

> They think that because we are Travelling people, if you go to them with your problems, you get no reply back. They treat us like scum – that's the truth.

Perceptions of discriminatory treatment in homelessness services were also found in a qualitative study of refugee access to social housing in Glasgow (Netto and Fraser, 2011). It is difficult to rule out the possibility of negative stereotyping on the part of at least some homelessness caseworkers relating to homeless people, ethnic minorities or both, that may be manifested as personal racism in their interactions with this client group.

Other gaps in service provision are reflective of deeply entrenched institutional racism against specific ethnic groups, including Gypsy Travellers. At the policy level, sites for parking caravans are included within the definition of a home (Scottish Parliament Equal Opportunities Committee, 2001). Those whose live in a caravan and are unable to park it are considered to be homeless (Scottish Executive, 2001). Such high level policy recognition accommodates different conceptualisations of homelessness between ethnic groups (Netto, 2006), a deep cultural attachment to travelling and the importance of possessing a caravan in order to travel. In the words of a Gypsy Traveller interviewed as part of Netto et al (2004)'s study,

> As long as you have a caravan, you can never be homeless... Homelessness is a state of mind, a state of soul. Unless people are allowed to make a home where they want to be, they won't be happy.

Examples of services that would support the travelling culture of Gypsy Travellers identified by specialist services were help with caravan damage or disrepair, or funding for purchasing caravans. However, at the level of practice, there is a lack of willingness to respond or support such lifestyles. The absence of these services indicates the difficulty of translating equal opportunities policies into practice, including where they have been publicly advocated within high level policy circles. As with the lack of responsiveness of mainstream agencies to the specific needs of other ethnic minority groups, lack of cultural sensitivity in this instance may be linked to a wider reluctance to depart from conventional norms of what constitutes a home, processes of home-making and service provision. Such reluctance may be viewed as manifestations of institutional racism which knowingly or unknowingly hinder access to homelessness services among ethnic minority communities.

Racial harassment and effectiveness of responses

A recurrent theme in studies of ethnic minority housing is the fear of and actual experience of racial harassment and its role in influencing housing-related decisions, including among asylum-seekers (Barclay et al., 2003), refugees (Netto and Fraser, 2011), Gypsy/Travellers (Craigforth, 2009; Netto et al, 2003a and 2003b) and other ethnic minority communities (Netto et al., 2001, 2011). This includes verbal or physical abuse and perceived danger to life from the local majority population. Concerns extend to the safety of children not only in the immediate neighbourhood (Netto and Fraser, 2009) but in schools in the catchment area (Netto et al, 2003a and b). Such concerns also influence parents' choice of accommodation. Indeed, in many cases, safety from the phenomenon was identified as the single most important factor in housing-related decision-making processes (Netto and Abazie, 2012). In the words of an individual who had recently gained refugee status and who was interviewed in Netto and Abaize's Glasgow-based (2012) study:

> I am very, very concerned about safe area. Very important to me because you know Glasgow does not like some minority groups.

Racial harassment, as defined by the Commission for Racial Equality (2006: 25), occurs when 'a person harasses another on grounds of race, ethnic or national origin' and 'when the conduct is 'unwanted' and has the effect or purpose of violating the other person's dignity or creating an intimidating, or offensive environment for that person" The definition also acknowledges that what is viewed as contributing towards an 'intimidating or offensive environment' is necessarily a subjective judgement on the victim's part. The victim-centred approach to racial harassment is also reflected in the Association of Chief Police Officers' (2005) definition of a racial incident. The benefit of this approach is that it counters any tendency of the bodies to which incidents are reported not to recognise a racial element. However, a major shortcoming of this definition is its failure to recognise that the vast majority of racial incidents are perpetrated by individuals from the majority White population against ethnic minorities. Indeed, Chahal (1999) has argued that blindness to this aspect of racist victimisation in official definitions contributes to ineffective policy and practice responses.

Evidence in support of the high relevance of fear of racial harassment in housing-related decisions can be found in studies of the phenomenon which reveal that most incidents occur near victims' homes (Chahal, 2007; Clark and Leven, 2000). Indicating that such acts may not be isolated incidents undertaken by lone perpetrators, in the field of criminology, racial harassment has been seen to reflect a local ethos of a perhaps influential tolerance of low-level racial hostility, which legitimises individual acts of racial harassment (Sibbitt, 1997; Webster, 2007). Interview accounts of ethnic minority individuals in Netto and Abazie's (2012) study indicate not only the repetitive nature of low level abuse in certain areas, but its pervasiveness:

> We have problems with neighbours who say it is not our place to be here. They tell us to go back. We get that a lot.

> A lot of people drink and come and kick at your door.

Reinforcing the pervasive nature of racial harassment, the data also reveal that, for some victims, the acts of harassment are not associated with a single perpetrator but with multiple ones ('a lot of people' or 'neighbours'). Such data concurs with that of the Scottish Crime Justice Survey (Clark and Leven, 2000) which found that around 60 per cent of individuals were victimised by three or more perpetrators. The data also demonstrate the predictability of ongoing victimisation and 'continuous insecurity' (Virdee, 1997). Both the pervasiveness of the phenomenon and its predictability indicate that ethnic minority individuals are likely to face difficulties in reporting regular low-level acts of harassment.

The reporting of racial harassment has continued to increase in Scotland (EHRC, 2010b). According to the then Strathclyde Policy Authority which covered the West of Scotland including the Glasgow City Council area, the rate of racist incidents between April to September in 2011/12 was 12.8 per cent per 10, 000 people, an increase of 5.8 per cent over the same period in the previous year. These rates are reflective of recording practices as well as actual numbers of racial incidents and include incidents outside the city as well as those within it. Such figures are of concern because they are indicative of ongoing interethnic conflict in some of the country's most deprived neighbourhoods. At the national level, hate crime statistics reveal that racial crime 'remains the most commonly reported hate crime' (Procurator Fiscal, 2015). In 2013 – 2014, there were 4,148 charges, more than twice the number for the other four categories of hate crime combined (that is, sexually aggravated crime, religiously aggravated crime and disability or transgender identity aggravation).

Complex social processes appear to be at work in places deprived of employment and opportunities for moving out of these areas (Amin, 1992; Robinson, 2008), including in Glasgow, the site for the research that this study draws on. New migrants typically live in economically disadvantaged and deprived neighbourhoods, with poor housing, high levels of unemployment, limited service provision and poor local facilities (Robinson, 2010). This can put a strain on local services, which may already be over-stretched (Robinson and Walshaw 2011). Individuals who are viewed as not 'belonging' to those neighbourhoods, might be perceived as contributing towards disadvantaged social-economic conditions, and seen as legitimate targets for abuse. However, as Robinson and Walshaw (2011) also point out, the new migrants may also bring a number of positive benefits, including filling gaps in the labour market, contributing to neighbourhood sustainability and viability of service provision. This study, along with other research, indicates the importance of paying attention to the local context in developing analyses of racism that are socially, politically and geographically located (Back, 1993; Netto, 2011a). As Netto (2011b) argues, it is important to identify attributes of places that enable individuals, including new migrants, to acquire both material and social capital and a sense of belonging.

Responses to racial harassment by social landlords

In the UK, housing organisations have been urged to take action against racial harassment by social landlords for more than two decades (cf CRE, 1987). Problems included under-reporting of racial incidents and the difficulty of implementing appropriate measures for supporting victims. Two of the main options identified for victims were to either 'stay put' or transfer to another property. Measures against perpetrators included legal actions that could be taken by the police or social landlords, including eviction by the latter; however, in a study carried out in Scotland, England and Wales, Lemos (2000) found that although many housing authorities offered security improvements to victims of racial harassment in social housing, few victims were transferred and action against perpetrators was rare.

In Scotland, the Housing (Scotland) Act 1985 gave social landlords the powers to introduce changes to tenancy agreements and to repossess properties from perpetrators of racial harassment. This is supported by human rights legislation which recognises the rights of individuals to peaceful enjoyment of their homes. Further, in relation to taking action against perpetrators of racial harassment living in social housing, the Equality and Human Rights Commission makes it clear that such action does not constitute an infringement of the Human Rights Act, if the action taken is 'lawful, *necessary and proportionate*' (EHRC, 2010b, p. 190; emphasis added). However, as we will see below, social landlords with little understanding of the impact of the phenomenon on ethnic minority communities may find it difficult to assess the necessity and proportionality of official responses.

Netto and Abazie's (2012) study revealed that many housing associations had policies in place for addressing racial incidents. In line with good practice guidance, many policies specified how victims and witnesses should be supported and the range of actions that could be taken against perpetrators.

Illustrating this, Glasgow Housing Association, Glasgow's largest housing association outlined a staged, escalatory victim-centred process for dealing with complaints of racial harassment beginning with interviews with the victim and warnings to the perpetrator, and proceeding to further action and possible eviction. Many organisations had also taken measures to publicise their policies on racial harassment to tenants. However, as the same study noted, such events-oriented responses appear to be heavily reliant on officer assessment of the severity of reported incidents. This is problematic, given the likelihood that the assessment involves individuals from the majority population, who may not have experienced racial harassment, judging the seriousness of acts inflicted on ethnic minorities. Further, as Netto and Abazie (2012) argue, policies based on the premise that action can be taken against individual perpetrators fall short in tackling more pervasive and recurrent forms of racism that may be operating at a local level. Significantly, not all housing organisations had policies on racial harassment or had taken measures to implement these effectively, including by training front-line staff on the duties of the organisation or other key agencies. Performance-monitoring systems for dealing with racial harassment were also lacking. Other persistent trends identified included the small number of transfers among victims and low threats of repossession and actual eviction of perpetrators. Indicating the pervasiveness of the problem in social housing estates, where housing officers were sympathetic to experiences of racist victimisation, they reported difficulties in accommodating people in alternative areas due to the shortage of accommodation in areas perceived by ethnic minorities to be 'safe'.

Summing up, the study found that while some good practice in tackling more serious acts of harassment was evident, wide policy and practice gaps remain. Further, some aspects of policies appear inherently flawed in tackling daily low levels of abuse. Netto and Abazie (2012) argue that while it might be necessary to take action against individual or household perpetrators of serious racial incidents, there is an urgent need for developing more 'place' based or area-based approaches to low level abuse. Such approaches would need to be grounded in the understanding that since complex and dynamic social processes give rise to such hostility, equally complex social processes, involving community development activities, are required to counter them. The implementation of both anti-racist and anti-poverty strategies at a local level plays an important role in supporting new migrants within existing communities, as well as in supporting established residents to accommodate new arrivals in the neighbourhoods concerned. This would require higher prioritisation of the issue by social landlords working with a range of community organisations and adequate resourcing. Within the current context of large scale displacement of people from Syria and other countries, this should involve higher levels of awareness of the specific needs and vulnerabilities of refugees compared to other migrants (Netto, 2011b). Community mobilisation can also play a role in challenging exclusionary discourses. At the local level, there is an urgent need to acquire greater understanding as to what kind of community development approaches work, how, for whom, and in what contexts (Robinson and Walshaw, 2011), and importantly, to ensure that community organisations have the capacity to carry out such work.

Conclusion

This chapter has explored the impact of racism on ethnic minorities' experiences of housing in Scotland in three major areas: access to the social rented sector, the provision of homelessness services and experiences of racial harassment and organisational responses to the phenomenon. It has shown the legacy of deeply entrenched institutional racism against ethnic minorities which inhibited access to the social rented sector and prevented them from benefiting from 'Right to Buy' policies, which was a major route to home ownership among the majority population in Scotland. By the time awareness had been raised of the need to counter discriminatory practices much of the better quality social housing stock had been sold. While it has been encouraging to note that some progress has now been made and blatant racial discrimination is now rare, research in this area has revealed the importance of continuing to be alert to exclusionary processes in terms of access to housing for ethnic minorities. When this is combined with racial disadvantage among ethnic minorities in the form of low levels of awareness of their rights to housing, illiteracy or fluency in English, the effects are exacerbated. Institutional racism in the social rented sector continues to be manifested in the persistence of allocation criteria that are indirectly discriminatory and in the lack of availability of appropriately sized accommodation for larger households. It is also evident in the lack of recognition of some housing organisations of the prevalence of racial harassment in some social housing estates.

In the planning and delivery of homelessness services, institutional racism takes the form of a lack of sensitivity to a range of specific needs that are associated with ethnic minority communities including those related to language, legal advice and specific provision for Gypsy Travellers...In some cases, racism, particularly in the case of that experienced by Gypsy Travellers stems from a failure to accommodate different conceptions of home in service provision other than that preferred by settled communities which is deemed to be superior to that preferred by this group, despite recognition of a caravan and a place to park it as constituting home in policy statements In other cases, the lack of sensitivity of homelessness services to ethnic minority groups may be viewed as lack of prioritisation of these issues within the context of informal organisational cultures operating within these organisations. Assuming that housing organisations are microcosms of Scottish society, such insensitivity may be viewed as a tendency within the wider society to either ignore or effectively downplay the specific needs of some of its ethnic minority communities. These exclusionary tendencies could be countered by paying more attention to improving the range and appropriateness of homelessness services. Such efforts, it might be argued, are particularly important given the lack of alternatives that may be available to the people concerned due to their typically limited material resources and the vital role that such provision can potentially play in improving the quality of life of Scotland's diverse communities.

Narratives of personal experiences of racial harassment in some social housing estates provide evidence not only of the existence of racism, but also of the challenges of tackling a phenomenon which is not experienced as sporadic or isolated but as pervasive. It has been argued that since complex processes in often socio-economically deprived communities contribute to the perpetration of racial harassment, long term resource intensive efforts are needed to counter the problem. Important first steps here may be the unpalatable recognition that racism is a 'live' phenomenon in the housing experiences of some of Scotland's ethnic minority communities, particularly those living in some social housing estates This may be difficult to acknowledge given the inclusive approach that Scottish politicians typically promote (Barker, 2015), but is essential. Closely associated with this would be a willingness to consider alternative responses to dominant policies for responding to racial harassment, where they exist, including a strong focus on community development activities and developing neighbourhood notions of 'place', which are not only inclusive of ethnically diverse communities, but celebratory of their existence. Such activities would need to be underpinned by greater efforts to address possible feelings of resentment, marginalisation and threat experienced by individuals from the majority population who live in some social housing estates that may be used to justify acts of racial harassment. It is likely that such efforts would need to be linked to wider strategies to reduce levels of poverty and deprivation within the majority population. New migratory flows of people, including refugees from Syria at the time of writing also indicate the timeliness of paying far greater attention to 'what works' in terms of creating more cohesive communities at the local level. It is likely that work in this area would i involve long established residents as well as new arrivals – including both economic migrants and refugees – to ensure that perceptions of marginalisation from social and political processes do not hinder integration efforts.

Overall, the chapter has shown that racism – institutional and personal, direct and indirect – influences ethnic minorities' experiences within the housing system in Scotland in specific ways. It has also shown that the forms of racism experienced by ethnic minorities can differ considerably, indicating the need for closer scrutiny of the relationship between institutional systems and processes and the experiences of different groups, including refugees and Gypsy Travellers. Sadly, it has also shown that, in some neighbourhoods, the experiences of some ethnic minorities reveal a high degree of racial hostility, which should be taken seriously not least because it is likely to be symptomatic of a wider dissatisfaction and sense of displacement among residents living in areas of deprivation.

CHAPTER 10

Changing the Race Equality Paradigm in Scotland's Public Sector

Carol Young

Introduction

THE COALITION FOR RACIAL EQUALITY AND RIGHTS (CRER) is a Scottish anti-racist organisation which works with partners, including public bodies, to tackle racial inequality. We take this approach because, whilst we believe that society as a whole bears the responsibility for tackling racial inequality, public sector institutions have particular influence and power which can be used to create wider change. Many of these institutions already invest significant time and effort in equality activities, but often with questionable impact. Race equality work is sometimes hampered by misconceptions about the causes of inequality, and by limited approaches to dealing with its consequences. Without a clear understanding of race and racism, even the most well-meaning efforts are likely to fail. This frustrating situation can only be reversed if institutions are willing to change their paradigm on race equality.

CRER works to inspire a new direction on race equality within public, social and organisational policy by supporting institutions to better respond to the challenges of tackling inequality and racism. This paper sets out some of the key areas where this support is needed, outlining key concepts which could be used to improve policy and practice. Many of the concepts explored here are long standing and will be familiar to readers, whilst some reflect more recent thinking around the causes and consequences of racial inequality.

Why do we need to change the race equality paradigm?

Fifty years after the introduction of the Race Relations Act 1965, Black and minority ethnic (BME) people in Scotland still face serious disadvantages including higher rates of poverty, lower rates of employment and a range of health inequalities in comparison to the ethnic majority population (Equality and Human Rights Commission, 2016). Despite this, race has largely fallen off the agenda (Operation Black Vote, 2014). Many people believe that Britain is essentially post-racial; that it has reached a point where race, racism and racial inequality are no longer significant issues (see, for example, Sayyid, 2010). There are also attempts to frame racial inequality as just another form of social class penalty (Heath and McMahon, 2000) whilst largely ignoring how race and class interact – for example, the different levels of advantage social class confers across ethnicities (Zuccotti, 2014). Outrage at racial discrimination in Britain is primarily now restricted to celebrity racism scandals and commentary on social media (CRER, 2014a). As unpleasant as it may be, this is not the primary dimension of racism affecting minority ethnic people in Britain. If anything, the popular fixation with these incidents detracts from the real structuring power of racism. The finger pointing opportunity they provide allows people to feel as though they oppose racism without actually having to do anything to address it in their own lives.

There's a perception that Scotland has less of a problem with racism than other areas of the UK, perhaps best summed up by the phrase 'we're all Jock Tamson's bairns.' But regardless of popular opinion, the statistics suggest otherwise. Between 2000 and 2013, the per capita rate of murders with a known or suspected racist element in Scotland was higher than in the rest of the UK – 1.8 murders per million people in the population compared to 1.3 (CRER, 2015a). In 2013–2014, 4,807 racist incidents were recorded by Police in Scotland (Scottish Government, 2015b). That's the equivalent of 92 incidents every week, without accounting for the many cases that go unreported.

The Scottish Government is currently developing a new Race Equality Framework, which is a positive move. However, this will be the first such document published since the Race Equality Statement 2008–2011 (Scottish Government, 2008). Public bodies are obliged to take action on race equality through the Scottish specific equality duties, yet the equality outcomes set in April 2013 often failed to address key inequalities for minority ethnic people (CRER, 2013a). Such inaction needs to be challenged. The lens through which race equality is viewed today is fundamentally flawed, and progress is stalling as a result. The first of the key areas this paper explores could shift this lens through helping institutions to better understand what racism is and how it operates.

Changing what we mean by 'racism'

Racism is a high profile issue, but there's very little public understanding of how it works in practice (Song, 2014a). Political and media commentary unhelpfully treats the term 'racism' as an insult to be aimed at individuals, a personality flaw or a social *faux pas*. No wonder, then, that public services and corporations are reluctant to consider the issue of institutional racism. A better understanding of racism in all its forms is needed. The basic terminology around race makes a good starting point on this journey for many institutions. Terms like racial, cultural and ethnic are often used interchangeably, which causes confusion. The current use of the term 'racial' has developed because disproved anthropological notions of racial difference have become embedded in the beliefs and behaviours of society; this is the social construct which underpins all forms of racism (Coates, 2013). 'Culture' describes how people are bound together by social customs, activities, beliefs, behavioural norms and values; this is sometimes but not always related to ethnicity. Ethnicity, on the other hand, describes how people are bound together by shared characteristics including language, culture, history, folklore, ideology, national origin, nationality or ancestry.

In our view, using these terms interchangeably can strip organisational messages of context and meaning, making them appear tokenistic and losing any positive intention behind them. The Equality Act 2010 contains its own definition of race. This focuses on colour, nationality and ethnic or national origins, prohibiting various types of racial discrimination. However, there is more to racism than unlawful discrimination, so the tendency of institutions to focus purely on legal compliance can be unhelpful. Acknowledgement of the broader structural, social and institutional aspects of racism is vital. Mirroring wider social attitudes, institutions and their staff often see the word 'racist' as a slur rather than an adjective to describe something which places the importance and value of one ethnic group's identity, culture, perspective or way of life above others. It begins with ethnocentrism – the practice of judging other cultures by the standards of their own – combined with racial stereotyping and a sense of superiority about the traditions, culture and practices of the dominant ethnic group (Barger, 2014). It's the assumption that the majority cultural viewpoint is the right way, the best way. Everything else is an anomaly. This tendency can certainly result in overt racism, which for example might take the form of hate speech or open discrimination. However, even seemingly obvious cases of racism can be contentious for some onlookers. It is common to see the intentions of the perpetrator questioned as a defence – perhaps they weren't being racist, but had some other problem with the person being targeted. This shows a fundamental misunderstanding of how racism operates. Knowing the weight that an accusation of racism carries, most people will think carefully before alleging it; they are also aware that, should they choose to do so, they may be quickly undermined. This means that both covert racism (subtle or less obvious forms) and some incidents of overt racism (more observable or apparent forms) can be difficult to challenge, even for those experiencing it (see, for example, Utt, 2011).

Racism and visibility

Overt racism occurs not because of the ethnicity of the person being targeted, but because of the perceptions of the person doing the targeting. Your likelihood of being targeted can vary according to how visible your ethnicity is; how 'different' you appear in their eyes (CRER, 2012). For people living in a majority white society, any skin colour other than white is a dead giveaway. It doesn't matter if someone was born into that society, grew up in it and have never known any other; the potential to be seen as 'different' stays with them for life. However, visibility is complex. Your skin colour can't be seen over the telephone, but your accent can lead to assumptions about your ethnicity. Your name on an application form may or may not make your ethnicity visible, depending on how it's perceived by the reader (Wykes, 2015). You could be white skinned, and still identifiably minority ethnic in many circumstances. Skin tone has not protected Jewish people, Irish people, Gypsy/Traveller communities or new European migrants from racism. Whiteness is about much more than skin colour, as we will explore in the following section.

We encourage the organisations we work with to ensure that experiences of racism are recognised appropriately. When someone believes that their ethnicity is the reason they're being treated badly, it's not acceptable for anyone else to judge otherwise. This is reflected in the definition of a racist incident as 'any incident which is perceived to be racist by the victim or any other person' (Macpherson, 1999).

Bias and privilege

Racism is not always easy to pinpoint, even for those on the receiving end (Touré, 2011). It runs on a spectrum, from hatred through to hidden bias, with tolerance somewhere in between. Tolerance may be preferable to intolerance, but it still implies that ethnic groups can choose to 'tolerate' each other rather than being able to live together as equals. Of course, living together as equals is a challenging goal. To work towards it, we require an understanding of what makes society unequal. Hidden bias is one factor at play in this; prejudice that is not deliberate but nonetheless affects attitudes and behaviour. In these cases, the person responsible has not consciously acknowledged how stereotypes affect their own perceptions and actions (Banaji and Greenwald, 2013).

Without a single hostile thought about someone from another ethnic background, people can still harbour racist attitudes and carry out racist actions as a result of hidden bias, which is also known as 'unconscious' bias. That description could arguably imply that it's something buried so deeply, people cannot be aware of it. In fact, developing an awareness of our underlying attitudes is vital to a genuinely anti-racist approach (Law, 2011). A term which acknowledges this more is 'implicit' bias, as used for example in implicit association testing which uses negative and positive associations to show racial bias (Harvard University, no date). Hidden bias isn't something that people are born with. It develops as children grow up in a society which promotes the viewpoint of the dominant ethnic group over all others. This shapes their attitudes, behaviours and ways of relating to each other (Vedantam, 2010). It's not only children who develop learned attitudes and behaviours around race, however, and these can be quite explicit as well as hidden.

For people in the ethnic majority, learned behaviour is one of many factors underpinning white privilege, the advantages which automatically apply to a person because they are white in a society designed around the world view of a white majority ethnic group (Guess, 2006). At its most basic, the advantage arises from white people being well represented in positions of power and, particularly for those in the majority ethnic group, the protection which whiteness provides them against the experience and threat of racism. The situation is maintained by structures and attitudes which replicate the power of the dominant group. Although it's an advantage they didn't ask for, white majority ethnic Scots carry it throughout their lives at the direct expense of their peers from minority ethnic backgrounds. White privilege is a product of white supremacy, entrenched in British cultural, social and political life as a key part of the ideological structures underpinning colonialism and imperialism. This still impacts life in Britain today – in our work, we argue that white privilege and institutional racism are the current outcomes of Britain's past deliberate adoption of white supremacy (Miles and Dunlop, 1987). This situation is not inevitable. White privilege, racism and hidden bias are socially constructed, and will reduce the more individuals and institutions actively challenge them.

Institutional racism

Contrary to the furore around Sir William Macpherson's (1999) use of the term in his report on the investigation of the murder of Stephen Lawrence, 'institutional racism' doesn't mean that a great number of individuals within an institution are racist (although that might also be true, in some instances). It's a far more subtle concept, which nonetheless has a deep and lasting impact on outcomes for minority ethnic people. We feel that it's vital for organisations to understand and acknowledge it.

Institutional racism arises from rules, customs, processes and practices which have been planned without regard to the potential impacts on people from minority ethnic groups. The impacts of the institution's work and the way it operates are racist, regardless of whether the people within the institution have racist attitudes themselves. Put simply, the decisions made within institutions reflect the preferences, priorities, social norms, values and needs that the decision makers share. If a majority of those decision makers are from the white majority population (not to mention also usually male, able-bodied etc.), then the institution will evolve to suit that type of person, creating gaps and barriers for everyone else (Flinders, Matthews and

Eason, 2011). Institutional racism can be difficult to legally challenge; in cases where there is a proven impact on someone in services or employment, it may be possible for them to make a claim under the 'indirect discrimination' provisions of the Equality Act 2010. However, institutional racism has broader implications which can't be rectified through legal means alone, so CRER's work with institutions aims to address this bigger picture.

Racism and the cycle of exclusion

Most people understand one or more aspects of racism, whether direct, institutional or hidden, but the way they link together to create a cycle of exclusion is less widely acknowledged (Brockmann, Butt and Fisher, 2001). Recruitment policies provide a clear example of how this cycle works. In our experience, policies to improve workforce diversity tend to hinge on encouraging applications from minority ethnic people. These policies are generally ineffective, because even where the level of applications from minority ethnic people is high, these candidates are much less likely to be appointed at interview stage (CRER, 2014b). The policy of encouraging applications is based on the assumptions of the majority ethnic managers instead of evidence about the experiences of minority ethnic applicants. This policy is intended to reduce racial inequality, but instead reflects institutional racism.

If a candidate has reached interview stage, this should mean that they meet the criteria for the job. So what is it that stops them from being appointed? In some cases direct racism may be responsible (Butler, 2012). Hidden bias, however, is potentially also a common factor (Peacock, 2014). Interviewers score candidates according to how much they agree with their answers and feel that they 'fit' with the organisational culture. Essentially, interviewers tend to appoint someone they believe is 'like them' (Colarelli, 2003). This perception can be skewed by hidden bias, which should be recognised and tackled. Both hidden bias and overt racism within interview processes ensure that under-representation in the workforce continues, which contributes to negative stereotypes about minority ethnic people in the workforce. These stereotypes then come full circle to feed into hidden or overt racist assumptions about who 'fits in'.

Recruitment processes are only one example of this cycle of exclusion. It can be seen in most areas where minority ethnic people experience worse outcomes – access to services or participation in political and civic life, for

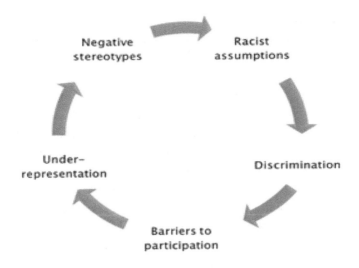

instance. To challenge this, organisations need to develop evidence based policies and practices with an understanding of racism in all of its forms, and without the blinkers of hidden bias.

Creating a better evidence base

Evidence based policy has slowly gained traction across the UK. In Scotland it has been a particular focus following the Christie Commission report on the future delivery of public services, published in 2011. In theory, evidence based policy should benefit everyone by ensuring that needs and circumstances of all are properly understood by policy makers. However, this depends on the breadth and quality of that evidence, how it's interpreted and whether it's acted upon. The principles of evidence based policy are arguably not being applied where minority ethnic communities are concerned. For example, the equality outcomes set by public bodies in Scotland in 2013 often had no obvious link to evidence on race equality. Where evidence was given, there were often concerns about its quality or whether it had genuinely influenced the outcomes (CRER, 2013a). If this can happen in a process directly relating to tackling racial inequality, serious doubts have to be raised about how well such evidence is used in everyday policy making. Without a better evidence base, flawed assumptions about the capacity, experience and needs of communities and individuals will continue to be made on a daily basis.

Selective use of evidence is a major part of the problem. Where evidence on race equality is mentioned in a policy context, it's often to applaud progress. For example, minority ethnic communities have particularly good outcomes in education and this fact is widely acknowledged (although it should be noted that there are often gender differences in attainment within minority ethnic groups). The problem is that this isn't leading to better representation in the workplace. Only 55.2 per cent of the non-white population aged 25-49 is in employment, compared to 72 per cent of the white population (Scottish Parliament Equal Opportunities Committee, 2016). Black and minority ethnic people are also more likely to be in low paid jobs, or clustered into particular occupations. It's clear that the progress in education is only half of a fairly bleak picture.

Sometimes, received wisdom is presented as evidence when research shows something to the contrary. For example, the common argument that language barriers are to blame for labour market disadvantages doesn't add up. Almost 85 per cent of Scotland's working age minority ethnic population have no problem with English language proficiency (National Records of Scotland, 2011), for example. So whilst language issues affect some individuals (many of whom are recent migrants who will rapidly develop English skills), the extent of employment inequalities such as higher rates of graduate unemployment (Tackey, Barnes and Khambhaita, 2011) show there must be other factors at play.

Explanations relating to personal capacity are still at the forefront of much public policy on tackling race equality. Our experience in working with public sector organisations has often shown that, where there is evidence of inequality, policy makers tend to assume that their own equality policies and practices will be effective and so attribute continuing inequality to external problems, possibly within minority ethnic communities. This is part of a wider mind-set that might be described as a 'deficit model' of racial inequality. This approach problematises people, downplays the strengths and assets they possess and at its worst essentially blames individuals for the disadvantages they face (Gorsky, 2010).

To avoid ineffective practice, it's necessary to move away from the deficit model and seek more robust evidence on racial inequality. However, gathering evidence is only the first step; using it effectively is another challenge altogether. Effective analysis of statistical evidence can be particularly difficult. Statistics are often not disaggregated by ethnicity, meaning that differences in outcome can't be accurately measured or addressed. Where they are disaggregated, BME communities are often treated as a homogenous group or grouped together in inconsistent ways (CRER, 2014b). This can disguise the real issues for specific communities and prevent practical action. Even where there is a degree of disaggregation by ethnicity, these inequalities can be missed. For example, looking at educational attainment, learners included in the 'Caribbean and Black: Other' category fare much worse than those in the African category, meaning that the common practice of amalgamating these into one 'Black / African / Caribbean' category hides the degree of inequality (ibid.).

Evidence and engagement

To tackle the effects of institutional discrimination, racism and hidden bias, gathering evidence from community involvement is often essential. This isn't just a matter of good practice. Some public sector bodies in Scotland and Wales are subject to Specific Equality Duties which require them to involve communities in specific parts of their equalities work, and in England case law has similar implications. Engagement should be undertaken as part of a wider process which also takes into account research and statistical evidence. Although communities can offer much expertise, they cannot be expected to know everything there is to know about racial inequality. What they can offer – their own knowledge and experience – should nevertheless be seen as an essential part of the evidence base.

Currently however, practice in engagement is at something of a crossroads. On one hand, there are examples of positive involvement between communities and institutions, from participatory budgeting to co-production (McGeachie and Power, 2015). On the other, community organisations are often deeply dissatisfied with the engagement they have with policy makers. Poorly handled or ineffective processes can actively damage community relations. Even in Scotland, where a set of National Standards for Community Engagement (Communities Scotland, 2005) and associated resources are available, tick box consultation exercises are all too common. In some cases, repeated community engagement exercises may even be used (whether consciously or not) as a stalling tactic to avoid taking action on the evidence already available. Whatever the engagement method, if the outcome turns out to be a foregone conclusion then communities have not been truly involved. Importantly, evidence from engagement needs to be interpreted with an understanding of racism and racial inequality. The deficit model sometimes operates within communities as well as institutions – community members may internalise negative messages and present them, even when these messages don't match their own experience (Kretzmann, 2010). The tendency for policy makers to listen to the loudest voices or rely on the 'usual suspects' becomes even more of a problem when internalised racism is at play.

Engagement processes also need to recognise that there are imbalances of power both within and between communities. Choosing not to explore conflicts within the engagement setting is patronising and counter-productive. Intercultural dialogue approaches can be useful in these situations; accepting difference of opinion and concentrating on the areas where people can agree, whilst respecting and valuing each contribution (British Council, no date). Engagement with minority ethnic communities must have visible results, be inclusive of all communities and be undertaken from a position of mutual trust and respect. True involvement, however, also requires a degree of power sharing. To achieve this, in our experience institutions will generally need to address issues with their own policy making hierarchy and power dynamics. This requires a degree of honesty and humility which policy makers may find challenging, but ultimately rewarding.

Understand the impact of 'difference'

The way that we view similarity and difference has a big part to play in tackling racism. Communities are brought together based on similarities and can be divided by difference. Individuals, meanwhile, are each vastly different. An important part of a more progressive approach to race equality in the public sector lies in recognising intersectionality; how the full range of characteristics someone possesses impacts their experience of inequality (Crenshaw, 2012). Much of the early prominent academic work on this by Kimberlé Crenshaw focused on how anti-discrimination law often fails to protect Black women whose experience is distinct from those of both white women and Black men (ibid). There are parallels to be made here with current approaches in the public sector, which tend to hinge on broad concepts of 'fairness' at the expense of a more nuanced view.

By talking about difference in basic terms without reflecting complex identities, institutions can unwittingly contribute to stereotyping (Kennedy, 2010). Not only do stereotypes fuel racist attitudes in the majority ethnic population, limiting opportunities, they also contribute to the internalised racism that makes it hard for people facing discrimination to effectively recognise and challenge it (Bivens, 2005). Racist social structures impact an individual's perception of their own power, potential, entitlements and behavioural roles. This actively reduces their ability to assert their rights and challenge those structures.

Internalised racism is experienced not just on an individual level, but often collectively. One example of this can be seen in the reluctance of communities to use particular services (Owuor and Nake, 2015). When communities express a feeling that a certain service is not seen as being 'for them', they are being manipulated into feeling that way by the environment that racist social structures have created. In our experience, this isn't about communities not wanting to use mainstream services or preferring to stay in their own spaces. It's about their perception of whether that environment is safe, based on generations of experience in similar environments where subtle (and less subtle) forms of racism were at play. In an ideal world, people would simply assert their right to use that service, with confidence. Internalised racism makes it psychologically difficult to do so (Owuor and Nake, 2015). When institutions and the individuals within them fail to respond properly to concerns about race equality issues, internalised racism is reinforced. Those who raised the concerns are made to feel that their views and experiences are irrelevant. Denying or downplaying inequalities is a form of racial microaggression, which again is closely linked to stereotypes.

Although the term 'microaggression' has developed a higher profile in recent years, it was first put forward in 1970 by Chester M Pierce. Racial microaggressions are subtle, regular interactions that reflect bias or stereotypes (similar to what is sometimes called 'everyday racism'). They can take the form of demeaning, disrespectful or insulting comments, which are often unintentional and therefore harder to challenge. Their impact builds over time to create a constant hostile environment for those on the receiving end (DeAngelis, 2009). Racial microaggressions begin with stereotypical assumptions. They can often be seen in the small talk people make, which might focus heavily on difference – where someone from a minority ethnic background is 'from', aspects of their appearance, religion or other cultural factors. They can be seen in the way people try to justify stereotypical attitudes to their minority ethnic friends by rejecting their difference – 'you're not like that, though', or worse still, 'I don't think of you as Black' (Torres, 2014).

A specific form of microaggression known as microinvalidation underpins this; microinvalidations occur when people downplay or dismiss concerns about racism (DeAngelis, 2009). When people are told that their objection to a racist joke is 'over-sensitive', that their feelings of being ignored by others might be 'a bit paranoid' or that their complaint about being overlooked for promotion is 'playing the race card', this has a massive impact on willingness to speak out (DeAngelis, 2009). This is true not just for the individual experiencing it, but for all others who witness it and the community at large. To ensure that complaints processes and workplace relations can work in everyone's interest, institutions must send a strong message that concerns will be taken seriously and addressed supportively.

Racism, integration and community cohesion

Part of the problem with creating more effective approaches to racial inequality is that tensions inevitably arise, including fear of creating a 'blame culture'. The tendency, then, is to try to avoid controversial topics. Sometimes concepts of inequality and racism are avoided in favour of positive messages about the importance of living and working together – about 'integrating' (Spencer, 2009). Broadly speaking, integration aims to create belonging and equality; to make minority ethnic communities more confident and resilient, and less isolated from the majority ethnic population. The problem is that this model of integration can't be sustainable where racism and exclusion exist (Feldham and Gidley, 2014). These factors actively create a lack of confidence, resilience and community cohesion. The fact that the onus always seems to be on minority ethnic communities to be the ones to 'integrate' makes this situation worse (Pilkington, 2009). Some of the current debate around this, particularly in regard to the nebulous concept of 'British values' and who is required to adhere to these, arguably veers far past integration and towards assimilation (Richards, 2014).

This rhetoric neatly avoids the need to tackle racism and exclusion in order to achieve cohesion. Community cohesion does not come about through cultural awareness training, or one-off opportunities to meet and mingle. It requires an environment where people from all communities can positively interact on an equal basis in neighbourhoods, workplaces, public services and spaces (James, 2008). This means improving representation, tackling stereotypes and breaking down barriers in all areas of life.

'Celebrating' diversity?

Many organisations in Scotland see 'diversity' themed activities as a core part of their work to promote equality. In our experience, the relationship between current concepts of diversity and stereotyping make this approach problematic at best, and damaging at worst. Negative stereotyping and the need to avoid it is understood in most policy environments, however what is less widely accepted is the need to actively challenge all stereotypes – positive ones included. Like negative stereotypes, positive stereotypes create an expectation of who people are and what they can be (Markman, 2013). They reinforce feelings of difference and 'otherness' between communities. Fostering good relations between different ethnic groups does require people to become comfortable with difference, and learning about traditions and practices linked to culture or ethnicity can be part of that process. However, there is a tendency in practice for these to be reduced to glamourous or romantic stereotypes; to become exoticised.

So many 'diversity' activities allow participants to sample traditional foods, watch traditional dances or view traditional artefacts without connecting with the people behind them. This reduces communities to traditional stereotypes. It may increase understanding on a theoretical level, but not on a personal level where it's most needed. To be successful, diversity activities need to enable participants to see similarities as well as differences. Most importantly, they have to demonstrate to people that the range of potential and personality for individuals from 'other' ethnic backgrounds is as wide and varied as their own. In the worst cases, these activities can actively promote stereotypes by presenting minority ethnic cultures from the majority ethnic perspective. For example, CRER has noted Scottish public bodies holding 'diversity' events featuring white British people wearing the traditional dress of other nations and approximating traditional dances, exoticising the cultures they're supposed to be 'celebrating.' Nothing about this approach can be helpful to good relations between ethnic groups. The whole concept of 'celebrating diversity' is contestable. It can be seen as simply replacing negative stereotypes with positive ones, effectively sweeping negativity under the carpet. Even if done with sensitivity, it can often ring hollow because it doesn't offer any answers to the range of structural inequalities people face (which are indeed diverse, but not to be celebrated) (Butcher, 2011).

Changing organisational culture and positive action

Minority ethnic groups face substantial disadvantages which can't be fully addressed by simply not discriminating. Social mobility doesn't seem to be the answer either; the barriers to social mobility remain even where communities have high educational attainment (CODE, 2014). The expectation that social mobility could resolve racial inequality is essentially part of the deficit model that needs to be rejected; rather than asking what more BME communities can do to achieve representation and progression within the workforce, senior managers should be asking what their organisation needs to do to make that happen. We believe that the best opportunity to reduce inequality is through changing the structures which maintain it. Public bodies have the power to make this happen through changing organisational cultures.

Where gaps exist and current practices are not closing them, positive action is needed. We advocate for this across the wide range of areas where minority ethnic people experience worse outcomes. Positive action counteracts institutional discrimination by adding specific activity to improve representation or address disadvantage in employment and career progression, in accessing services or in civic participation (Government Equalities Office, 2010 and 2011). However, only limited forms of positive action are permitted by the Equality Act 2010. The activity must be proportionate and only undertaken in order to address disadvantage or under-representation. Where the law arguably falls short is in the provision that positive action generally can't result in 'more favourable' treatment of any group (except in relation to disability). Perceptions of what might be 'more favourable' vary, which can discourage organisations from taking positive action. Positive action should mitigate disadvantage; this necessarily means that the advantages the current system confers to white people will be lessened, which some perceive as treating minority ethnic people 'more favourably' rather than simply creating a more level playing field.

BskyB are one of the few high-visibility organisations in the UK to take ambitious approaches to positive action, including offering direct entry to senior jobs. Importantly, they began this partly because of feedback from minority ethnic staff who found existing approaches to capacity building through skills development patronising and unnecessary (Sweeney, 2014). In our experience, much of the 'capacity building' activity which is touted as positive action is done without any evidence of need or evaluation to establish its success. This is the deficit model in action; the assumption that minority ethnic people are less 'skilled', and that they can somehow work their way out of disadvantage. Using an evidence-based approach should increase the success of positive action programmes. Appropriate activities can be planned through identifying gaps and inequalities, exploring causes and possible solutions (Equality and Human Rights Commission, 2010a). Unfortunately, institutions seem reluctant to take meaningful, evidence based forms of positive action. Fear of tokenism may be partly to blame for this, however the popular understanding of 'tokenism' itself has racist implications (Muhs, Niemann, González, and Harris, 2012).

Avoiding tokenism

Tokenism as we understand it in the race equality movement occurs where activities are designed to create the appearance of equality without actually tackling barriers or improving practice (Kanter, 1977). For example, if an organisation with low diversity in its senior ranks appoints a new minority ethnic member of the management team, tokenism could be at play if we see that person being valued less than other managers and used as a token representative of diversity. The organisation may decline to promote other minority ethnic staff, and we might suspect they feel they've 'already got one'.

In the popular mindset, however, that appointment would be deemed tokenistic based on the racist assumption that the best person for the task was probably white. If a new worker from the majority ethnic population is ineffective in their role, there will be no suspicion that their ethnicity helped them to get the job. Tokenism is only ever brought into the equation where the candidate is from a group at risk of discrimination (including those who are female, gay or disabled, for instance).

A less obvious form of tokenism (in the true sense) can be seen in how some public bodies identify priorities for action on race equality. For example, in recent years CRER has noted waves of public sector activity focused on Polish, Roma and Gypsy/Traveller communities. Tackling inequalities facing specific communities is laudable; it's essential to recognise the diversity of experience and need between and within minority ethnic communities. However, efforts can become tokenistic when narrowly focused activities are chosen at the expense of wider anti-racist work, especially where the outcomes are not clear. There is some concern, in fact, that organisations might deliberately choose a narrow focus in order to avoid looking at the bigger picture. This trend can be seen in the work done to set equality outcomes in 2013; many public authorities in Scotland mentioned race equality directly only in relation to either Refugees and Asylum Seekers or Gypsy/Travellers (CRER, 2015b).

Challenging policy-making hierarchies

Our experience in working with public bodies suggests that mismatched relationships between senior and operational staff often hamper equality work. Senior figures may enthusiastically demonstrate leadership on equality, for example, but lack the expertise needed to put their ethos into action. At the same time, there may be people further down the chain of command who specialise in equality but don't have the authority to drive improvement. Because of this mismatch, equality initiatives driven from below often aren't understood by management, whilst management may propose activities which sound good in theory but are impractical or ineffective in practice. Personnel changes worsen this; if there isn't a shared understanding of what works or is desirable, it's very difficult to pick up the thread once the person driving change is gone. The end result is that organisations often invest significant time and energy planning equality work only to eventually water down or abandon those plans. These failures are symptomatic of the power hierarchies which underpin racial inequality and block progress. Those with influence and responsibility need to empower equality specialists to fulfil their potential. This is especially important when their work aims to challenge persistent inequalities, which can be a hard sell in environments that favour the status quo.

Learning from the past, working for the future

The fact that racial inequality is entrenched in many areas of life is not fresh news. Nevertheless, it bears repeating because progress until now has been painfully slow (Equality and Human Rights Commission, 2016). In our view, a lack of persistence has potentially stalled advancements in many areas. The fact that much race equality work is undertaken on a short-term basis with little evaluation makes lasting progress impossible. This is hampered partly by a reliance on voluntary sector inputs which are subject to funding cycles of one to three years, for example through Local Authority funding or the Scottish Government's Equality Fund.

Meanwhile in the public sector, successive equality duties have required action to address inequality. This has been the case since 2002, and yet there is still not a firm understanding of what works and doesn't work for race equality. Actions and outcomes have been set according to the trends of the time and very few institutions have managed to evidence progress (Fyfe, MacMillan, Bruce, Finlay and Hewitt, 2013). Partly in response to this, the current Scottish specific public sector equality duties have an emphasis on equality mainstreaming (embedding equality throughout the organisation's strategy and functions) and progress reporting (Equality and Human Rights Commission, 2013). The duties also have a focus on outcomes. If properly implemented, these can be a strong driver for advancing equality. Rather than measuring success by outputs (i.e. what has been done within the organisation), equality outcomes identify the changes institutions want to see in the lives of people facing inequality. This means that the outcomes can only be achieved by demonstrating real progress on race equality.

To demonstrate that progress, in our view it's necessary to link all activity on race equality to evaluation and monitoring. Organisations should be regularly analysing the impact of their work through longitudinal qualitative and quantitative indicators. Over time, this would make it possible to detect the impact of policy, practice and positive action with a degree of certainty. The common practice of using statistics simply to demonstrate that there's still a problem is not good enough. Statistics also need to be used in planning continued action and in showing measureable improvements. Ironically, we find that organisations sometimes cite evidence gaps as a reason for inaction and yet still fail to act on the evidence they do have. Despite decades of research, reviews and recommendations, progress on race equality remains limited. Lack of evidence is arguably less of a problem than the response to existing evidence, which has been inconsistent, lacking in long-term commitment and leadership.

Conclusion

2015 marked the 50th anniversary of the Race Relations Act 1965. In this period of austerity, which worsens inequality (Runnymede, 2015), there is a real danger of stalling the progress made since then. We believe that public sector organisations have a responsibility to take action to avoid this. This means finding new ways to work which reject the deficit model and tokenistic or stereotypical interpretations of diversity. The key concepts outlined in this paper which we use in supporting public bodies can inform that change, however challenging the status quo takes boldness and hard work; this needs to come from within the organisation itself. Inevitably, creating equality requires those who currently hold power to share that power with people who have previously been disadvantaged by it. This is a much harder approach to 'sell' to organisations than softer forms of race equality work which focus on capacity building and simple non-discrimination. However, by setting out the case for change in simple terms that relate directly to organisations and their work, this resistance can be overcome. We believe that these organisations can make genuine, measurable progress by changing their paradigm on race equality.

Race, Ethnicity and Employment in Scotland

Jatin Haria

Introduction

AS CAROL YOUNG explained in the previous chapter, the Coalition for Racial Equality and Rights (CRER) is a Scottish anti-racist organisation which works to eliminate racial discrimination and promote racial justice across Scotland. We view employment inequality as a major contributor to the continuing disadvantage faced by Black and minority ethnic communities in Scotland. Despite long-standing legislation outlawing racism in employment practices, and many short-term projects that have attempted to deal with the issues, the disparity in employment outcomes for white and non-white people in Scotland is still great, and does not show signs of diminishing.

Evidence suggests that positive interaction between people from different ethnic backgrounds can help erode prejudicial attitudes and build cohesive and integrated communities. This interaction can take place in neighbourhoods and communities (where people live), in social and cultural arenas (where people gather for leisure) and in employment (where people work). Of these three aspects, achieving integration in the workplace *should* be the easiest, and even if the premise behind contact theory (Allport, 1954) is disputed, having a representative workforce can only lead to fairer outcomes, not just for the minority ethnic employees, but also for the clients and customers of the employer. However, there is ample evidence that people from Black and minority ethnic backgrounds continue to suffer disadvantage in the labour market (for the details of what is known, see Annex 1). Some of this is down to structural discrimination in the labour market and some to direct racial discrimination by employers. The disadvantage in employment often leads to a knock-on effect, including increased poverty amongst people from Black minority ethnic communities, and a lack of provision of appropriate services. Whilst it would be unusual for employers to confess to direct racial discrimination, CRE research into the private sector labour market in 2000 found that a quarter of employers with no equality programme in place believed that formal equality policies were 'divisive' and when asked if they would initiate a racial equality programme, the majority of respondents said 'No' even if they were convinced it would reap commercial benefits (CRE, 2000);

The legal requirements

Much of equality and employment legislation is reserved to Westminster, but urgent and major action is needed to address the gross racial inequalities in the Scottish labour market if Scotland is truly to become the equal egalitarian nation it wants to become. The need to eliminate racial discrimination in employment has been legally recognised ever since the Race Relations Act 1968 which made it illegal to refuse employment to a person on the grounds of colour, race, ethnic or national origins. The revised 1976 Act placed an additional general statutory duty on local authorities to:

> ...make appropriate arrangements with a view to securing that their various functions are carried out with due regard to the need – (a) to eliminate unlawful racial discrimination; and (b) to promote equality of opportunity, and good relations, between persons of different racial groups (Race Relations Act, 1976).

Following the Macpherson Inquiry into the murder of Stephen Lawrence (1999), the Act was further amended in 2000 to place public authorities (not just local authorities) under new statutory duties to *promote* race equality. The aim was to ensure public authorities *proactively* provide fair and accessible services, and improve equal opportunities in employment. In relation to achieving fair employment practices, the Act required all listed public bodies to monitor by racial group for staff in post, and applications for employment, promotion and training. Employers with over 150 staff were also required to monitor uptake of training, results of performance appraisals, numbers involved in grievances and disciplinary action and reasons for staff leaving their employment. The monitoring data was required to be published annually. These requirements were largely unchanged by the revised Scottish Specific Public Sector Equality Duties that came in as a result of the Equality Act 2010, with the important addition that public bodies are now also required to *use* the gathered information to better perform the general equality duty and to detail the *progress* they have made in gathering and using this information (SSPSED, 2013).

The general public sector equality duty (section 149 of the Equality Act 2010) came into force on 5 April 2011, applies to public bodies and others carrying out public functions and requires organisations subject to it to have due regard to the need to:

- Eliminate unlawful discrimination, harassment and victimisation
- Advance equality of opportunity between different groups
- Foster good relations between different groups

It supports good decision-making by ensuring public bodies consider how different people will be affected by their activities, helping them to deliver policies and services which are efficient and effective; accessible to all; and which meet different people's needs. The Equality Duty is supported by specific duties, set out in regulations which came into force in Scotland on 27 May 2012. The Scottish Specific Public Sector Equality Duties apply only to those public bodies that are listed in the regulations, and now number some 250 organisations (for the requirements placed on these bodies, see Annex 2).

The current situation

Data on the ethnic origin of employees in Scotland's workforce has always been difficult to obtain. Many employers just do not gather such data, and sample sizes in national studies such as the ONS Labour Force survey often do not allow for meaningful disaggregated data on ethnicity to be analysed. Despite having duties to collect employee monitoring information since 2002, public bodies in Scotland are still struggling to record the ethnic make-up of their workforces (CRER, 2014b). It was partly due to these concerns that the Scottish Specific Public Sector Duties (as outlined above) had such an emphasis on employee data gathering from public sector employers. However, although some 250 listed public bodies in Scotland are legally obliged to publish information on the ethnicity of their employees in post and those going through recruitment and related processes, these bodies are of varying sizes, and have varying recruitment needs and processes. Even when they have published the required data (and not all do so), there is no standard template for recording the data. Different organisations record on different timeframes, and some publish actual numbers whilst others only give percentages of staff in each ethnic category. Furthermore, the employment data for all of the listed bodies are not gathered together in one place. Therefore, there is no overview of public sector employment in Scotland with regard to racial equality. Combining the data across the whole public sector in Scotland would make it possible to examine racial equality issues on a wider scale; a scale where something definitive can be said about ethnicity and employment in Scotland's public sector.

To rectify this problem, in 2012, CRER attempted was to do just this; i.e. to gather together and amalgamate all data in relation to ethnicity and employment in Scotland's public sector. We believe this was the first time this had been attempted in Scotland. 165 organisations were surveyed, using Freedom of Information (FOI) legislation; we understood that employment data for most education authorities, community justice authorities and licensing boards were combined with the local council data so these were not separately approached. In our analysis, we only looked at responses to our FOI requests; in some cases it may well have been that the relevant data could have been available from elsewhere.

Many organisations publish the data many months after it has been (internally) collated, so a decision was taken to seek data for the financial year 2011/12. For the majority of organisations contacted our FOI request would have imposed no additional burden; it already being a legal requirement that the requested data was both held and published (albeit, at that time under the Specific Race Equality Duties). The vast bulk of organisations to which we sent our FOI requests were cooperative and fully supported the aims of the project; however, it was necessary to return to the majority of them in order to seek clarification on the data provided and/or to ask for the data to be provided in a usable format. It was a disappointment to find the data records held by public bodies to be in such poor shape.

Most organisations could provide some data for basic staff numbers, i.e. those actually in post. For other data categories (e.g. applications, or people leaving) only a sample of the provided information could be used; the data either not being provided or even available, or it being of too poor quality for analysis. In many cases, the numbers being referred to were too low for any meaningful analysis to be conducted (even when this data was amalgamated across a number of organisations), and the poor quality of data provided also meant that no meaningful ethnicity analysis could be conducted for the uptake of training opportunities or for applications for promoted posts.

It would have been useful to have an analysis based on all the individual ethnicity categories as used in the 2011 Census. However, the level of disaggregation by ethnicity is dependent upon the data supplied. In order to maximise the number of institutions utilised for analysis, it was necessary to combine data upwards to a level of the poorest quality available, and therefore at the minimal level of disaggregation, namely as 'All white' and 'All Non-white'. In this context 'white' refers to all white ethnicities, including white Scottish, white British, white UK and all 'white Other' categories. The 'All Non-white' refers to all other ethnicities, including 'Mixed' ethnicities. We remain aware of the on-going discussions about the appropriateness of terminologies used, especially around the use of 'non-white'. Additionally, it should be borne in mind that when looking at ethnicity, no indication is given of nationality or place of birth. Similarly, appearance (skin colour) is not always synonymous to ethnicity, despite some of the labels used in Census categories.

Finally, it must be pointed out that the analysis published tells us the position on the ground as reported by the data available from listed public bodies; it does not tell us why the position has arisen. Nonetheless, the overall picture shown does point to certain trends in relation to issues regarding ethnicity and public sector employment in Scotland; trends that flag up areas of serious concern and call for further research and deeper analysis, and for action to ensure fair employment for people of all ethnicities in Scotland.

The research (CRER, 2014b), showed that across the public sector for staff in post, the figure for non-white staff varied from 0.8 per cent (in Fire and Rescue Services) to 7.3 per cent in Higher Education institutions, with an overall average of 2.7 per cent for the whole of the sector. Ethnic origin data was not known or not gathered for 23.7 per cent of all employees, ranging (perhaps unsurprisingly) from 2.5 per cent unknown in organisations with fewer than 150 employees to 31.7 per cent of staff in the National Health Service. This continues to be a cause for concern, not least because in the main public bodies have had a duty to collect such information from 2002 onwards. The numbers with unknown ethnicity actually increased from the 2010/11 figure and shows that the situation did not improve on a year-to-year basis. Of particular concern was the fact that in the NHS, information on the ethnicity of staff was missing for about a third of the workforce – this in an industry where knowledge of the ethnicity of service users (i.e. patients) is of arguably more importance than in any other sector, and therefore calls into question how staff can be asking for ethnicity information from patients if they themselves are not being asked for their own information, and more so if they themselves are reluctant to divulge this information to their employers. Even the Scottish Government had no knowledge of the ethnicity of 20.9 per cent of its workforce.

However, it should be borne in mind that detailed analysis and comparison to demographic data for Scotland is not possible as the ethnicity data provided may be skewed by factors such as the recruitment of overseas staff in organisations such as academic institutions or the NHS. Data for job applicants showed that the overall proportion of all non-white applicants exceeded their proportion within the Scottish population, perhaps debunking the myth that Black and minority ethnic people do not apply for public sector jobs. However, there was a wide variation between the sectors, with 1.8 per cent of non-white applicants for jobs in Fire and Rescue, and 23.9 per cent of non-white applicants for posts in the HE sector (although again no analysis is available to determine if this figure was skewed by applicants from overseas).

The 2011/12 data for applicants who are then shortlisted was relatively on par when looking at the public sector as a whole (in that the same percentage of white and non-white people who applied were also shortlisted) although this parity was entirely due to the relative high success rate of the non-white category within the NHS. For all other sectors, the disparity between the percentage of applicants from Black and minority ethnic backgrounds and the percentage subsequently shortlisted was stark (for example, in Police Forces, 27.8 per cent of white applicants were shortlisted, but only 19.4 per cent of non-White applicants were). The inequality of outcomes for black and minority ethnic short-listed candidates being appointed compared to their white counterparts was even more blatant. It would be reasonable to assume that candidates who have been shortlisted have met the minimum requirements of the person specification for advertised posts, so certain factors (e.g. experience or qualification requirements) can be discounted for in attempting to explain the difference in outcomes. But there must be reasons as to why, for example, as our research found, only 17.7 per cent of non-white people interviewed for local authority jobs were appointed, compared to a figure of 31.9 per cent for white interviewees.

The compounded disparity between white and non-white applicants who are shortlisted and then appointed leads to a situation where (according to the 2011/12 data) 7.1 per cent of all white applicants for public sector posts went on to be appointed, but where only 4.4 per cent of non-white applicants got appointed. This figure is at its starkest in large public sector organisations – where Black and minority ethnic applicants only had a 1.1 per cent chance of being subsequently appointed, compared to 8.1 per cent for their white counterparts. Even within local authorities, white applicants are almost three times more likely to be successful in securing a post than non-white applicants – 6.1 per cent compared to 2.1 per cent. Whilst the above analysis concentrated on data available for the period 2011/12, more recent analysis has shown similar trends and outcomes (see for example, Mejka, 2015, or CRER, forthcoming, 2016).

The lack of meaningful action

The data paints a bleak picture in relation to race and employment in Scotland. From time to time, Government and other stakeholders acknowledge that there is a problem and set up short-term working groups and draw up action plans to try and tackle the problem:

- in 2006, the (then) Scottish Executive established a Strategic Group on BME labour market participation which set an aspiration to eliminate racial inequality in the labour market by 2013;
- also in 2006, the (then) Equal Opportunities Commission in Scotland published its report on the 'employment of visible ethnic minority women in Scotland';
- the 2008 Scottish Government Race Equality Statement committed to negotiate with public sector bodies and set targets for the employment of Black and minority ethnic people by March 2011;
- from 2008 till 2010, Glasgow Works had an ethnic minority sub-group, had appointed a Policy manager to take the race agenda forward and had developed an action plan to tackle labour market inequalities in the city.

And the above are just examples of initiatives in Scotland – many issues raised by UK-wide activities and research would also have a direct bearing on the Scottish position. However, despite all of this effort, and all of the above initiatives having concluded their work, the position of Scotland's Black and minority ethnic communities in relation to the labour market continues to remain bleak, and in some cases is even getting worse. Calling for additional short-term ad hoc interventions will be unlikely to change things.

In addition, where action is supported, it tends to be focused on supply-side issues, as if the issue was that all Black and minority ethnic people cannot speak English, are poorly skilled or lack educational qualifications. Undoubtedly, these issues will be a factor for some people, but the issue of poor skills and qualifications are not race specific issues. For sure, for newer migrants, there may be issues relating to a need for ESOL provision, recognition of their overseas qualifications, or a lack of UK-based work experience, etc., but as the data shows, this affects only a minority of people from Black and minority ethnic communities in Scotland. Scotland's Black and minority ethnic communities could be the source of youthful and well-qualified workers instead of then being – as is currently all too often the case – unemployed or under-employed.

It is easy for employers and public authorities to look only at supply-side issues as in the main they can either say it is not their problem or throw some money at some voluntary sector group and assume that is the issue dealt with. This is highlighted, for example, in relation to a question asked in 2015 in the Scottish Parliament (PQ S4W-24413) by John Mason MSP on what the Scottish Government has done to improve the employment rate for Black minority ethnic people. The only answer given by Annabelle Ewing MSP, the Minister for Youth and Women's Employment, was that 'we (have) provided over £5.2million over the period 2012/15 to support organisations working with ethnic minority communities to develop and improve their employability skills and access to employment'. To give another example, COSLA in its 2011 response to the Government consultation on the then proposed specific equality duties, stated that 'in the case of recruitment often the issue is not discrimination but ensuring that those with a disability of from BME communities have the relevant skills and experience for particular jobs'.

Dealing with institutionalised racial discrimination in the labour market is not an easy topic to take on, but unless we begin to do so then the current situation will remain unchanged. Notwithstanding the general requirement on all employers to not discriminate on racial grounds, it is generally accepted that the public sector need to be more proactive in pushing for equality and equal outcomes. In employment, the Scottish Specific Duties require listed bodies to, each year, gather information on the composition, recruitment, development and retention of their employees, *and* to detail the progress they have made in gathering and using the information they have collected. Whilst most bodies do now publish details on the composition of their workforce (albeit with a large percentage of unknown or declined data) it often proves difficult to obtain the information on applicants, exits, promotions, etc., and near enough impossible to find bodies that have published any information on how they have (or plan to) use the data.

A thorough analysis of public bodies' performance in meeting the (reporting requirements of the) Scottish Specific Equality Duties was conducted by the Equality and Human Rights Commission in September 2015 (EHRC, 2015). This found that 89 per cent of public bodies examined had published some employee information, but only 64 per cent published information on staff recruitment by ethnicity; this figure dropped to just 43 per cent for those who provided any ethnicity data on staff development (e.g. training, promotions, etc.). The report found that 73 per cent of public bodies were assessed as having some information on how they are using the employee data, but did not provide additional information on how this was being used or what protected characteristics were specifically examined.

The lack of any sustained focus or meaningful action on this issue was the main catalyst that led CRER, amongst a few others, to lobby for the Scottish Parliament Equal Opportunities Committee to launch a formal inquiry into the matter. This was agreed in spring 2015, with an open call for evidence issued which resulted in over 50 submissions, over a third of which were from public bodies. Six evidence sessions were held, with invitations to attend issued to a wide range of sectors, including academics, the EHRC, representatives of public bodies, trades unions, race equality groups and the Cabinet Secretary for Social Justice. A session with a small number of private sector employers was held in camera and a further four meetings of the committee were held in private to consider the draft report (Scottish Parliament, 2015).

The final report 'Removing Barriers: Race, Ethnicity and Employment' (Scottish Parliament, 2016) was launched in January 2016, and makes 17 recommendations for action by the Scottish Government. It asks for the Scottish Government to show leadership on this issue and asserts that 'without confronting existing practices, we cannot address any underlying racism and discrimination that the evidence confirms exists'. At the time of writing, a response from the Government was still awaited.

Confronting existing practices

Confronting existing practices requires a change from the standard ways of doing things. This requires the elimination of racist practices and procedures. One of the key measures talked about, especially when referring to improving employment outcomes, relates to positive action. However, the Equality Act 2010 only permits very limited positive action activities to be taken, and positive discrimination in recruitment and promotion is all but illegal. Most positive action initiatives (when these can be found) are aimed at capacity building and skills development and as we have argued above, whilst these are certainly necessary for some, especially for newer migrants, for most Black and minority ethnic people in Scotland a more pressing matter is the elimination of direct and institutional racism.

A specific action allowed under the Equality Act 2010 is often referred to as the 'tie-break' – where, given two equal candidates, employers can legitimately opt for one who has a protected characteristic that is under-represented in their workforce, However, we do not know of any situation where this has been utilised in Scotland in favour of a Black and minority ethnic applicant. Tie-break options may be more viable when an employer is recruiting a pool of potential applicants – e.g. if the Scottish Fire Service has some set basic criteria that it requires of all potential fire-fighters, it could create a pool of all who meet this basic standard, and it may be possible to use the tie-break method to ensure that the pool was ethnically mixed – we accept that even this model may be challenged in an employment tribunal, but such an initiative may help them improve on the 0.45 per cent BME workforce that they have as of December 2014. The Scottish Government could use a similar model for its graduate entry programmes.

There are other measures that would also help improve BME employment rates – e.g. some research has shown that merely having a Black and minority ethnic person on an interview panel improves the employment rate of BME candidates; the (re)-establishment of BME employee forums might help with retention rates; the setting of BME employment targets so that HR managers can be incentivised and held to account for their actions; always going for open recruitment (as opposed to word of mouth, or sub-contracting to employment agencies that may not share the same ethos of equality as the employer; taking steps to include a greater number of BME people as interns and work experience placements; and providing detailed feedback to all applicants on why they failed to make the cut). Asking equality-related questions at all interviews may also help improve the culture of organisations in that appointing more people who believe in tackling discrimination can only be a good outcome for all.

Recently, it is being said more and more that the problem is one of unconscious bias. We believe in the statement that it (unconscious bias) is racism by another name, and only seems to become unconscious when people are found out. In any case, if the outcome is differential treatment on the grounds of race it is still unlawful. The proposed devolved powers contained in the Scotland Bill currently going through the UK Parliament which will allow 'provision that supplements or is otherwise additional to provision made by (the Equality Acts 2006 and 2010); (and) in particular, provision imposing a requirement to take action that the Acts do not prohibit' may allow the Scottish Parliament and the Scottish Government to impose some of the above suggestions for meaningful positive action to be adopted in Scotland (Scotland Bill 2015–16, 2016).

Conclusion

Notwithstanding the above, even utilising positive action measures can only go so far. The real need is to deal with institutional, structural and direct racism, by organisations and individual employers. If we accept that in the main Black and minority ethnic people are equally competent as their white counterparts, then it should follow that they should be afforded equality of outcome in the recruitment and selection process. Quotas based on ethnicity are surely the best way to ensure equality of outcome, at least in the short term. Although currently illegal, the law is capable of being amended when enough pressure is placed upon it (for example, it was made legal to opt for women-only short-lists for candidate selection). There is not just a lack of recognition of the problem, there is a lack of any urgency to do anything about it and there is a lack of any leadership on this issue in Scotland.

There really is a 'no problem here' attitude. Scotland's complacency, especially by its large public sector employers, is of great concern. The figures showing white applicants in some public bodies are almost three times more likely to be successful in securing a post than non-white applicants clearly show that the positive action that is in place is in fact positive discrimination in favour of white people! That *is* the problem.

Annex 1: Race, Ethnicity and Employment: the evidence

- The 2011 Census recorded 4 per cent of the Scottish population as being from a (non-white) minority ethnic origin (National Records of Scotland, 2013);
- In terms of educational attainment, the average tariff score achieved was higher for *all* non-white school leavers than for white Scottish pupils (SPICe, 2015);
- Despite the better (on average) educational attainment (at school), and their subsequent higher participation rate in higher or further education, non-white groups aged 25-49 have a significantly lower employment rate (55.2 per cent) than their white counterparts (72 per cent), and a higher unemployment rate (7.9 per cent compared to 5.5 per cent) (ibid);
- Despite common mythology, the self-employment rate for white and non-white groups aged 16/24 and 25/49 are not significantly different (1.6 per cent and 1.3 per cent for 16/24, and 8.9 per cent vs 9.6 per cent for 24/49-year-olds) (ibid).
- From Census 2011 data, around 60 per cent of people of Pakistani origin, the largest non-white minority ethnic group in Scotland, were born in the UK, and many of the remaining 40 per cent will have lived (and been educated) in the UK for a lengthy period of time; (National Records of Scotland, 2013).
- The 2009 Department for Work and Pensions Test for Racial Discrimination in recruitment practices, which matched job applications from white and minority ethnic applicants found that in towns across the UK, including in Glasgow, applicants with minority ethnic sounding names were 21 per cent more likely to be rejected than those with 'white' sounding names (Wood et al, 2009).

Annex 2: Regulation 6 of the Scottish Specific Public Sector Equality Duties

Duty to gather and use employee information:

(1) A listed authority must take steps to gather information on –
   (a) the composition of the authority's employees (if any); and
   (b) the recruitment, development and retention of persons as employees of the authority, with respect to, in each year, the number and relevant protected characteristics of such persons.

(2) The authority must use this information to better perform the equality duty.

(3) A report published by the listed authority in accordance with regulation 3 must include –
   (a) an annual breakdown of information gathered by it in accordance with paragraph (1) which has not been published previously in such a report; and
   (b) details of the progress that the authority has made in gathering and using that information to enable it to better perform the equality duty.

CONCLUSION

No Problem Here?

Maureen McBride and Minna Liinpää

THE PHRASE 'NO PROBLEM HERE' refers to the once-powerful myth that Scotland did not have a problem with racism or anti-immigration attitudes compared to England. Not only did this occlude the experiences of racialised minorities and prevent the development of robust responses to discrimination and inequality, it also had a considerable impact on the policy field. As Williams and De Lima (2006) have argued, it has led to what they term a 'laissez-faire politics' with regard to race equality. We very much accept that in recent years this myth has been challenged from several positions. Important advocacy work (from organisations such as CRER, Bemis, CEMVO), though historically underfunded and under resourced, has helped to put pressure on the Scottish Government to develop its policy response to the various forms of racial inequality. The Scottish Government also recently showed its formal commitment to tackling racism and racial inequality, and published its Race Equality Framework for Scotland 2016–2030 – although nothing was put in place for five years after the previous Race Equality Statement 2008–2011 came to an end. Nonetheless, as Meer points out (2016: 4):

> The Framework document itself shows that there has been a sincere effort to reflect on the successes and limitations of prevailing race equality approaches in Scotland, and an attempt to identify gaps in data and other kinds of practice-based knowledge that might hinder the delivery of effective race equality strategies.

With this context in mind, the policy-oriented chapters in this collection (by Haria, Meer, Netto, and Young) are much-needed contributions to a critical dialogue vis-à-vis the political and policy field. Moreover, more recent academic work has started to pose a challenge to the silence within academia relating to racism and related aspects of Scotland's history such as its disproportionate role in the Empire and involvement in the slave trade (Mullen, 2009; Devine 2011; Devine 2015; Morris, 2016).

Our argument then is that Scotland does have a problem with racism despite the fact that, within both academia and local and central Government, there remains a complacency regarding racism and its structuring power. This became evident in the aftermath of the 'Brexit' vote of 23 June 2016, in which 51.9 per cent of UK voters opted to leave the European Union following a referendum which was dominated by the topic of immigration. The 'Leave' campaign was very much shaped by right-wing, anti-immigrant rhetoric, which appeared to be bound up in a re-imagining of English and/or British nationalism. A racialised frame was used by particular elite members, such as UKIP's Nigel Farage, to co-opt working class support for a Leave vote. Virdee (2017: 2) argues that this 'helped cohere and then shift those parts of the working class most invested in understanding the "white working class" as the main victims of globalisation firmly into the camp of the anti-immigrant right wing'. Although there is some reason to be cautious regarding the statistics given the small number of reported crimes, there is no doubt that in the aftermath of the referendum there was an increase in racist and xenophobic rhetoric and behaviours, and there were claims of surges in racially-motivated hate crimes (*The Independent,* 15 February 2017). However, what is important to note is that Scotland was believed to have bucked such a trend.

While England and Wales saw a 27 per cent increase in reported hate crimes, Scotland was the only police force area in the UK where the number of recorded hate crimes fell. This was explicitly linked to Scotland's majority Remain vote, as in Scotland 62 per cent of voters opted to Remain part of the European Union, compared to 46.6 per cent in England. From some perspectives, this demonstrated the growing chasm between Scotland and England in relation to, among other things, attitudes towards immigration. This has helped to reinforce a sense of difference, a notion of an inclusive, progressive, 'civic' Scottish nationalism, epitomised by the frequent pro-immigration statements made by the Scottish Government, which are in stark contrast to the negative rhetoric emanating from the UK Government. However, as De Lima contends, 'positive policy discourses on immigration and the role of migrants are not enough' – rather, 'if discrimination of Scotland's minority ethnic groups is to be addressed, migration policies need to foreground social justice considerations' and not merely highlight the benefits of migration based on 'economic stability' arguments (2012: 98). Moreover, Scotland's majority Remain vote has been used to justify calls for a second referendum on Scottish independence, with First Minister Nicola Sturgeon claiming that given that there has been 'a significant and material change in the circumstances that prevailed in 2014', the Scottish Parliament should have the right to hold another referendum on the question of breaking away from Britain (*The Independent*, 13 March 2017).

We believe that in the post-Brexit context, the 'no problem here' myth in Scotland has been given a new lease of life. Regardless of the fact that research data reveals much convergence between the Scottish and English populations in terms of their attitudes towards race, immigration and national belonging (see Runnymede Trust 2016), there is a sense of 'Scottish exceptionalism' – that *we* are different from the English – which appears to shape much of the political, media, and public consciousness. This is undoubtedly elite-led, but discourses evident in some print media and even more so on social media suggests that this notion of 'exceptionalism' has significant popular appeal.

In terms of its focus, this collection dwells on definitional and analytical issues vis-à-vis racism, and the different modalities of racism. As argued by Sivanandan (1983: 2), 'racism does not stay still' – instead, 'it changes shape, size, contours, purpose, function—with changes in the economy, the social structure, the system and, above all, the challenges, the resistances to that system'. Thus, it is crucial to consider different modalities of racism and the ways in which 'new' or 'cultural' racism (Taguieff, 1990) – especially Islamophobia – has become a central feature of contemporary political and media discourses. While not a new phenomenon, racism against Roma communities has especially gained more traction since the accession of Eastern European countries to the European Union in 2004 and 2007. We hope that although some of the chapters provide in-depth analysis of the experiences of particular social groups, the volume as a whole offers a comparative focus, highlighting the overlap, continuities and discontinuities in terms of how racism affects different groups.

Moreover, this collection sought to locate contemporary debates on racialisation and racism and place them in an appropriate historical context: the '*longue durée*' of Scottish history. We alluded earlier to how, in

Scotland, as in Britain as a whole, aspects of the past are played down to suit a narrative of progress and inclusivity. This of course includes underplaying Scotland's disproportionate role in the British Empire. Gilroy (2004) argues that the relationship between 'white Britain' and its immigrant populations is profoundly shaped by the legacy of the British Empire. This is no less the case in Scotland, however in Scotland the largest migrant groups were mostly 'white'. As such, chapters 3 and 4 respectively focus on a specific aspect of Scotland's imperial past: the Irish Catholic experience in Scotland. Both chapters reflect on the fact that the Irish Catholics were a racialised group subject to similar processes of negative stereotyping and discrimination as faced by newer migrants today. This is not only missing in much of the academic work on sectarianism in Scotland, it is also marginalised in racism studies because of the predominance of colour-coded understandings of racism. Yet an understanding of how Irish Catholics were racialised historically and de-racialised over time, though in various ways still occupying and experiencing a sense of 'outsider status', reveals how racialisation and racism changes over time, and that we have to be alive to the possible legacy of historic inequalities.

Finally, some may wonder what about anti-English sentiment in Scotland? During the 2014 independence referendum, Jeremy Paxman famously argued that the referendum was fuelled by anti-English hatred (Harrison, 2014). Additionally, there is academic research which has pointed to a strain of anti-English sentiment leading in some instances to forms of discriminatory behaviour (see e.g. Watson, 2003; McIntosh et al, 2004; Hussain and Miller, 2006). However, there is little evidence to suggest that the existence of such anti-English rhetoric is encoded in the institutional structures of Scottish society in the way that, say, anti-Catholic Irish racism was and anti-Muslim racism still is, leading in both cases to observable and systemic patterns of inequality across a range of socio-economic indicators. In this sense, it would be misleading to analyse anti-Englishness through the prism of racism. According to Omi and Winant (1994: 162), racism is 'a fundamental characteristic of social projects which create or reproduce structures of domination based on essentialist categories of race'. While our starting point is that any attempt to stigmatise individuals or groups on the basis of their nationality or ethnicity is unacceptable, we also believe that the English in Scotland are not subject to *structures of exclusionary domination,* nor have they ever been historically. As Song (2014: 109) warns, uncritical use of the term 'racism', 'fails to differentiate between quite disparate forms of racialisation, by lumping all racialised phenomena under its umbrella'. We argue that this it is equally pertinent in Scotland to challenge what Song (2014) terms 'a culture of racial equivalence'. It is the responsibility for those who research and write on the question of 'race' in Scotland to recognise, critically assess, and conceptualise the operation of power relations in examples of racialisation and racism.

We write this contribution in a moment when the Scottish political and social context is in flux. In order to think through the implications for race, class and nationalism in this changing context, this collection provides a much needed critical discussion of these themes in Scotland both historically as well as contemporaneously. Importantly, the contributions from academics, activists and anti-racist organisations have sought to challenge and criticise the dominant narrative of 'Scottish exceptionalism': rather than Scottishness being characterised by 'innate inclusiveness', racism works differently in Scotland. We hope they open up a debate that has been shut down for too long. There is no room for complacency.

Bibliography

About Homecoming Scotland (2014), available at: http://www.visitscotland.org/business_support/ advice_materials/toolkits/homecoming_scotland_2014/about_homecoming.aspx [Last Accessed 20/4/2015].

Advisory Group on Tackling Sectarianism in Scotland (2013) *Independent Advice to Scottish Ministers and Report on Activity 9 August 2012 –15 November 2013*. Edinburgh: Scottish Government.

Allen, T. [1994] (2012) *The Invention of the White Race, Volume 1: Racial Oppression and Social Control*. London: Verso.

Allport, G.W. (1954). *The Nature of Prejudice*. Cambridge, MA: Perseus Books.

Althusser, L. (2014) *On The Reproduction of Capitalism: Ideology and Ideological State Apparatus*. London: Verso.

Amnesty International (2013) 'Hungary: Murder convictions are 'wake-up call' over hate crimes against Roma', *Press Release*, Tuesday 6 August. Available at: https://www.amnesty.org/en/latest/ news/2013/08/hungary-roma-trial-verdict/ [Last accessed 13/3/2016].

Anderson, B. [1982] (2006) *Imagined Communities: Reflections on the Origin and Spread of Nationalism*. London: Verso.

Anstead, A. (2013) 'The stereotypes used against Eastern Europe are as old as they are wrong', *New Statesman*, 17 May. Available at: http://www.newstatesman.com/economics/2013/05/stereotypes-used-against-eastern-europe-are-old-they-are-wrong [Last accessed 13/3/2016].

Appiah, K. A., (1995) 'Race' in *Critical Terms for Literary Study*, edited by Frank Lentricchia and Thomas Mclaughlin. Second edition, Chicago: University of Chicago Press.

Association of Chief Police Officers (ACPO) (2005) *Hate Crime: Delivering a Quality Service – Good Practice and Tactical guidance* London: ACPO.

Astier, H. (2014) 'France's Unwanted Roma', BBC *News Magazine*. Friday 13 February. Available at: http://www.bbc.co.uk/news/magazine-25419423 [Last accessed 13/3/2016].

Back, L. (1993) 'Race, identity and nation within an adolescent community in South London', *New Community* 19: 217-33.

Balibar, E., and Wallerstein, I. (1991) *Race, Nation, Class: Ambiguous Identities*. London: Verso.

Balibar, E. (1991) 'Racism and Nationalism' in E. Balibar and I. Wallerstein (eds.) *Race, Nation, Class: Ambiguous Identities*. London: Verso.

Balibar, E., (1991) 'Racism and Politics in Europe Today', *New Left Review* 186 (March-April): 5-19.

Banaji, M. and Greenwald, A. (2013) *Blindspot: Hidden Biases of Good People*. New York: Delacorte Press.

Bannerji, H. (1998) 'Politics and the Writing of History' in R. Roach Pierson and N. Chaudhuri (eds.) *Nation, Empire, Colony: Historicizing Gender and Race*, Bloomington. Ind.: Indiana University Press.

Banton, M. (2000) 'The Idiom of Race: A Critique of Presentism' in L. Back and J. Solomos (eds.), *Theories of Race and Racism*. New York: Routledge.

Barclay, A., Bowes, A., Ferguson, I., Sim, D. and Valenti, M. (2003) *Asylum Seekers in Scotland*. Edinburgh: Scottish Executive.

Barger, K. (2014). *Ethnocentrism: What is it? Why are people ethnocentric? What is the problem? What can we do about it?* Available from: http://www.iupui.edu/~anthkb/ethnocen.htm [Last accessed 19/2/2016].

Barker, F. (2015) *Nationalism, Identity and the Governance of Diversity: Old Politics, New Arrivals*. Palgrave Macmillan: Basingstoke.

Barker, M. (1981) *The New Racism: Conservatives and the Ideology of the Tribe*. London: Junction Books.

Barth, F. (1969) *Ethnic Groups and Boundaries: The Social Organization of Culture Difference*, Oslo: Universitetsforlaget.

Bauman, Z. (1992) 'Blood Soil and Identity', *Sociological Review*, vol. 40. no. 4: 675–701.

BBC News (2015a) 'Man sentenced over MSP Humza Yousaf's racist abuse', 16 June. Available at: http://www.bbc.co.uk/news/uk-scotland-glasgow-west-33147598 [Last accessed 08/08/2015].

BBC News (2015b) 'Nicola Sturgeon: Scotland ready to take in 1,000 refugees', 4 September. Available at: http://www.bbc.co.uk/news/uk-scotland-scotland-politics-34146653 [Last accessed 20/11/2015].

BBC Scotland (2009) 'Scots urged to face 'slave past'', 21 October. Available at: http://news.bbc.co.uk/1/hi/scotland/highlands_and_islands/8318723.stm [Last accessed 1/6/6/2015].

Bechhofer, F., and D. McCrone (2012) 'Changing Claims in Context: National Identity Revisited', *Ethnic and Racial Studies*, 37 (8): 1350–1370.

Beider, H. and Netto, G. (2012) 'Minority Ethnic Communities and Housing: Access, Experiences and Participation' in G. Craig, K. Atkin, R. Flynn and S. Chattoo, (eds.) *Understanding 'Race' and Ethnicity: Theory, History, Policy, Practice*. Policy Press: Bristol.

Belfast Telegraph (2011) 'PSNI base bomb alert is linked to Neil Lennon campaign'. Available at: http://www.belfasttelegraph.co.uk/news/northern-ireland/psni-base-bomb-alert-is-linked-to-neil-lennon-campaign-28611306.html [Last accessed 8/1/2016].

Bhandari, K. (2013) 'Imagining the Scottish nation: tourism and homeland nationalism in Scotland', *Current Issues in Tourism* (July): 1-17.

Billig, M. (1995) *Banal Nationalism*, London: Sage.

Billig, M. (2002) 'Henri Tajfel's 'cognitive aspects of prejudice' and the psychology of bigotry', *British Journal of Social Psychology*, vol. 41, no. 2: 171-188.

Bivens, D. K. (2005). 'What is Internalized Racism?', in M Potapchuk and S. Leiderman (eds.), *Flipping the Script: White Privilege and Community Building*. Silver Spring, MD: MP Associates.

Bourdieu, P. (1991) *Language and Symbolic Power*. Cambridge: Polity Press.

Bourdieu, P. (2014) *On the State: Lectures at the College de France 1989–1992*. Cambridge: Polity Press.

Bourdieu, P. and Wacquant, L. J. D. (1992) *An Invitation to Reflexive Sociology*. Chicago, IL: University of Chicago Press

Bowes, A.M., Dar, N.S., and Sim, D.F. (1997) 'Pakistanis and Social Rented Housing: A Study in Glasgow' in A. M. Bowes and D. F. Sim (eds.) *Perspectives on Welfare*. Aldershot: Ashgate.

Boyle, M. (2011) *Metropolitan Anxieties: On the Meaning of the Catholic Adventure in Scotland*, Farnham: Ashgate.

Bradley, J. (1995) *Ethnic and Religious Identity in Modern Scotland: Culture, Politics and Football*, Aldershot: Avebury.

Bradley, J. (1996) 'Symbol of prejudice: Football and the Catholic Community in Scotland', *Patterns of Prejudice*, vol. 30, no. 3: 35-48.

Bradley, J. (2006) 'Sport and the Contestation of Ethnic Identity: Football and Irishness in Scotland', *Journal of Ethnic and Migration Studies*, vol. 32, no. 7: 1189–1208.

Briggs, B. (2012) 'Revealed: Abuse of Roma at Glasgow job centre 'routine', *The Scotsman*, Sunday 20 May 2012. Available at: http://www.scotsman.com/news/scotland/top-stories/revealed-abuse-of-roma-at-glasgow-job-centre-routine-1-2306203 [Last accessed 13/3/2016].

British Council and Institute for Community Cohesion (no date). *Intercultural Dialogue Toolkit*. Available from: http://www.cohesioninstitute.org.uk [Last accessed 23/2/2016].

Brockmann, M., Butt, J. and Fisher, M. (2001) 'The Experience of Racism: Black Staff in Social Services', *Research Policy and Planning*, 19:2. Available at: http://ssrg.org.uk/wp-content/uploads/2012/02/rpp192/article1.pdf [Last accessed 13/3/2016].

Brubaker, R. (1996) *Nationalism Reframed: Nationhood and the National Question in the New Europe*, Cambridge: Cambridge University Press.

Brubaker, R. (2004) 'The Manichean Myth: Rethinking the Distinction between "Civic" and "Ethnic" Nationalism' in H. Kriesi, K. Armingeon, H. Siegrist, and A. Wimmer (eds.), *Nation and National Identity*, West Lafayette, Indiana: Purdue University Press.

Brubaker, R. and Cooper, F. (2000) 'Beyond "Identity"', *Theory and Society*, vol. 29, no. 1: 1-47.

Bruce, F. (2010) *Showfolk: An Oral History of a Fairground Dynasty*. Devon: NMSE Publishing Ltd.

Bruce, S. (1988) 'Sectarianism in Scotland: a Contemporary Assessment and Explanation', *The Scottish Government Yearbook*, Edinburgh: Unit for the Study of Government in Scotland: 150-165.

Bruce, S., Glendinning, T., Paterson, I. and Rosie, M. (2004) *Sectarianism in Scotland*. Edinburgh: Edinburgh University Press.

Bruce, S., Glendinning, T., Paterson, I. and Rosie, M. (2005) 'Religious discrimination in Scotland: Fact or Myth?' *Ethnic and Racial Studies*, 28:1, pp.1466-4356.

Burke, E. [1792] (1999) 'Letter to Sir Hercules Langrishe', in I. Kramnick (ed.), *The Portable Edmund Burke*. Harmondsworth: Penguin.

Butcher, M. (2011). *Managing Cultural Change: Reclaiming Synchronicity in a Mobile World*. Farnham: Ashgate.

Butler, V. (2012). *All Party Parliamentary Group on Race and Community - Ethnic Minority Female Unemployment: Black, Pakistani and Bangladeshi Heritage Women*. London: Runnymede.

Cairney, P. (2016) The 'Scottish approach' to policy and policymaking: what issues are territorial and what are universal? *Policy & Politics*, 44 (3), 333–50.

Campsie, A. (2017) 'Should Glasgow's "slavery streets" be renamed?', *The Scotsman*, 20 February 2017. Available at: http://www.scotsman.com/news/should-glasgow-s-slavery-streets-be-re-named-1-4371826 [Last accessed 3/11/2017].

Carlyle, T. [1839] (1899) *Chartism*. London: Chapman and Hall.

Cathain, M. S. O. (2007) *Irish Republicanism in Scotland, 1858–1916: Fenians in Exile*. Dublin: Irish Academic Press.

Chattoo, S. and Atkin, K. (2012) 'Race, ethnicity and social policy: theoretical concepts and the limitations of current approaches to welfare' in G. Craig, K. Atkin, S. Chattoo and R. Flynn (eds.), *Understanding 'Race' and Ethnicity: Theory, History, Policy, Practice*. Policy Press: Bristol.

Chatwin, B. (1987) *The Songlines*. London: Jonathan Cape.

Christie, C. (2011) *Commission on the Future Delivery of Public Services*. Edinburgh: Public Services Commission.

Church of Scotland (1923) *The Menace of the Irish Race to Our Scottish Nationality*. Edinburgh: Church of Scotland.

Clark, C. (1998) 'Counting Backwards: the Roma 'Numbers Game' in Central and Eastern Europe', *Radical Statistics* 69. Available at: http://www.radstats.org.uk/no069/article4.htm

Clark C. (1999) 'Race', Ethnicity and Social Security: The Experience of Gypsies and Travellers in Britain'. *Journal of Social Security Law*, vol. 6, no. 4: 186-202.

Clark, C. (2006) 'Defining ethnicity in a cultural and socio-legal context: the case of Scottish Gypsy-Travellers', *Scottish Affairs* 54: 39-67.

Clark, C. and Greenfields, M. (2006) *Here to Stay: the Gypsies and Travellers of Britain*. Hatfield: University of Hertfordshire Press.

Clark, C. (2014) 'Glasgow's Ellis Island? The integration and Stigmatisation of Govanhill's Roma population', *People, Place and Policy*, vol. 8, no. 1: 34-50.

Clark, C. (2015) 'Integration, Exclusion and the Moral 'Othering' of Roma Migrant Communities in Britain' in V. Cree, G. Clapton and M. Smith (eds.) *Revisiting Moral Panics*. Bristol: Policy Press.

Clark, C. and Campbell, E. (2000) 'Gypsy Invasion: a critical analysis of newspaper reaction to Czech and Slovak asylum-seekers in Britain, 1997', *Romani Studies*, vol. 10, no. 1: 23-47.

Clark, C. and Taylor, R. (2014) 'Is Nomadism the problem? The social construction of Gypsies and Travellers as perpetrators of 'anti-social' behaviour in Britain', in S. Pickard (ed.), *Anti-Social Behaviour in Britain: Victorian and Contemporary Perspectives*. Basingstoke: Palgrave.

Clark, I. and Leven, T. (2000) *The 2000 Scottish Crime Survey: Analysis of the Ethnic Minority Booster Sample*. Edinburgh: Scottish Executive.

Coates, T. (2013) 'What we mean when we say race is a social construct'. *The Atlantic*, 15 May. Available at: http://www.theatlantic.com/national/archive/2013/05/what-we-mean-when-we-say-race-is-a-social-construct/275872/ [Last accessed 13/3/2016].

CoDE (2014) *Addressing Ethnic Inequalities in Social Mobility*. Manchester: CoDE. Available at: http://www.ethnicity.ac.uk/medialibrary/briefings/policy/code-social-mobility-briefing-Jun2014.pdf [Last accessed 13/3/2016].

Cohen, S. (2011) *Folk Devils and Moral Panics*. London: Routledge.

Colarelli, S. (2003) *No Best Way: An Evolutionary Perspective on Human Resource Management*. Santa Barbara: Praeger Publishing.

Colley, L. (1996) *Britons: Forging the Nation, 1707-1837*. New Haven: Yale University Press.

Commission for Racial Equality (1987) *Living in Terror*. London: CRE.

Commission for Racial Equality (2000) *Equal Opportunities and Private Sector Employment in Scotland*. London: CRE.

Commission for Racial Equality (2006) *Statutory Code of Practice on Race Equality in Housing*. London: CRE.

Communities Scotland (2005) *National Standards for Community Engagement*. Edinburgh: Scottish Executive.

Cooney, J., 1982. *Scotland and the Papacy: Pope John Paul II's Visit in Perspective* Edinburgh: Paul Harris.

Craig, C. And O'Neil, M. (2013) 'It's time to move on from 'race'? The official invisibilisation of minority disadvantage', *Social Policy Review 25*, pp: 93-112.

Craigforth Household Survey (2009) *Accommodation Needs Assessment of Gypsies/Travellers in Grampian 2008–2009*. Aberdeen: Moray and Aberdeenshire Councils.

Crenshaw, K. (2012) *On Intersectionality: The Essential Writings of Kimberlé Crenshaw*. Jackson: Perseus.

Coalition for Racial Equality and Rights (2012) *Scottish Identity and Black and Minority Ethnic Communities in Scotland*. Glasgow: CRER.

Coalition for Racial Equality and Rights (2013a) *Equality in Glasgow: Public Bodies and the Equality Duties*. Glasgow: CRER.

Coalition for Racial Equality and Rights (2013b) *State of the Nation 2013: Education*. Glasgow: CRER.

Coalition for Racial Equality and Rights (2014a). *Racist is an adjective, not an insult*. Glasgow: CRER.

Coalition for Racial Equality and Rights (2014b). *State of the Nation 2014: Employment*. Glasgow: CRER.

Coalition for Racial Equality and Rights (2015a). *Ten true things we need to say about racism in Scotland*. Glasgow: CRER.

Coalition for Racial Equality and Rights (2015b). *Public Sector Equality Duty portal*. Available from: http://www.crer.org.uk/public-sector-equality-duty [Last accessed 22/2/2016].

CRER (2016) 'State of the Nation: ethnicity and employment in Scotland's public sector', Glasgow: CRER.

Crown Office and Procurator Fiscal Service (COPFS) (2016) *Hate Crime in Scotland 2015-16*. Available at: http://www.copfs.gov.uk/images/Documents/Equality_Diversity/Hate%20Crime%20in%20 Scotland%202015-16.pdf

Curtis, L. (1984) *Nothing but the same old story: the roots of anti-Irish racism*, London: Information on Ireland.

Dalton, M. and Daghlian, S. (1994) *Barriers to Access: Black Applicants and Housing Association Tenure*, Research Paper No 9. Glasgow: SEMRU.

Davidson, N., Liinpää, M., McBride, M., and Virdee, S. (2015) 'Racism: from the Labour Movement to the Far-right', *Ethnic and Racial Studies*, vol. 38, no. 3: 446-451

DeAngelis, T. (2009) 'Unmasking Racial Microaggressions', *Monitor on Psychology*, vol. 40, no. 2. Available at: http://www.apa.org/monitor/2009/02/microaggression.aspx [Last accessed 13/3/2016].

De Beauvoir, S. (1956) *The Second Sex*, London: Jonathan Cape.

Delgado, R and Stefancic, J. (1993) 'Critical Race Theory: An Annotated Bibliography', *Virginia Law Review*, 79 (2): 461–516.

De Lima, P. (2012) 'Migration, Race and Racism' in G. Mooney and G. Scott (eds.) *Social Justice and Social Welfare in Contemporary Scotland*. Bristol: Policy Press.

Denholm, A. (2014) 'Teaching of slavery in schools branded tokenism', *The Herald*, 9 January. Available at: http://www.heraldscotland.com/news/home-news/teaching-of-slavery-in-scots-schools-branded-tokenism.23126288 [Last accessed 1/6/2015].

De Swaan, A. (2015) *The Killing Compartments: The Mentality of Mass Murder*, New Haven: Yale University Press.

Devine, T. M. (1991) *Irish Immigrants and Scottish Society in Nineteenth and Twentieth Century Scotland*. Edinburgh: John Donald Publishers.

Devine, T. M. (ed.) (2000) *Scotland's Shame? Bigotry and Sectarianism in Modern Scotland*, Edinburgh: Mainstream Publishing Company.

Devine, T. M. (2003) *Scotland's Empire: The Origins of the Global Diaspora*, Harmondsworth: Penguin Books.

Devine, T. M. (2008) 'The End of Disadvantage? The Descendants of Irish-Catholic Immigrants in Modern Scotland since 1945', in M. Mitchell (ed.), *New Perspectives on the Irish in Scotland*. Edinburgh: John Donald Publishers.

Devine, T. M. (2012) *The Scottish Nation: A Modern History*, Harmondsworth: Penguin Books.

Donald, P., Gosling, S., Hamilton, J., Hawkes, N., McKenzie, D. and Stronach, I. (1995) '"No Problem Here": Action Research against Racism in a Mainly White Area', *British Educational Research Journal*, vol. 21, no. 3: 263-275.

Dowie, D. (1996) *Ethnic Minority Housing in Glasgow: Scottish Homes Glasgow District Office Development Fund Strategy*. Glasgow: Scottish Homes.

Du Bois, W.E.B. [1935] (1992) *Black Reconstruction in America, 1860-1880: an Essay Towards a History of the Part which Black Folk Played in that Attempt to Reconstruct Democracy in America, 1860-1880*. New York: Free Press.

Duffy, J. (2013) 'Life on the Edge of Society', *The Herald*, Saturday 26 October. Available at: http://www.heraldscotland.com/news/home-news/life-on-the-edge-of-society.22524867 [Last accessed 13/3/2016].

Duffy, J. (2014a) 'Examining the slave trade over tea and cake', *The Herald*, 19 January. Available at: http://www.heraldscotland.com/news/home-news/examining-the-slave-trade-over-tea-and-cake.23208394 [Last accessed 1/6/2015].

Duffy, J. (2014b) 'Why Scotland must face up to slave trade past', *The Herald*, 6 July. Available at: http://www.heraldscotland.com/news/home-news/why-scotland-must-face-up-to-slave-trade-past.24677369 [Last accessed 1/6/2015].

Duffy, J. (2015) 'Destitute and penniless: 'no warning' benefit sanctions imposed in nearly 300,000 cases', *The Sunday Herald*, Sunday 1 November. Available at: http://www.heraldscotland.com/news/13928559.Destitute_and_penniless___no_warning__benefit_sanctions_imposed_in_nearly_300_000_cases/ [Last accessed 13/3/2016].

Duncan, T. (1996) *Neighbour's Views of Official Sites for Travelling People*. York: Joseph Rowntree Foundation. Available at: https://www.jrf.org.uk/report/neighbours-views-official-sites-travelling-people [Last accessed 13/3/2016].

Edward, M. (1993) *Who Belongs to Glasgow: 200 years of Migration*. Glasgow: Glasgow City Libraries.

Edwards, O. D. (2014) *Burke and Hare*. Second edition, Edinburgh: Birlinn.

Elias, N. (2012) *On the Process of Civilisation: Sociogenetic and Psychogenetic Investigations, Collected Works of Norbert Elias*, Vol. 3. Dublin: University College Dublin Press.

Elias, N. (2013) *Studies on the Germans: Power Struggles and the Development of Habitus in the Nineteenth and Twentieth Centuries, Collected Works of Norbert Elias*, vol. 11. Dublin: University College Dublin Press

Elias, N. and Dunning, E. (2008) *Quest for Excitement Sport and Leisure in the Civilizing Process, Collected Works of Norbert Elias*, vol. 7. Dublin: University College Dublin Press.

Elias, N. and Scotston, J. (2008) *The Established and the Outsiders, Collected Works of Norbert Elias*, vol. 4. Dublin: University College Dublin Press.

Equality Act (2010).

Equality and Human Rights Commission (2010a) *Starter Kit: Positive Action for Service Providers*. London: Equality and Human Rights Commission.

Equality and Human Rights Commission (2010b) *The First Triennial Review*, Equality and Human Rights Commission: London.

Equality and Human Rights Commission (2013) *Technical Guidance on the Public Sector Equality Duty: Scotland*. London: Equality and Human Rights Commission.

Equality and Human Rights Commission (2015) *Measuring Up? Report 4: Performance – a report of public authorities*. London: Equality and Human Rights Commission.

Equality and Human Rights Commission (2016) *Is Scotland Fairer?* London: Equality and Human Rights Commission.

Essed, P. (1991) *Understanding Everyday Racism: An Interdisciplinary Theory*. University of Amsterdam,

European Network Against Racism (2014) 'Violence against Roma on the rise, says Amnesty', Tuesday 8 April. Available at: http://www.enar-eu.org/Violence-against-Roma-on-the-rise [Last accessed 13/3/2016].

European Roma Rights Centre (2014) 'Czech Republic must put an end to Unlawful Segregation of Romani Children', *Press Release*, Wednesday 12 November. Available at: http://www.errc.org/article/czech-republic-must-put-an-end-to-unlawful-segregation-of-romani-children/4330 [Last accessed 13/3/2016].

Fekete, L. (2004) 'Anti-Muslim racism and the European security state', *Race and Class*, vol. 46, no. 1: 3-29.

Feldham, D. and Gidley, B. (eds.) (2014) *Integration, Disadvantage and Extremism*. London: Pears Institute and COMPAS.

Finn, G. (1990) 'Prejudice in the History of Irish Catholics in Scotland'. Paper presented at the 24th History Workshop Conference, Glasgow College of Technology/Glasgow Caledonian University.

Finn, G. P. T. (2003) '"Sectarianism": A Challenge for Scottish Education', in T. G. K. Bryce & W. M. Humes (eds.), *Scottish Education: Post-Devolution*. Second Edition, Edinburgh: Edinburgh University Press.

Finn, G. and Uygun, F. (2008) *'Sectarianism' and the Workplace: Report to the Scottish Trades Union Congress & the Scottish Government*. Department of Educational & Professional Studies, University of Strathclyde.

Fisher, P. and Nandi, A. (2015) *Poverty across Ethnic Groups through Recession and Austerity* Available at: https://www.jrf.org.uk/report/poverty-across-ethnic-groups-through-recession-and-austerity [Last accessed 25/9/2015].

Flinders, M., Matthews, F. and Eason, C. (2011). 'Public Appointments are Still Male, Pale and Stale'. Available from: http://www.blogs.lse.ac.uk [Last accessed 22/2/2016].

Flint, J. and Powell, R. (2013) 'Scottish Enlightenment and the Sectarian Civilising Offensive', in J. Flint and J. Kelly (eds.) *Bigotry, Football and Scotland*. Edinburgh: Edinburgh University Press.

Forsyth, R. (2008) 'Irish Government raises Rangers 'Famine' Chant with Alex Salmond', *Telegraph*. Available at: http://www.telegraph.co.uk/news/uknews/2964710/Irish-Government-raises-Rangers-famine-chant-with-Alex-Salmond.html [Last accessed 1/11/2015].

Foster, R. (1988) *Modern Irish History 1600- 1972*. London: Allen Lane.. s.l.:s.n.

Foucault, M. (2007) *Security, Territory, Population: Lectures at the College de France 1977- 1978*. London: Palgrave.

Fraser, D. (2015) 'Welcome to Scotland?', *BBC News*, Available at: http://www.bbc.co.uk/news/uk-scotland-31796146 [Last accessed 1/11/2015].

Fyfe, A., MacMillan, K., Bruce, C., Finlay, J. and Hewitt, E. (2013) *Public Sector Equality Duty: Implementation of Scottish Specific Duties*. Edinburgh: Scottish Government.

Gallagher, T. (1987) *Glasgow: The Uneasy Peace*, Manchester: Manchester University Press.

Gallagher, T. (2013) *Divided Scotland: Ethnic Friction and Christian Crisis*. Glendaruel: Argyll Press.

Garavelli, D. (2017) 'Dani Garavelli: Facing up to slavery in second city of empire', *The Scotsman*, 24 September 2017. Available at: http://www.scotsman.com/news/dani-garavelli-facing-up-to-slavery-in-second-city-of-empire-1-4568273 [Last accessed 3/11/2017].

Gibbons, L. (ed.) (1996) *Transformations in Irish Culture*. Cork: Cork University Press.

Gilroy, P. (1987) *There Ain't No Black in Union Jack*. London: Routledge.

Goldberg, T. G. (2006) 'Racial Europeanization', *Ethnic and Racial Studies*, 29 (2), pp. 332-64.

Goodall, K., McKerrell, S., Markey, J., Millar, S.R., and Richardson, M.J. (2015) 'Sectarianism in Scotland: A "West of Scotland" Problem, a Patchwork or a Cobweb?', *Scottish Affairs*, vol. 24, no. 3: 288-307.

Gordon, P. and Newnham, A. (1985) *Passport to Benefits? Racism in Social Security* London: Child Poverty Action Group and The Runnymede Trust.

Gorsky, P. (2010) *Unlearning Deficit Ideology and the Scornful Gaze*. Fairfax: EdChange.

Gosset, T. (1997) *Race: The History of an Idea in America*. New York: Oxford University Press.

Government Equalities Office (2010) *Quick Start Guide to Positive Action in Service Provision*. London: Government Equalities Office.

Government Equalities Office (2011) *Quick Start Guide to Positive Action in Recruitment and Promotion*. London: Government Equalities Office.

Guess, T. J. (2006) 'The Social Construction of Whiteness: Racism by Intent, Racism by Consequence', *Critical Sociology*, vol. 32, no. 4: 649-673.

Guardian (2015) 'First Syrian refugees arrive in Glasgow to low-key welcome', 17 November. Available at: http://www.theguardian.com/uk-news/2015/nov/17/syrian-refugees-arrive-glasgow-scotland [Last accessed 28/11/15].

Guy, W. (2015) 'Why Roma Migrate', *Open Democracy*, 30 June. Available at: https://www.opendemocracy.net/beyondslavery/will-guy/why-roma-migrate [Last accessed 13/3/2016].

Hall, S. (2007) 'Whose heritage? Un-settling 'The Heritage', re-imagining the post-nation' in L. Smith (ed.) *Cultural Heritage: Critical Concepts in Media and Cultural Studies, Vol 2*. New York: Routledge.

Hamilton, D. (2012) 'Scotland and the Eighteenth-Century Empire', in T.M. Devine and J. Wormald (eds.) *The Oxford Handbook of Modern Scottish History*. Oxford: Oxford University Press.

Hamilton-Smith, N., Malloch, M. and Ashe, S. (2015) 'Public Processions and Social Context: Challenges in the Search for Community Impact', *Scottish Affairs*, 24:3, pp.308-327.

Hancock, I. (2000) 'The Consequences of anti-Gypsy Racism in Europe', *Other Voices: The (e)Journal of Cultural Criticism*, vol. 2, no. 1, available at: http://www.othervoices.org/2.1/hancock/roma.php [Last accessed 13/3/2016].

Handley, J. D. (1945) *The Irish in Scotland*. Cork: Cork University Press.

Harrison, J. (2014) 'Paxman: "a head of steam in Scotland for hating the English"'. *The Herald*. 1 June 2014. Available at: http://www.heraldscotland.com/news/13163227.Paxman__a__head_of_steam_in_Scotland_for_hating_English_/ [Last accessed: 4 June 2017]

Harvard University (No date). *Project Implicit*. Available from: http://www.implicit.harvard.edu [Last accessed 22/2/2016].

Heath, A and McMahon, D (2000) *Ethnic Differences in the Labour Market: The Role of Education and Social Class Origins*. Oxford: University of Oxford.

Herald (2014) "I am a victim of anti-Irish racism' says Scots writer.' Available at: http://www.heraldscotland.com/news/13140070._I_am_a_victim_of_anti_Irish_racism_says_Scotswriter/ [Last accessed on 1 October 2015].

Herald Scotland (2015) 'Community reps: report into Irish-Scots significantly flawed.' Available at: http://www.heraldscotland.com/news/13203224.Community reps report into Irish Scots significantly flawed/ [Last accessed on 12 September 2015].

Hepple, B. (2011) *The New Legal Framework*. Hart Publishing.

Hickman, M. J. (1995) *Religion, Class and Identity*. Aldershot: Avebury.

Hickman, M. (1998) 'Reconstructing Deconstructing "Race": British political Discourses about the Irish in Britain', *Ethnic and Racial Studies*, vol. 21, no. 2: 288-307.

Homecoming Scotland (2010) Homecoming Scotland 2009: A Year of Celebration. Published by Event Scotland and the Scottish Government. Available at: http://www.eventscotland.org/resources/downloads/get/42.pdf [Last accessed 20/4/2015].

Hopkins, P. (2010) 'Young Muslim Men in Scotland: Inclusions and Exclusions', *Children's Geographies*, vol. 2, no. 2: 257-272.

Hopkins, P., Botterill, K., Sanghera, G. and Arshad, R. (2015), 'Faith, Ethnicity, Place: Young People's Everyday Geopolitics in Scotland'. Available at: https://research.ncl.ac.uk/youngpeople/outputs/finalreport/Faith,%20Ethnicity,%20Place%20final%20report.pdf

House of Commons (2015) EEA *migrants: access to social housing* (England) Available at: http://www.parliament.uk/briefing-papers/SN04737.pdf [Last accessed 13/3/2016].

Hussain, A. and Miller, W. (2006) *Multicultural Nationalism: Islamaphobia, Anglophobia and Devolution*. Oxford: Oxford University Press.

Ignatieff, Michael (1993) *Blood and Belonging: Journeys into the New Nationalism*. London: BBC Books and Chatto & Windus.

The Independent (2016) 'David Cameron prompts backlash by announcing plans to teach Muslim women English', 18 January. Available at: http://www.independent.co.uk/news/uk/home-news/backlash-as-david-cameron-announced-plans-to-teach-muslim-women-english-a6818496.html [Last accessed 08/03/2015].

The Independent (2017) 'Hate crimes rise by up to 100 per cent'. The Independent. 15 February. Available at: http://www.independent.co.uk/news/uk/home-news/brexit-vote-hate-crime-rise-100-per-cent-england-wales-police-figures-new-racism-eu-a7580516.html [Last accessed 10/6/2017].

The Independent (2017) 'Nicola Sturgeon announces second Scottish referendum'. *The Independent*. 13 March 2017. Available at: http://www.independent.co.uk/news/uk/politics/second-scottish-independence-live-referendum-nicola-sturgeon-brexit-speech-second-indy-ref-2-uk-eu-a7626746.html [Last accessed 21 June 2017].

Irish Independent (2014) 'Racism probe after Glasgow cabbie tells brothers to stop speaking Irish'. Available at: http://www.independent.ie/irish-news/racism-probe-after-glasgow-cabbie-tells-brothers-to-stop-speaking-irish-29900818.html [Last accessed 7/8/2015].

Islamic Human Rights Commission (ISHR) *Environment of Hate: The New Normal for Muslims in The UK*. London: IHRC.

Jacobson, M. F. (1998) *Whiteness of a Different Colour: European Immigrants and the Alchemy of Race*. Cambridge, Massachusetts: Harvard University Press.

James, M. (2008) *Interculturalism: Theory and Policy*. London: Baring Foundation.

Jinga, I. (2014) 'Romanians do not recognise this thief stereotype – and neither do the British', *The Guardian*, 18 February. Available at: http://www.theguardian.com/commentisfree/2014/feb/18/romanians-thief-stereotype-british-people-daily-mail-rudi-roma-romanian [Last accessed 13/3/2016].

Jobcentre Plus (2008) *Race, Disability and Gender Equality Schemes 2008-2011*. London: Department for Work and Pensions.

Jobcentre Plus (2010), *Jobcentre plus Race, Disability and Gender Equality Schemes Annual Progress Report 2009-10*, London: Department for Work and Pensions.

Jovanovic, Z. (2015) 'Why Europe's 'Roma Decade' Didn't Lead to Inclusion', *Voices: Open Society Foundation*, Monday 21 September. Available at: https://www.opensocietyfoundations.org/voices/why-europe-s-roma-decade-didn-t-lead-inclusion [Last accessed 13/3/2016].

Kanter, R.M. (1977) 'Some Effects of Proportions on Group Life: Skewed Sex Ratios and Responses to Token Women', *American Journal of Sociology,* vol. 82, no. 5: 965-990.

Kauffman, E. P. (2008) 'The Orange Order in Scotland since 1860: A Social Analysis', in M. Mitchell (ed.), *New Perspectives on the Irish in Scotland*. Edinburgh: John Donald.

Kearton, Antonia (2005) 'Imagining the "Mongrel Nation": Political Uses of History in the Recent Scottish Nationalist Movement', *National Identities*, vol. 7, no. 1: 23-50.

Keating, M. (2005) *The Government of Scotland*. Edinburgh: Edinburgh University Press.

Kelly, J. (2007) 'Hibernian Football Club: The Forgotten Irish?', *Sport in Society*, vol. 10, no. 3: 514-536.

Kelly, J. (2010) '"Sectarianism" and Scottish Football: Critical Reflections on Dominant Discourse and Press Commentary', *International Review for the Sociology of Sport*, vol. 46, no. 4: 418-435.

Kennedy, A. (2010). 'Genuine celebrations: Including cultural experiences in the program', *Putting Children First* 33 (March): 17-19. Available at: http://ncac.acecqa.gov.au/educator -resources/pcfarticles/genuine_celebrations_cultural_experiences_mar10%20.pdf [Last accessed 13/3/2016].

Kidd, C. (2003) 'Race, Empire and the Limits of Nineteenth Century Scottish Nationhood', *Historical Journal,* December, 46:4, pp.873- 892.

Kidd, C. (2006) *The Forging of Race: Race and Scripture in the Protestant World 1600- 2000*. Cambridge: cambridge University Press.

Kiely, R., Bechhofer, F., and McCrone, D. (2005) 'Birth, Blood and Belonging: Identity Claims in Post-devolution Scotland', *Sociological Review*, vol. 35, no. 1: 150-171.

Kirchgaessner, S. (2015) 'Rome pledges to dismantle Roma ghettos after court ruling', *The Guardian*, Tuesday 21 July. Available at: http://www.theguardian.com/world/2015/jul/21/rome-pledges-dismantle-roma-ghettos-court-ruling-italy [Last accessed 13/3/2016].

Knox, R. (1850) *The Races of Men*. London: Henry Renshaw.

Kretzmann, J. P. (2010) 'Asset-based Strategies for Building Resilient Communities', in Reich, J.W., Zautra, A. & Hall, J.S. (eds.) *Handbook of adult resilience*. New York: Guilford Press.

Kyriakides, C., Virdee, S. and Modood, T. (2009) 'Racism, Muslims and the National Imagination', *Journal of Ethnic and Migration Studies*, 35:2, pp.289-308.

Law, A. (2015) 'Sectarianism, criminalisation and the civilising process in Scotland', in Croall, H. Mooney, G. and Munro, M (eds.), *Crime, Justice and Society in Scotland*, London: Routledge.

Law, A. and Mooney, G. (2011) 'The Decivilizing Process and Urban Working Class Youth in Scotland', *Social Justice*, vol. 38, no. 4: 106-126.

Law, B. M. (2011). 'Retraining the Biased Brain', *Monitor on Psychology*, vol. 42, no. 9. Available at: http://www.apa.org/monitor/2011/10/biased-brain.aspx [Last accessed 13/3/2016].

Law, I. (2009) *Racism and Ethnicity: Global Debates, Dilemmas and Directions*. London: Routledge.

Leadbetter, R. (2013) 'Shocking truth of Scotland's role at "very heart" of slavery', *The Herald*, 3 October. Available at: http://www.heraldscotland.com/news/home-news/shocking-truth-of-scotlands-role-at-very-heart-of-slavery.25489540 [Last accessed 1/6/2015].

Leask, D. (2014a) 'Warning: Scam of barefoot begging', *Evening Times*, 2 January. Available at: http://www.eveningtimes.co.uk/news/13270646.Warning__Scam_of_barefoot_begging/ [Last accessed 13/3/2016].

Leask, D. (2014b) 'Barefoot cheek or serious need?' *Evening Times*, 10 January. Available at: http://www.eveningtimes.co.uk/news/13271190.Barefoot_cheek_or_serious_need_/ [Last accessed 13/3/2016].

Lebow, N. (1973) 'British Historians and Irish History', *Eire-Ireland*, vol. 8, no. 4: 3-38.

Leith, M. S. (2008) 'Scottish National Party Representations of Scottishness and Scotland', *Politics*, vol. 28, no. 2: 83-92.

Lemos, G. (2000) *Racial Harassment: Action on the Ground*. London: Lemos and Crane.

Liégeois, J-P. (1994) *Roma, Gypsies, Travellers*. Strasbourg: Council of Europe Press.

Lipsky, M. (1980) *Street-level Bureaucracy: Dilemmas of the Individual in Public Services*. New York: Russell Sage Foundation.

Lord Advocate's Guidelines on the Offensive Behaviour at Football and Threatening Communications (Scotland) Act 2012. http://www.copfs.gov.uk

Lorimer, D. (1996) *The Victorians and Race*. Aldershot: Ashgate

Low Pay Commission (2013) *National Minimum Wage: Low Pay Commission Report 2013*, Cm 8565. London: The Stationery Office. Available at: http://www.lowpay.gov.uk/lowpay/report/pdf/9305-BIS-Low_Pay-Accessible6.pdf [Last accessed 2/7/2013].

Mac an Ghaill, M. (2001) 'British Critical Theorists: The production of the conceptual invisibility of the Irish diaspora', *Social Identities*, vol. 7, no. 2: 179-202.

MacEwan, M. (1980) 'Race Relations in Scotland: ignorance or apathy?', *New Community*, 8, 266-274.

MacEwen, M.; Dalton, M.; and Murie, A. (1994) *Race and Housing in Scotland: A Literature Review and Bibliography*. Edinburgh: Edinburgh College of Art/Heriot Watt University, Research Paper 58.

Macguire, C. and Bator-Skorkiewicz, A. (2014) 'Pierwszy Minister Alex Salmond: O Niepodleglosci Szkocji', *Emigrant Magazine*, (August). Available at: http://issuu.com/emigrantmagazyn/docs/emi-grant_august_2014_web/1 [Last accessed 20/4/2015].

Mackenzie, J.M. (1993) 'Essay and Reflection: On Scotland and the Empire', *International History Review*, vol. 15, no. 4: 714-739.

MacMillan, J. (2011) 'Is it now officially OK to sing anti-Irish, anti-Catholic hate songs in Scottish football stadiums?' *Telegraph*. Available at: http://blogs.telegraph.co.uk/culture/jmacmillan/100052373/is-it-now-officially-ok-to-sing-anti-irish-anti-catholic-hate-songs-in-scottishs-football-stadiums/ [Last accessed 1/1/2015].

Macpherson, W. (1999) *The Stephen Lawrence Inquiry: Report of an Inquiry by Sir William Macpherson of Cluny*. London: Home Office.

Malik, L. (2009) *From Fatwa to Jihad: The Rushdie Affair and its Legacy*. London: Atlantic Books.

Malik, K. (1996) *The Meaning of Race: Race, History and Culture in Western Society*. New York: New York University Press.

Mandler, P. (2000) *History, Religion and Culture: British Intellectual History 1750-1950*. Cambridge: Cambridge University Press.

Mann, B. (1992) *The New Scots: The Story of Asians in Scotland*. Edinburgh: John Donald.

Markman, A. (2013). *The Pain of Positive Stereotypes*. Available from: www.psychologytoday.com [Last accessed 22/2/2016].

Martin, A.E. (2012) *Alter-Nations: Nationalisms, Terror and the State in Nineteenth Century Britain and Ireland*. Columbus: The Ohio State University Press.

McCall, C. (2015) 'How severe are the cuts facing Scottish councils?', *The Scotsman*, Thursday 15 October. Available at: http://www.scotsman.com/news/politics/how-severe-are-the-cuts-facing-scottish-councils-1-3918039 [Last accessed 13/3/2016].

McCallum, I. (2013) *The Celtic, Glasgow Irish and the Great War: The Gathering Storms*. Glasgow: Ian McCallum.

McClaren, R. (2016) 'Travellers site in St Cyrus branded a risk to life', *The Courier*, Friday 19 February. Available at: http://www.thecourier.co.uk/news/local/angus-the-mearns/travellers-site-in-st-cyrus-branded-a-risk-to-life-1.924978 [Last accessed 13/3/2016].

McCrone, D. (2001) *Understanding Scotland: the Sociology of a Stateless Nation*. London: Routledge.

McGeachie, M. and Power, G. (2015) *Co-production in Scotland – a Policy Overview*. Glasgow: Scottish Co-Production Network.

McIntosh, I., Sim, D., and Robertson, D. (2004) 'It's as if you're some alien…': Exploring English Attitudes in Scotland, Sociological Research Online, 9(2). Available online: http://www.socresonline.org.uk/9/2/mcintosh.html [Last accessed 15/6/2017].

McKenna, K. (2015) 'We Scots must face up to our slave trading past', *The Guardian*, 22 November. Available at: http://www.theguardian.com/commentisfree/2015/nov/22/scots-must-face-up--to-slave-trading-past [Last accessed 29/2/2016].

McLaren, S. (2017) 'The slave trade made Scotland rich. Now we must pay our blood-soaked debts.' 13 January. *The Guardian*. Available at: https://www.theguardian.com/commentisfree/2017/jan/13/slave-trade-slavery-scotland-pay-debts [Last accessed 15/6/2017].

McVeigh, R. (1997) 'Theorising Sedentarism: The Roots of Anti-nomadism' in T. Acton (ed.), *Gypsy Politics and Traveller Identity*. Hatfield: University of Hertfordshire Press.

Mearns Leader (2015) 'One less hurdle for St Cyrus Travellers' site', *The Mearns Leader*, 22 December. Available at: http://www.mearnsleader.co.uk/news/local-headlines/one-less-hurdle-for-st-cyrus-travellers-site-1-3981443 [Last accessed 13/3/2016].

Meer, N. (2010) 'The impact of European Equality Directives upon British Anti-Discrimination Legislation', *Policy & Politics*, 38(2), 197-215.

Meer, N. (2013) 'Race, Culture and Difference in the Study of Antisemitism and Islamophobia', *Ethnic and Racial Studies*, 36 (3), 385-398.

Meer, N. (2014) *Race and Ethnicity*. London: Sage.

Meer, N. (2015) 'Looking up in Scotland? Multinationalism, multiculturalism and political elites', *Ethnic and Racial Studies*, 38 (9), 1477-1496.

Mejka, W. (2016) 'Equality – If Not Now, When?' Available at: http://www.equality-ifnotnow-when.blogspot.co.uk [Last accessed 4/3/2016].

Meltzer, B.N. and Musolf, G.R. (2002) 'Resentment and *ressentiment*', *Sociological Inquiry*, vol. 72, no. 2: 240-55.

Mennell, S., Elliott, M., Stokes, P.A., Rickard, A., and O'Malley Dunlop, E. (2000) 'Protestants in a Catholic State – A Silent Minority in Ireland', in T. Inglis, Z. Mach, and R. Mazanek (eds.) *Religion and Politics: East-West Contrasts from Contemporary Europe*. Dublin: University College Dublin Press.

Merton, R. (1968) *Social Theory and Social Structure*. New York: The Free Press.

Miles, R. (1982) *Racism and Migrant Labour*. London: Routledge and Kegan Paul.

Miles, R. (1989) *Racism*. London: Routledge.

Miles, R. (1993) *Racism after Race Relations*. London: Routledge.

Miles, R. and Brown, M. (1989) *Racism*. Second edition, London: Routledge.

Miles, R. and Dunlop, A. (1987) 'Racism in Britain: The Scottish Dimension', in P. Jackson (ed.), *Race and Racism: Essays in Social Geography*. London: Allen and Unwin.

Mills, C. W. (1959) *The Sociological Imagination*. Oxford: Oxford University Press.

Mitchell, M. J. (1998) *The Irish in the West of Scotland, 1797–1848*. Edinburgh: John Donald.

Mitchell, M. (2008) 'Irish Catholics in the West of Scotland in the Nineteenth Century: Despised by Scottish workers and controlled by the Church?', in M. Mitchell (ed.), *New Perspectives on the Irish in Scotland*. Edinburgh: John Donald.

Modood, T., Berthoud, R., Lakey, J., Nazroo, J., Smith, P., Virdee, S., & Beishon, S. (1997). *Ethnic minorities in Britain: Diversity and dis-advantage: The fourth national survey of ethnic minorities*. London: Policy Studies Institute.

Money, R. (2007) 'Executive slave trade booklet sparks criticism from anti-racism group', *The Herald*, 24 March. Available at: http://www.heraldscotland.com/executive-slave-trade-booklet-sparks-criticism-from-anti-racism-group-1.827376 [Last accessed 1/6/2015].

Montagu, A. [1942] (1997) *Man's Most Dangerous Myth: The Fallacy of Race*. Sixth edition, Walnut Creek, California: AltaMira Press.

Morris, M. (2014) 'Robert Burns: Recovering Scotland's Memory of the Black Atlantic', *Journal for Eighteenth-Century Studies*, vol. 37, no. 3: 343-359.

Morris, M. (2016) 'Multidirectional Memory, Many-Headed Hydras and Glasgow' in K. Donington, R. Hanley and J. Moody (eds.) *Britain's History and Memory of Transatlantic Slavery: Local Nuances of a 'National Sin'*. Liverpool: Liverpool University Press.

Mosse, G. (1995) 'Racism and Nationalism', *Nations and Nationalism*, vol. 1, no. 2: 163–173.

Muhs, G.G., Niemann, Y.F., González, C.G. and Harris, A.P. (eds.) (2012). *Presumed Incompetent: The Intersections of Race and Class for Women in Academia*. Utah: Utah State University Press.

Mullen, S. (2009) 'Ae Fond Kiss and Then We Sever!' *Variant* 35: 8-10.

Mullen, S. (2017) 'The Politics of Glasgow and Slavery', *Cable*, Issue 5 November 2017. Available at: https://www.cablemagazine.scot/the-politics-of-glasgow-and-slavery/ [Last accessed 3/11/2017].

Murray, B. (1998) *The Old Firm: Sectarianism, Sport, and Society in Scotland*. Edinburgh: John Donald.

Mycock, A. (2012) 'SNP, Identity and Citizenship: Re-Imagining State and Nation, *National Identities*, vol. 14, no. 1: 53-69.

Nairn, T. [1977] (2003) *The Break-up of Britain: Crisis and Neo-nationalism*. Third edition, London:Verso.

National Library of Scotland (no date). 'Scotland and the Slave Trade'. Available at: http://www.nls.uk/collections/topics/slavery#scotland [Last accessed 29/2/2016].

National Records of Scotland (2011). *Scotland's Census 2011*. Available at: http://www.scotlandscensus.gov.uk/ [Last accessed 23/2/2016].

Nelson, B. (2012) *Irish Nationalists and the Making of the Irish Race*. Princeton: Princeton University Press.

Netto, G. (2006) 'Vulnerability to Homelessness: Use of Services and Homelessness Prevention in Black and Minority Ethnic Communities', *Housing Studies*, vol. 21, no. 4: 581-603.

Netto, G. (2011a) 'Refugee Housing Pathways, Identity Negotiation and "Place"', *Housing Theory and Society*, vol. 28, no. 2: 123-143.

Netto, G. (2011b) 'Strangers in the City: Addressing Challenges to the Protection, Housing and Settlement of Refugees', *International Journal of Housing Policy*, vol. 11, no. 3: 285-305.

Netto, G. and Abazie, H. (2012) 'Racial Harassment in the Social Rented Sector: The Case for a Community Development Approach', *Urban Studies*, vol. 50, no. 4: pp. 674-690.

Netto, G., Arshad, R., de Lima P., Almeida Diniz, F., MacEwen, M., Patel, V. and Syed, R. (2001) *Audit of Research on Minority Ethnic Issues in Scotland from a 'Race' Perspective*. Scottish Executive: Edinburgh.

Netto, G., Fancy, C., Lomax, D., Satsangi, M. and Smith H. (2003a) *Improving Understanding of the Housing Circumstances of Minority Ethnic Communities in Aberdeenshire and Moray*. Edinburgh: Communities Scotland.

Netto, G., Fancy, C., Lomax, D., Satsangi, M. and Smith, H. (2003b) *Improving Understanding of the Housing Circumstances of Minority Ethnic Communities Aberdeen City*. Edinburgh: Communities Scotland.

Netto, G., Fancy, C., Pawson, H., Lomax, D., Singh, S. and Power, S. (2004) *Black and Minority Ethnic Communities and Homelessness in Scotland*. Edinburgh: Scottish Executive.

Netto, G., Sosenko, F. and Bramley, G. (2011) *Review of Poverty and Ethnicity in Scotland*. Joseph Rowntree Foundation. Available at: http://www.jrf.org.uk/publications/review-poverty-and-ethnicity-scotland [Last accessed 13/3/2016].

Netto, G., Fitzpatrick, S., Sosenko, F. and Smith, H. (2015) *International lessons on Tackling Extreme Housing Exclusion*. Joseph Rowntree Foundation.

Nicholls, C. M., Arthur, S., and Creegan, C. (2010) *Perceptions of Unfair Treatment in the Public*. London: Government Equalities Office, HMSO.

Nietzsche, F. [1887] (1996) *On the Genealogy of Morals: A Polemic*. Oxford: Oxford University Press.

Niro, B. (2003) *Race*. London: Palgrave Macmillan.

Omi, M. and Winant, H. (1994). Racial formation in the United States: from the 1960s to the 1990s. New York; London: Routledge.

Operation Black Vote (2014) UK *Political Leaders: Don't Shame Us!* London: Operation Black Vote.

Ormston, R., Curtice, J., McConville, S. and Reid, S. (2011), *Scottish Social Attitudes Survey 2010: Attitudes to Discrimination and Positive Action*. Scottish Centre for Social Research (ScotCen)

Ormston, R., Curtice, J., Hinchliffe, S. and Marcinkiewicz, A. (2015) 'A Subtle but Intractable Problem? Public Attitudes to Sectarianism in 2014', *Scottish Affairs*, vol. 24, no. 3: 266-287.

Owuor, J. and Nake, J. (2015) *Internalised Stigma as a Barrier to Access to Health and Social Care Services by Minority Ethnic Groups in the UK*. London: Race Equality Foundation.

Paradies, Y., Priest, N. Jehonathan B., Truong, M., Gupta, A., Pieterse, A., Kelaher, M. and Gee, G. (2013) 'Racism as a Determinant of Health: A Protocol for Conducting a Systematic Review and Meta-analysis', *Systematic Reviews*, vol. 2, no. 85. Available at: http://systematicreviewsjournal.biomedcentral.com/articles/10.1186/2046-4053-2-85 [Last accessed 13/3/2016].

Paterson, L. (2000a) 'The Social Class of Catholics in Scotland', *Journal of the Royal Statistical Society: Series A*, vol. 163, no. 3: 363-379.

Paterson, L. (2000b) 'Salvation through Education? The Changing Social Status of Scottish Catholics', in T. M. Devine (ed.), *Scotland's Shame? Bigotry and Sectarianism in Modern Scotland*. Edinburgh: Mainstream.

Paterson, L., Simpson, L., Barrie, L. and Perinova, J. (2011) *Unequal and Unlawful Treatment: Barriers faced by the Roma community in Govanhill when Accessing Welfare Benefits and the Implications of Section 149 of the Equality Act, 2010*. Oxford/Glasgow: Oxfam Law into Practice Project/Govanhill Law Centre. Available at: http://www.govanlc.com/UUTR.pdf [Last accessed 13/3/2016].

Paxton, R. O. (2005) *The Anatomy of Fascism*. Harmondsworth: Penguin.

Peacock, A. (2014) *HR Bias in Recruitment for Law Firms*. Available from: http://www.graftonhaymes.co.uk. [Last accessed 23/2/2016].

Phillips, D. and Harrison, M. (2010) 'Constructing an Integrated Society: Historical Lessons for Tackling Black and Minority Ethnic Housing Segregation in Britain'. *Housing Studies*, vol. 25, no. 2: 221-235.

PIEDA (1995) *Second Study of Consumer Preferences in Housing*, Edinburgh: Scottish Homes.

Pierce, C. (1970) 'Offensive Mechanisms'. In F. Barber (ed.), *The Black Seventies*. Boston: Porter Sargent.

Pilkington, A. (2009) 'From Institutional Racism to Community Cohesion: the Changing Nature of Racial Discourse in Britain', *Sociological Research Online*, vol. 13, no. 3. Available at: http://www.socresonline.org.uk/13/3/6.html [Last accessed 13/3/2016].

Pinfold, J. (2007) *The Slave Trade Debate: Contemporary Writings For and Against*, Oxford: Bodleian Library.

Pittock, M. (2008) *The Road to Independence*. London: Reakton.

Platt, L. (2007) *Poverty and Ethnicity in the UK*. Available at: https://www.jrf.org.uk/report/poverty-and-ethnicity-uk [Last accessed 25/9/2015].

Poole, L. and Adamson, K. (2008) *Report on the Situation of the Roma Community in Govanhill*, Glasgow, Glasgow/Paisley: Oxfam and the University of the West of Scotland. Available at: http://archive.scottish.parliament.uk/s3/committees/equal/inquiries/migration/subs/SEGlasgowCHCP1.pdf [Last accessed 13/3/2016].

Poole, L. (2010) 'National Action Plans for Social Inclusion and A8 migrants: The case of the Roma in Scotland'. *Critical Social Policy*, vol. 30, no. 2: 245-266.

Powell, R. (2013) 'The Theoretical Concept of the "Civilizing Offensive" *(beschavingsoffensief)*: Notes on its Origins and Uses', *Human Figurations: Long-term Perspectives on the Human Condition*, vol. 2, no. 2. Available at: http://hdl.handle.net/2027/spo.11217607.0002.203 [Last accessed 13/3/2016].

Procurator Fiscal (2015) 'Hate crime in Scotland'. Available at: http://www.copfs.gov.uk/images/Documents/Equality_Diversity/Hate%20Crime%20in%20Scotland%202013-14.pdf [Last accessed 25/9/2015].

Raab, C. and Holligan, C. (2012) 'Sectarianism: Myth or Social Reality?', *Ethnic & Racial Studies*, 35 (11), 1-21.

Race Relations Act (1976). Available at: http://www.legislation.gov.uk/ukpga/1976/74 [Last accessed 15/6/2017].

Ranulf, S. (1964) *Moral Indignation and Middle Class Psychology: A Sociological Study*. New York: Schoken Books.

Reid, I. (2013) 'He's Back! But Scotland's National Demon Never Left: Revisiting Media Representations of Neil Lennon and Narratives of Bigotry', in J. Flint and J. Kelly (eds.), *Bigotry, Football and Scotland*, Edinburgh: Mainstream.

Reid, I. (2008) 'An Outsider in our Midst': Narratives of Neil Lennon, Soccer and Ethno-religious Bigotry in the Scottish Press', *Soccer and Society*, vol. 9, no. 1:.64-80.

Reilly, P. (2000) 'Kicking with the Left Foot: Being Catholic in Scotland' in T.M Devine (ed.), *Scotland's Shame? Bigotry and Sectarianism in Modern Scotland*. Edinburgh: Mainstream.

Renan, E. (1990) 'What is a Nation?', in H. K. Bhabha (ed.), *Nation and Narration*. London: Routledge.

Research Report No 607, A report of research carried out by National Centre for Social Research on behalf of the Department for Work and Pensions. http://www.natcen.ac.uk/our-research/research/a-test-for-racial-discrimination-in-recruitment-practice-in-british-cities/ [Last accessed 15/6/2017].

Richards, B. (2014) 'In the Debate about Britishness, it is Important to Distinguish Between Two Different Types of Social Cohesion'. Available at: http://blogs.lse.ac.uk/politicsandpolicy/british-ness-and-social-cohesion/ [Last accessed 22/2/2016].

Robinson, D. (2008) 'Community Cohesion and the Politics of Communitarianism', in J. Flint and D. Robinson (eds.), *Community Cohesion in Crisis? New Dimensions of Diversity and Difference.* Bristol: Policy Press.

Robinson, D. (2010) 'Neighbourhood Effects of New Immigration', *Environment and Planning*, vol. 42, no. 10: 2451-2466.

Robinson, D and Walshaw, A. (2011) 'New Migration, Neighbourhood Effects and Community Change'. Available at: https://www.shu.ac.uk/research/cresr/sites/shu.ac.uk/files/new-migration neighbourhood-effects.pdf [Last accessed 25/9/2015].

Rodger, J. (2008) *Criminalising Social Policy: Anti-social Behaviour and Welfare in a De-civilised Society.* Cullompton: Willan.

Rosenblatt, P. C. (2014) *The Impact of Racism on African American Families: Literature as Social Science.* Farnham: Ashgate Press.

Rosie, M. (2004) *The Sectarian Myth in Scotland: of Bitter Memory and Bigotry.* Basingstoke: Palgrave Macmillan.

Rosie, M. (2008) 'Protestant Action and the Edinburgh Irish', in M. Mitchell (ed.), *New Perspectives on the Irish in Scotland.* Edinburgh: John Donald Publishers.

Rosie, M. (2015) 'The Sectarian Iceberg?' *Scottish Affairs*, vol. 24, no. 3: 328-350.

Ross, D. (2016) 'Historians: Pupils should be taught about Scotland's role in the slave trade', *The Herald*, 16 January. Available at: http://www.heraldscotland.com/news/14213248.Historians_pupils_should_be_taught_about Scotland's_role_in_the_slave_trade/ [Last accessed 29/2/2016].

Ross, P. (2011) 'Scotland's 4,000 Show Folk are finding times hard, but all are determined to keep their wagons rolling', *Scotland on Sunday*, 29 May. Available at: http://www.scotsman.com/lifestyle/ scotland-s-4-000-showfolk-are-finding-times-hard-but-all-are-determined-to-keep-their-wagons-rolling-1-1667111 [Last accessed 13/3/2016].

Runnymede Trust (2015) *The 2015 Budget: Effects on Black and Minority Ethnic People.* London: Runnymede Trust.

Salmond, A. (2013) 'Preface' in SNP's *Scotland's Future: Your Guide to an Independent Scotland.* Edinburgh: Scottish Government.

Salmond, A. (2014a) Glasgow Caledonian University Speech (New York campus). Delivered on 7 April. Available at: http://news.scotland.gov.uk/Speeches-Briefings/Glasgow-Caledonian-University-speech-b45.aspx [Last Accessed 20/4/2015].

Salmond, A. (2014b) Morning Call, BBC Radio Scotland. Broadcast on 29 August.

Sayyid, S. (2010) *Do Post-racials Dream of White Sheep?* Leeds: Centre for Ethnicity and Racism Studies.

Scheler, M. (1972) *Ressentiment. New York: Schocken Books.*

Scotland Bill (2015-16) Available at: http://www.publications.parliament.uk/pa/bills/cbill/2015-2016/0003/16003.pdf *[Last accessed 13/3/2016].*

The Scotsman (2016) "Hate crimes in Scotland 'fell after brexit vote'", 22 September 2016. http://www.scotsman.com/news/hate-crimes-in-scotland-fell-after-brexit-vote-1-4237818 [Last accessed 15/6/2017].

Scottish Executive (2001) *Helping Homeless People: An Action Plan for Prevention and Effective Responses.* Homelessness Task Force Final Report Edinburgh: Scottish Executive.

Scottish Government (2003) *Asylum Seekers in Scotland the Impact of Dispersal – Service Providers Perspectives.* Available at: http://www.gov.scot/Publications/2003/02/16400/18350 [Last accessed 13/3/2016].

Scottish Government (2008) *Race Equality Statement 2008-2011.* Edinburgh: Scottish Government.

Scottish Government (2014a) *Analysis of the 2011 Census data.* Available at: http://www.scotlandscensus.gov.uk/housing-and-accommodation [Date accessed 25 September 2015].

Scottish Government (2014b) *Scottish Crime and Justice Survey of 2012/13: Main Findings*, Edinburgh: Scottish Government.

Scottish Government (2015a), 'Analysis of Equality Results from the 2011 Census – Part 2'. Available at: http://www.gov.scot/Publications/2015/03/8716/0 [Last accessed 15/6/2017].

Scottish Government (2015b) *Racist Incidents Recorded by the Police in Scotland, 2013-14. Scottish Government.* Available at: http://www.gov.scot/Publications/2015/11/7911 [Last accessed 15/6/2017].

The Scottish Household Survey (2015) *Scotland's People Annual Report: Results from 2014 Scottish Household Survey.* Available at: http://www.gov.scot/Publications/2015/08/3720/4 [Last accessed 15/6/2017].

Scottish Parliament (2016) *Removing barriers: race, ethnicity and employment.* Available at: http://www.parliament.scot/parliamentarybusiness/CurrentCommittees/96080.aspx [Last accessed 15/6/2017].

Scottish Government (2015a) *Report on the operation of the Offensive Behaviour at Football and Threatening Communications (Scotland) Act 2012,* Edinburgh: Scottish Government.

Scottish Government (2015b) *Racist Incidents Recorded by the Police in Scotland, 2013-14.* Edinburgh: Scottish Government.

Scottish Government (2015c) *Analysis of Equality Results from the 2011 Census - Part 2* (Chapter 2: Gypsy/Travellers). Edinburgh: Scottish Government. Available at: http://www.gov.scot/Publications/2015/03/8716 [Last accessed 13/3/2016].

Scottish Government (2015d) *SCORE (Scottish Continuous Recording System) Annual Summary Report 2014-2015.* Available at: http://www.gov.scot/Publications/2015/06/5064/1 [Last accessed 25/9/2015].

Scottish Government Social Research (2011) *An Evaluation of Football Banning Orders in Scotland.* Edinburgh: Scottish Government.

Scottish Government Social Research (2013) *Religiously Aggravated Offending in Scotland, 2012-1.* Edinburgh: Scottish Government.

Scottish Parliament Equal Opportunities Committee (2001) *Inquiry into Gypsies/Travellers and Public Sector Bodies - 1st report.* Edinburgh: Scottish Parliament.

Scottish Parliament (2012) *Equal Opportunities Committee 3rd Report, 2012 (Session 4) Gypsy/Travellers and Care.* Edinburgh: Scottish Parliament. Available at: http://www.scottish.parliament.uk/S4_EqualOpportunitiesCommittee/Reports/eor-12-03w-rev2.pdf [Last accessed 13/3/2016].

Scottish Parliament (2013) *Equal Opportunities Committee 1st Report, 2013 (Session 4): Where Gypsy/Travellers Live.* Edinburgh: Scottish Parliament. Available at: http://www.scottish.parliament.uk/S4_EqualOpportunitiesCommittee/Reports/eor-13-01w.pdf [Last accessed 13/3/2016].

Scottish Parliament Equal Opportunities Committee (2015) *Race, Ethnicity and Employment: Evidence Received.* Available at: http://www.scottish.parliament.uk/parliamentarybusiness/CurrentCommittees/89972.aspx [Last accessed 4/3/2016].

Scottish Parliament Equal Opportunities Committee (2016) *Removing Barriers: Race, Ethnicity and Employment.* Edinburgh: Scottish Parliament.

Scottish Refugee Council (2012) *Asylum in Scotland: The Facts.* Available at: http://www.scottishrefugeecouncil.org.uk/ [Last accessed 20/12/2015].

Sibbitt, R. (1997) *The Perpetrators of Racial Harassment and Racial Violence.* Home Office Research Study 176. London: Home Office.

Sikh Channel (2014) Sikh Channel Special: 'Scotland Referendum Debate', 6 September. Available at: https://www.youtube.com/watch?v=7xkBqViFZBU [Last accessed 20/4/2015].

Silverman, M. (1993) *Deconstructing the Nation, Immigration, Racism and Citizenship in Modern France.* London: Routledge.

Simmel, G. (1908) *Soziologie: Untersuchungen über die Formen der Vergesellschaftung.* Leipzig: Duncker and Humblot.

Siraj, A. (2011) 'Meanings of Modesty and the Hijab amongst Muslim Women in Glasgow, Scotland', *Gender, Place & Culture: A Journal of Feminist Geography,* vol. 18, no. 6: 716-731.

Sivanandan, A. (1983) 'Challenging racism: strategies for the [19]80s', *Race and Class,* vol. 25, no. 2: 1-11.

Skills Development Scotland (2016) Modern Apprenticeship Statistics Full Year Report 2015/16. Available at: https://www.skillsdevelopmentscotland.co.uk/media/41664/modernapprenticeship-statistics-quarter-4-2015-16-2-1.pdf [Last accessed 15/6/2017].

Smith, A. (2005) 'Civic and Ethnic Nationalism' in P. Spencer and H. Wollman (eds.) *Nations and Nationalism: A Reader.* Edinburgh: Edinburgh University Press.

Smith, A. (2014) 'Statues in the park are not just figures from the past', Manchester Policy Blogs: Ethnicity. Available at: http://blog.policy.manchester.ac.uk/featured/2014/04/statues-in-the-park-are-not-just-figures-from-the-past/ [Last accessed 29/2/2016].

Smyth, J. (ed.) (2000) *Revolution, Counter-Revolution and Union: Ireland in the 1790s*. Cambridge: Cambridge University Press.

Social Marketing Gateway (2013) *Mapping the Roma Community in Scotland: Final Report*. Glasgow: The Social Marketing Gateway. Available at: http://www.gov.scot/resource/0043/00434972.pdf [Last accessed 13/3/2016].

Song, M. (2014a) *Challenging a Culture of Racial Equivalence*. London: Runnymede Trust.

Song, M. (2014b) 'Challenging a Culture of Racial Equivalence', *British Journal of Sociology*, vol. 65, no. 1: 107-129.

Spencer, S. (2011) *Policy Primer: Integration*. Oxford: Migration Observatory.

SPICe Briefing (2015) *Ethnicity and Employment*. Edinburgh: Scottish Parliament.

Stenhouse, D. (2004) *On the Make: How the Scots took over London*. Edinburgh: EUP

Strachan, G. (2013) 'Travellers' arrival angers Arbroath', *The Courier*, Friday 21 June. Available at: http://www.thecourier.co.uk/news/local/angus-the-mearns/travellers-arrival-angers-arbroath-1.105051 [Last accessed 13/3/2016].

Strathclyde Police (2011) *Diversity Report*. Glasgow: Strathclyde Police.

Sue D. W. (2007) 'Racial Microagression in Everyday Life', *American Psychological Association*, 62 (4), 271-286.

Sweney, M. (2014) 'BSkyB to take 20% of talent from Black, Asian or other minority backgrounds', *The Guardian*, 18 August. Available at: http://www.theguardian.com/media/2014/aug/18/bskyb-20-percent-talent-black-asian-ethnic-minority [Last accessed 13/3/2016].

Swift, R., 2001. 'Thomas Carlyle, "Chartism", and the Irish in Early Victorian England'. *Victorian Literature and Culture*, vol. 29, no. 1: 67-83.

Tackey, N.D., Barnes, H. and Khambhaita, P. (2011) *Poverty, Ethnicity and Education*. York: Joseph Rowntree Foundation.

Taguieff, P.A. (1990) 'The New Cultural Racism in France', *Telos* 83, pp.109-122.

Taguieff, P-A. (2001) *The Forces of Prejudice on Racism and its Doubles*. Minneapolis: University of Minnesota Press.

The University of Edinburgh (2014) The Global Migrations of the Scottish People since c.1600: Issues, Debates and Controversies. Programme. Available at: http://www.shca.ed.ac.uk/documents/GlobalMigrationsBrochure.PDF [Last accessed 3/11/2017].

Third, H., Wainwright, S. and Pawson, H. (1997) *Constraint and Choice for Minority Ethnic Home Owners in Scotland*. Edinburgh: Scottish Homes.

Torres, A. (2014). *Microaggression*. Available at: http://www.nationalreview.com [Last accessed 23/2/2016].

Touré (2011). 'The Most Racist Thing That Ever Happened to Me'. *The Atlantic*, 14 September. Available at: http://www.theatlantic.com/national/archive/2011/09/the-most-racist-thing-that-ever-happened-to-me/245019/ [Last accessed 13/3/2016].

Trevor-Roper, H. (1983) 'The Invention of Tradition: The Highland Tradition of Scotland', in E. J. Hobsbawm and T. Ranger (eds.), *The Invention of Tradition*, Cambridge: Cambridge University Press.

Urquhart, F. (2013) 'Traveller caravan camp in Aberdeen school field', *The Scotsman*, 12 June. Available at: http://www.scotsman.com/news/traveller-caravan-camp-in-aberdeen-school-field-1-2963567 [Last accessed 13/3/2016].

Utt, J. (2011) *Post-racial = more covert in our racism?* Available from: http://www.changefromwithin.org [Last accessed 19/2/2016].

Vedantam, S. (2010) *The Hidden Brain: How Our Unconscious Minds Elect Presidents, Control Markets, Wage Wars, and Save Our Lives*. New York: Spiegel & Grau.

Verrips, K. (1987) 'Noblemen, Farmers and Labourers: A Civilizing Offensive in a Dutch Village', *Netherlands Journal of Sociology*, vol. 23, no. 1: 3-17.

Virdee, S. (1997) 'Racial Harassment' in T. Modood, R. Berthoud, J. Lakey, J. Nazroo, P. Smith, S. Virdee and S. Beishon (eds.), *Ethnic Minorities in Britain*. Policy Studies Institute: London.

Virdee, S. (2014) *Racism, Class and the Racialized Outsider*. Basingstoke: Palgrave Macmillan.

Virdee, S. (2017) 'The second sight of racialised outsiders in the imperialist core', *Third World Quarterly*. Available at: http://dx.doi.org/10.1080/01436597.2017.1328274 [Last accessed 15/6/2017].

VisitScotland (2014) 'Uniquely Scottish'. Available at: http://www.visitscotland.com/about/arts-culture/ uniquely-scottish/ [Last Accessed 20/4/2015].

Visram, R. (1995) *The History of the Asian Community in Britain*. London: Pluto Press.

Wade, M. (2014) 'Scotland must face up to role in slavery', *The Times*, 11 January. Available at: http:// www.thetimes.co.uk/tto/news/uk/scotland/article3972379.ece [Last accessed 1/6/2015].

Waiton, S. (2013) 'The New Sectarians', in J. Flint and J. Kelly (eds.) *Bigotry, Football and Scotland*. Edinburgh: Edinburgh University Press.

Waiton, S. (2016) 'Criminalizing Songs and Symbols in Scottish Football: how anti-sectarian legislation has created a new 'sectarian' divide', *Soccer & Society*, (early electronic release, 21 January). Available at: http://www.tandfonline.com/doi/abs/10.1080/14660970.2015.1133413

Walker, G. (2001) 'Identity Questions in Contemporary Scotland: Faith, Football and Future Prospects', *Contemporary British History*, vol. 15, no. 1: 41-60.

Walls, P. and Williams, R. (2003) 'Sectarianism at work: accounts of employment discriminating against Irish Catholics in Scotland', *Ethnic and Racial Studies*, vol. 26, no. 4: 632-661.

Watson, M. (2003) *Being English in Scotland*. Edinburgh: Edinburgh University Press.

Watt, N. (2015) 'Illegal immigrants to UK face eviction without court order under new laws', *The Guardian*, Tuesday 4 August. Available at: http://www.theguardian.com/uk-news/2015/aug/03/ illegal-immigrants-face-eviction-without-court-order-under-plans-to-discourage-migrants [Last accessed 13/3/2016].

Weber, M. [1904] (1946) 'The Protestant Sects and the Spirit of Capitalism', in H.H. Gerth and C.W. Mills (eds.) *From Max Weber: Essays in Sociology*, New York: Oxford University Press.

Webster, C. (2007) *Understanding Race and Crime*. Oxford: Oxford University Press.

What's On Glasgow, 'Emancipation Acts'. http://www.whatsonglasgow.co.uk/event/010407-emancipation-acts/ [Last accessed 1/6/2015].

Williams, C., and de Lima, P. (2006) 'Devolution, multicultural citizenship and race equality: From laissez-faire to nationally responsible policies', *Critical Social Policy*, 26 (3), pp.498-522.

Wood, M., Hales, J., Purdon, S., Sejersen, T. and Hayllar, O. (2009) *A Test for Racial Discrimination in Recruitment in British Cities*. London: Department for Work and Pensions.

Wykes, E. (2015) 'Invisible Names and Visible Privileges: The Racialisation of Names'. Available at: http://www.discoversociety.org [Last accessed 22/2/2016].

Zimmerman, K. A. (2015). *What is Culture?* Available at: http://www.livescience.com [Last accessed 22/2/2016].

Zuccotti, C. (2014) *Do Parents Matter? Occupational Outcomes among Ethnic Minorities and British Natives in England and Wales (2009-2010)*. London: University of London.

Xenos, N. (1996) 'Civic Nationalism: Oxymoron?' *Critical Review: A Journal of Politics and Society*, vol. 10, no. 2: 213-231.

Yousaf, H. (2014) 'The Not Just White Paper', *Scottish Left Review* 80 (January/February): 10-11.

Notes on Contributors

ALLAN ARMSTRONG is a retired teacher and author of *From Davitt to Connolly, 'Internationalism from Below' and the Challenge to the* UK *State and British Empire, 1889–95* and *The Ghost of James Connolly – James Connolly and Edinburgh's New Trade Union, Labour and Socialist Movements (1890–96)*. He also contributed to *Unstated – Writers on Independence and Scotland and the Easter Rising*. Allan is a communist, republican, freethinker, secularist and Scottish internationalist and on the Editorial Board of *Emancipation & Liberation* (http://republicancommunist.org/blog). He is a supporter of the Radical Independence Campaign, the Republican Socialist Alliance, and the Campaign for a European Republican Socialist Party.

COLIN CLARK teaches sociology and social policy at the University of the West of Scotland (UWS). His research is mainly located within the fields of Romani studies and Ethnic and Racial Studies, with a special interest in issues of identity, migration and citizenship. Colin has published widely in these areas and supervises a number of PhD students. Outside of UWS, Colin sits on the Board of Directors of the Glasgow based anti-racist organisation the Coalition for Racial Equality and Rights (CRER) and he is also a Trustee of the Roma Rights group Friends of Romano Lav (FORL). Colin tweets as @ profcolinclark.

NEIL DAVIDSON lectures in Sociology at the University of Glasgow. He is the author of 6 books, including the Deutscher-Prize winning *Discovering the Scottish Revolution* (2003), *How Revolutionary Were the Bourgeois Revolutions?* (2012 and 2017) and, most recently, *Nation-States: Consciousness and Competition* (2016). Neil is a member of RISE and continues to support the Radical Independence Campaign.

PAUL GOLDIE is a second year PhD student in the University of Glasgow. Prior to this he completed a Masters in Equality and Human Rights. His current research focuses on the experiences of women from an Irish Catholic background growing up in the west of Scotland. More broadly, Paul's research interests include racism, nationalism and human rights.

JATIN HARIA is the Executive Director at the Coalition for Racial Equality and Rights (CRER), an anti-racist social policy charity that works to address issues of structural racism across Scotland (www.crer.org.uk). In previous lives, Jatin has served on the Commission for Racial Equality (CRE) Scotland Advisory Board, the Scottish Executive's Race Equality Advisory Forum and the STUC General Council, and was a founder member of the STUC's Black Workers' Committee. In 2016, Jatin acted as the lead representative in Zaffir Hakim's Employment Tribunal case against the STUC where the STUC were found guilty of unfair dismissal and victimisation.

ALEX LAW is Professor of Sociology at Abertay University. His recent publications include *Social Theory for Today: Making Sense of Social Worlds* (2014).

MINNA LIINPÄÄ is a PhD Researcher at the University of Glasgow. Her research is funded by the ESRC and the Centre on Dynamics of Ethnicity (CODE) based jointly at the universities of Glasgow and Manchester. Minna's current research focuses on nationalism, post-colonialism, identity, ethnicity and racism. She is using the Scottish independence referendum as a case study in order to explore and interrogate the ways in which nationalist narratives are constructed and mobilised from above, and interpreted, experienced and potentially challenged by ethnic minorities from below.

MAUREEN MCBRIDE is a PhD Researcher at the University of Glasgow. Maureen's research is intended to develop a more theoretically-informed approach to the study of sectarianism in Scotland than the current mainstream scholarship offers. Utilising the Offensive Behaviour at Football and Threatening Communications Act (2012) as a case study, she explores how people make sense of new hierarchies of belonging and exclusion that have emerged in contemporary society and places and aims, thus developing a critical framework which places power and inequality at the centre of analysis. Her publications include 'Can new legislation succeed in wiping out the sectarian problem in Scotland?' (in *Scottish Association for the Study of Offending Journal*, 2014), and a report for the Scottish Government entitled 'What works to reduce prejudice and discrimination? A review of the evidence' (2015).

NASAR MEER is Professor of Race, Identity and Citizenship at the University of Edinburgh and a Royal Society of Edinburgh Research Fellow (2014–2019). He has a longstanding interest in race, identity and citizenship. His publications include: *Islam and Modernity* (ed., 2017); *Interculturalism and Multiculturalism: Debating the Dividing Lines* (co-ed, 2016); *Citizenship, Identity and the Politics of Multiculturalism: The Rise of Muslim Consciousness* (2015, 2nd Edition); *Racialization and Religion* (ed., 2014), *Race and Ethnicity* (2014) and *European Multiculturalism(s): Religious, Cultural and Ethnic Challenges* (co-edited, 2012). In 2016 he was awarded the Royal Society of Edinburgh's Thomas Reid Medal. www.nasarmeer.com

GINA NETTO is a Reader/Associate Professor at The Urban Institute at Heriot Watt University, Edinburgh. Her research interests are focused on migration, ethnicity and poverty. Recent work includes two Joseph Rowntree Foundation commissioned studies, *International Lessons on Tackling Extreme Housing Exclusion* (2015) and *In-Work Poverty, Ethnicity and Informal Workplace Cultures* (2013). Academic outputs include papers in *Urban Studies, Sociology, Policy and Politics, Housing Studies, Housing Theory and Society, International Journal of Housing Policy, Social Policy and Administration, Journal of Mental Health, Public Health, Journal of Public Health and Health Promotion International*. Gina is currently co-editing a themed section on 'Migrants in the Labour Market' for *Social Policy and Society*.

JIM SLAVEN is an Edinburgh based writer, activist and founding member of the James Connolly Society. With 30 years' experience of anti-racist and anti-sectarian work his research looks at the intersection between race, nation and class. He has written widely on Scottish and Irish culture and politics. He is founder of 107 Cowgate, whose events and tours explore Edinburgh's history and future from a working class perspective. He is currently working on a project to use artistic approaches and techniques to develop open dialogue and create social change. He tweets at: @JimSlaven.

SATNAM VIRDEE is Professor of Sociology at the University of Glasgow and founding Director of the Centre for Research on Racism, Ethnicity and Nationalism (CRREN). He is a historical and political sociologist with research interests in racism, class and historical capitalism. He is the author and co-author of five books, including most recently *Racism, Class and the Racialized Outsider* (Palgrave Macmillan, 2014). A new book entitled *Stretching Marxism, Situating Racism* will appear in 2019.

CAROL YOUNG is Senior Policy Officer for the Coalition for Racial Equality and Rights. Carol's remit at CRER includes research, policy work and development and delivery of equality publications, resources and training. Her work focuses on embedding equalities into organisational policy and practice from an anti-racist perspective. She has a particular interest in race equality within employment and educational contexts, and in the operation of Scotland's Public Sector Equality Duties. Her background is in cross-strand equality work within the voluntary and public sectors.

Luath Press Limited

committed to publishing well written books worth reading

LUATH PRESS takes its name from Robert Burns, whose little collie Luath (*Gael.*, swift or nimble) tripped up Jean Armour at a wedding and gave him the chance to speak to the woman who was to be his wife and the abiding love of his life. Burns called one of the 'Twa Dogs' Luath after Cuchullin's hunting dog in Ossian's *Fingal*. Luath Press was established in 1981 in the heart of Burns country, and is now based a few steps up the road from Burns' first lodgings on Edinburgh's Royal Mile. Luath offers you distinctive writing with a hint of unexpected pleasures.

Most bookshops in the UK, the US, Canada, Australia, New Zealand and parts of Europe, either carry our books in stock or can order them for you. To order direct from us, please send a £sterling cheque, postal order, international money order or your credit card details (number, address of cardholder and expiry date) to us at the address below. Please add post and packing as follows: UK – £1.00 per delivery address; overseas surface mail – £2.50 per delivery address; overseas airmail – £3.50 for the first book to each delivery address, plus £1.00 for each additional book by airmail to the same address. If your order is a gift, we will happily enclose your card or message at no extra charge.

Luath Press Limited
543/2 Castlehill
The Royal Mile
Edinburgh EH1 2ND
Scotland
Telephone: +44 (0)131 225 4326 (24 hours)
email: sales@luath. co.uk
Website: www. luath.co.uk